Redemption
and
Recovery

Redemption
and
Recovery

**Further Parallels of Religion and
Science in Addiction Treatment**

DANIEL E. HOOD

Transaction Publishers
New Brunswick (U.S.A.) and London (U.K.)

Library of Congress Catalog Number: 2011018269
ISBN: 978-1-4128-4252-5

Printed in the United States of America

Library of Congress Cataloging-in-Publication Data

Hood, Daniel E.
  Redemption and recovery: further parallels of religion and science in addiction treatment / Daniel E. Hood.
    p. cm.
  Includes bibliographical references and index.
  ISBN 978-1-4128-4252-5
  1. Drug addiction—Treatment—United States. 2. Drug addiction—Treatment—Religious aspects. 3. Substance abuse treatment facilities—United States. 4. Drug addiction—Treatment—United States—Case studies. 5. Drug addiction—Treatment—Religious aspects—Case studies. 6. Substance abuse treatment facilities—United States—Case studies. I. Title.
  HV5825.H663 2011
  616.86'06—dc23
                        2011018269

Contents

Preface and Acknowledgments

The research project that culminated in this book and its predecessor (Hood 2011a) began when I was in graduate school. The idea originated in a seminar at CUNY Graduate School under the eminent drug researcher Charles Winick. That was in the post crack era of the late 1990s while Clinton was still in the White House and "faith-based" programs got little public notice or government support; separation of church and state was still assumed proper political doctrine. Some of the earliest research for this book was done during that period, but more of it lopped over into the Bush years when faith-based organizations had begun to gain more traction on the political playing fields. The early drafts of the books were written as faith-based organizations gained increasing legitimacy and funding from the Bush Administration to deal with various social problems, including drug addiction.

Addiction Treatment and *Redemption and Recovery* are now being published as we begin what may (or may not) be a new political era. We have yet to see whether the Obama regime will continue the Bush era support for faith groups. The President has not cut off their funding, but he has also sent some signals that he (also?) favors harm reduction—an approach that challenges current forms of "use reduction" drug treatment, whether sectarian or secular. Whatever the new folks in the White House do, faith-based organizations will continue to do "their thing," as they attempt to apply their ancient (and not so ancient) principles to the social problems they feel called to address.

This book and its predecessor are attempts, first, to describe and, second, to understand what it is faith-based and non faith-based drug "treatments" (particularly "drug-free" rehabilitation programs) do for and to their clients. The descriptions are based on the words and actions of the participants and the staff of the two programs in question; the understanding is a specifically sociological one that is grounded in a particular ethnographic outlook.

These books have several goals, which I hope become clear in the reading. One goal, in particular, is to tell the stories of the *subjects* of these works. They are the residents of two particular residential programs that serve people with drug problems. I have chosen to call the programs Redemption House and Recovery House. If I agreed to tell their stories publicly and without alteration, they (particularly the residents of Recovery House) agreed to share them with me. That is the deal we made with each other, pure and simple. That is one reason you will find some rather lengthy quotes in the following pages. Without this bargain, there would be no story to tell, no book to write. To the degree possible given the demands of the social science discipline and the publishing business—both legitimate operations in my view—these are their books and their story. And that is why they come first in the acknowledgments that follow.

The Residents

Early on in the time I spent participating in Recovery House treatment process, I found myself in an orientation seminar on "gratitude." I was sitting in a circle with about fifty other participants while the leader roamed about the center of the circle. At brief intervals he would stop and point to someone who was then expected to identify something he or she was grateful for. When he suddenly thrust his finger in my direction, I was flabbergasted. I had been busy "observing" and did not expect to be asked to participate so soon or so directly! I had no idea how to respond, but mumbled something feeble about agreeing with the person just ahead of me.

I now know how to respond. I am "eternally" and "globally" grateful to the men of Redemption House and the men and women of Recovery House who graciously provided the substance of this ethnography. Despite the fact that they were experiencing a particularly tense and confusing period in their lives, almost without exception they allowed a complete stranger to intrude on their privacy. They were patient with my naïve questioning and polite whenever I pressed them to "tell me more about that." Almost from day one, most residents included me in their discussions, encounters, prayers, meals, and recreation, as if I belonged. Stereotypes about "drug addicts" suggest that they are incapable of empathy or consideration for others, that they are narcissistic and lacking in basic social skills. In my experience, nothing could be further from the truth. Throughout my stays at Redemption House and Recovery House, I was shown precisely the kind of friendliness, kindness, and consideration these stereotypes suggest would be missing.

My only regret about this project is that many, if not most, of its dramatis personae will not have access to its results. The vast majority of the men and women who people this ethnography no longer have any connection with the treatment programs. That is only one of the failings of conventional drug rehabilitation.

It was a great privilege to be allowed into the lives and thoughts of the residents and staff members of these two programs. Most of the residents I got to know to varying degrees have moved back into the street life they hoped to escape. Some few are building new lives and careers for themselves, perhaps as staff members of these or other rehabilitation facilities. I wish all of them all the best, and hope that the results of their good work reflected in these pages can contribute to improving the lot of people in their circumstances in the future. God bless them all, every one.

Sociological and Other Influences

At the New School for Social Research in the 1970s, Benjamin Nelson taught me the importance of the study of religion "in all times and climes" to an understanding of human social life in general. Ben emphasized locating sociological work amidst "particular peoples in particular places," by which he meant not basing it on straw men or models, but on actual people inhabiting actual social worlds. Throughout this work, both research and writing, I have tried to keep these bits of "directorial advice" in mind.

Space does not allow me to do more than mention various other distinguished sociologists who even more directly influenced this work. Charles Winick, M. Herbert Danzger, and Harry G. Levine at the CUNY Graduate Center were most prominent in this regard. I am indebted to these three men for sharing with me their time, their knowledge, and their enthusiasm for learning as a vocation.

Jack Levinson, Lynn Zimmer, John P. Morgan, MD (honorary sociologist), William Kornblum, Sidney Aronson, Emil Osterreicher, Stephen Steinberg, J. R. Burkholder, Charles Lawrence, and Ernest Kilker were influential in shaping my sociological imagination in general and/or this book in particular. Robert Saute, a CUNY colleague, proofread this entire second volume. Non-sociologists who contributed in various important ways include Edward P. Augsburger, David Pavlick, William T. Hunter, Jr., Sharon Stancliff, C. Carlson, Elizabeth Carson, and especially Henry Sindos. I am deeply grateful for the contributions of each of these friends, colleagues, and mentors.

My knowledge of the therapeutic community's self-understanding was assisted in important ways by a graduate seminar and several informal discussions with George DeLeon, (then) Director of the Center for Therapeutic Community Research. Jerome Carroll was also instrumental in providing access to the therapeutic community that is central to this study.

Most important, I am happily indebted for the constant love and support of my wife, Linda, and my son, Michael. They were emotionally sustaining throughout this project, and continue to provide the central grounding for my life. Linda also did yeo(wo)man's work as proof reader at the earliest stages of writing and as PC technical advisor throughout the process.

I am also grateful for financial support. A Harold M. Proshanky Fellowship from the City University of New York supported a portion of my earliest participant observations. I did the research on harm reduction as treatment alternative while I was a Drug Policy Fellow at the Lindesmith Foundation (now Drug Policy Alliance) funded by the Open Society Institute (grant #10000335).

I also want to thank the people at Transaction Publishers. First, Irving Louis Horowitz, executive editor, saw the importance of the issues taken up in this book, when other editors and publishers could not. Also, the Transaction staff, especially Jennifer Nippins, Andrew McIntosh, and Larry Mintz were most helpful and gracious in guiding a novice author through the process of producing not one, but two publishable manuscripts.

Finally, two people provided me with special entreé to the different, yet similar, worlds of Recovery and Redemption: Vito Tomanelli and Jack Roberts. Without their access and insight, none of what follows would have been possible. My conversations with David Mapes were also crucial; he was a fount of information and always gracious with his time. I hope I have done justice to the trust these men afforded me, despite their various disagreements with my analyses and conclusions about their worlds. I am sincerely grateful to each of them.

While all of the people mentioned here made significant contributions to this volume, for which I am most appreciative, any and all errors it contains are my responsibility alone.

Introduction

This book is a companion volume to *Addiction Treatment: Comparing Religion and Science in Application,* published by Transaction earlier this year. It is based on the same comparative ethnography of two drug-free residential programs for people with drug-use problems. One program is religious, or faith-based, the other claims to be grounded in science and empirical research. The chapters that appear here were integral parts of the original five hundred-plus page manuscript that I submitted to Transaction. The editors were initially excited about the manuscript as a whole, but considerations of size and pricing eventually dictated that not all chapters would make it under a single cover. Thus a two-book approach was initiated. The first book, *Addiction Treatment,* focuses on detailed descriptions of the two focal programs, which I dubbed Redemption House and Recovery House, and the central "treatment" process of personal conversion or identity transformation.[1]

The decision to publish my manuscript as two books required some compromises and, indeed, sacrifices be made in the integrity of the larger ethnographic manuscript. These can only be corrected by reading the two volumes in concert. However, I believe that each book provides crucial insights into the operations of drug treatment and training (as the faith-based programs prefer to be called) that can be found nowhere else, at least in book form or in such detail. It is also possible to read each of the essays in this book independently since each approaches a single topic within the larger whole. This will be easier and more rewarding if you know a little bit about the parameters of the larger study and its general thrust or argument. This will be the main task of this Introduction: to provide the reader who has no knowledge of the previous volume with what might be called an extended abstract of its plan, program, and findings. In the conclusion to this volume, I will provide the chapter scheme for the original manuscript so that those who wish to, may read—or at least—know the nature of the "whole" argument. But first let me describe in outline the book you hold in your hand.

Recovery and Redemption

The chapters in this volume focus less on treatment process than did the earlier book. Only two chapters (4 and 5) in this volume deal directly with process. Other chapters here focus on (a) the clients of the two programs and (b) the comparative success and failure of these programs and their general types. The first client-focused chapter ("Resident Demographics") looks at who the program residents are and what their lives were about *prior* to seeking treatment or training. It does this through a process I call contextualized demographics. This consists of comparing detailed background stories of two central characters—one from either House—as well as several other "minor" characters in less detail. My purpose is to demonstrate the profound and broad similarities between the clients of faith-based and secular or science-based approaches to drug treatment. This proposition continues a major theme of the entire project and flies in the face of widely accepted dogma—at least within the drug treatment industry and treatment research community—that religious- and science-based programs serve very different clientele as well as different purposes (Langrod et al. 1972; Marlatt 1988).

The other client-focused chapter ("Resident Accounts") describes the similarities between the two sets of residents as well as the two programs of transformation they are enduring via the clients' tales of deprivation and depravity that supposedly influenced their current situation in a drug treatment or training facility. Using a grounded theory approach (Glaser and Strauss 1967), it was a relatively simple matter to organize under the very same general categories these sad tales (Goffman 1961) that residents use at both Houses to account for their present degraded status and stigmatization. The supposedly radically different people (largely men) in the two supposedly categorically different programs (scientific vs. religious) use almost identical vocabularies of motive (Mills 1940) to account for their presence in treatment or training. Not only this, but they also had the very same opinions of what accounts for success (and failure) in overcoming their demons (Redemption House) or their disease (Recovery House) and attaining the same goal of sobriety equally prescribed by both programs, perfection in abstinence. Once again, my data lends itself to the interpretation that not only are the two programs of personal transformation largely identical, except in their separate rhetorics (the story of the first volume), but they are, if anything, even more alike in the clientele they attract and (a bit less so) in the consciousness they seek to induce among them.

As I said, two chapters here deal with treatment and training process. The first of these (Chapter 3) is an in-depth look at the role of religion—or "spirituality"—in the self-described empirical and science-based program at Recovery House. This chapter describes how religion found its way back into the therapeutic community (TC) form of treatment (Recovery House), after its banishment in the early 1960s by the TC's originator, Charles Dederich. This chapter on "Religion in Recovery House" analyzes how the TC staff uses Higher Power spirituality both to "nihilate" (i.e., negate) any interference by "outside" religious forces and as a tool for inducing conformity to its central message and program (its orthodoxy) among its clientele. This twelve-step doctrine of a Higher Power is analyzed sociologically, and its self-definition as a tolerant "non-religion" is debunked.

Chapter 4, the other process chapter, looks at what happens to the residents of Redemption House and Recovery House as they prepare to graduate and meet the hostile—or merely indifferent—world outside. This chapter is based on a smaller sample than the rest of the study, in part due to the small percentage of graduates produced by both programs and in part due to my lack of access to them. Nevertheless, this "Reentry" chapter looks in particular at the ways both programs do and do not prepare their graduates for success (and failure!) in abstinent sobriety amidst a decidedly non-abstinent world. Again, the basic assumptions that underlie treatment and training are demonstrated to be virtually identical and the "techniques" they teach their clientele almost equally similar. In addition, this chapter looks closely at the attempt of at least one success- ful graduate to gain the status of "normality" in his everyday life, beyond the stigma of both addiction and recovery. In so doing, he challenges many of the basic assumptions of America's treatment industry about both addiction and recovery, including its sacrosanct notion of the necessity of perfect abstinence with zero tolerance for any relapse in thought, word, or deed.

The final chapter of this volume addresses the question of comparative success and failure of drug treatment vs. discipleship training; of science vs. religion in the application of addiction solutions. After a somewhat less than strictly mathematical analysis of the various statistical surveys that attempt to assess (or prove) success rates of both types of programs, I suggest that there is little agreement about what successful treatment means and, thus, what the rates of success are. Moreover, to the degree that my analysis has any valid- ity (which I agree is questionable in strict statistical and definitional terms), I conclude that both programs appear to have virtually identical rates of suc- cess and failure. Further, I suggest that those rates compare favorably with the success of religious conversion in other contexts (revivals, proselytizing sects). In sum, success is minimal and failure the norm at all sorts of addiction treatment programs. In this regard, at least, I suggest that the claim "treatment works," which has become a watchword for both the treatment industry and the treatment research community, is the practical equivalent of the evangelical Christian's clarion call: "Jesus saves."

Each of the chapters in this volume demonstrates in its particular "realm" the two major themes developed in the earlier book, namely that these religious and scientific applications of addiction solutions are doing the same things with, for, and to their clients (who are also virtually the same people). They simply designate their process and techniques by different vocabularies and justify them via different rationale systems. One program uses a religious or theological rationale for its training procedures; the other uses the language and discourse of empirical science and mental health to justify its procedures. The second theme is that they are both largely unsuccessful in solving the drug and other problems of their clients, despite some spectacular successes in individual cases (examples of which I discuss) and despite their own claims to the contrary.

In regard to the issue of justifications, I argue the secular, supposedly scientific program is more obfuscatory than the religious and therefore has something, perhaps much, to learn from them. Redemption House understands itself as offering a choice of "selves" or identities or consciousnesses to its clients. Its clients can choose to be drug-involved with the world or to be disciples of Jesus (or at least most of them can) and attain heaven. There is no pathological determinism or medical imperative involved. Recovery House, on the contrary, offers not so much a choice as a necessity: health or illness. Science and medicine are as much or more widely taken for granted as cultural authorities than is religion today. This is much different than some two centuries ago when the idea of addiction was "discovered" (Levine 1978) and treatments were subsequently developed, most of the original ones under religious auspices (Baumohl 1987).

While drug involvement at Redemption House is a real choice—though seen as morally wrong and eternally disastrous—at Recovery House it is not a choice but a disease (or emotional disorder), one that the state has the right to insist be treated, with or without the volition of the individual. Thus, not only does the state criminalize drug "possession," but Recovery House and similar programs of treatment medicalize what is essentially a socially unacceptable form of behavior, especially when engaged in by already despised groups (minorities, the poor, or disaffected youth) (Conrad and Schneider 1985). By medicalizing behavior, therapeutic authorities "widen the net" of the criminal justice system and expand the state's direct domination of selected dissident groups. In this sense, so-called science-based, drug-free treatments like Recovery House use science as an ideological screen for programs of social control and correction (Habermas 1970). Because they have lost much of their cultural authority, programs like Redemption House and Teen Challenge (its erstwhile parent organization) must remain almost entirely voluntary, depending much more exclusively on persuasion to affect their conversions, at least for the time being. Who knows what changes might attend government funding of faith-based programs as these ancient authorities attempt to reassert control in the public sphere? While I do not analyze the political situation in any detail, the fact that Redemption House operates in much the same way as Recovery House, sheds considerable light on the nature of the latter's "science- and research-based" procedures. The use of religious metaphors at Redemption House to explain and justify much the same process that occurs at Recovery House (with much the same level of success) calls into question many, if not all of the "scientific" assumptions on which our "addiction and treatment science" is based.

The Programs and Process

Both programs at the heart of this book and its predecessor are located in similar south Bronx neighborhoods some two dozen blocks apart. Both programs are what we commonly call "rehabs." They are in-patient or residential programs in which clients—or residents, as I prefer—are housed, fed, and sometimes clothed twenty-four hours per day, seven days per week for up to a year (sometimes more) or until they prove worthy of graduation or they "split" (leave the program without authorization of the staff). The vast majority of residents fit the latter category; up to 50 percent leave within the first three to six months. Both programs condemn such splitees to certain relapse into drug use and provide them no assistance and little in the way of referral to other types of programs (e.g., harm-reduction services like needle exchange or methadone maintenance) when they leave. Splitees are told explicitly and didactically that when they leave they are doomed to relapse and either return eventually to treatment or training or die as a result of their renewed drug use. While relapse is common in these circumstances, it may well be only temporary, since many who misuse drugs outlive such behaviors, with or without treatment. Some of the latter, we know, are abstinence program splitees (Courtwright, et al. 1989).

Both programs, as detailed in *Addiction Treatment*, attempt to "rehab" their clients via a personal transformation accomplished by similar processes and techniques. Among these are: "encapsulation" and "discourse deprivation" (cutting residents off from outside influences, ideas, and interactions, especially from "the street"); constant surveillance and ideological indoctrination ("bombing" or "showering" with program rhetoric 24/7) about the dangers of the "disease" or "sinful nature" that results in drug using symptoms; and the necessity of accepting the program's "blueprint" for correction and personal reclamation. The rhetorical showers occur daily in both formal (e.g., in classroom and seminar training) and informal settings (via peer pressure from more assimilated clients and surveillance and reprimand by staff members). The programs call their blueprints for successful training (at Redemption House) or treatment (at Recovery House) and subsequent sobriety "Christian living" or "Right living," respectively. These paradigms for success consist of virtually the same set of directions, in particular: do not return to previous social environments and networks ("people, places, and things") and do create new social networks via a local evangelical congregation (Redemption House) or a local chapter of Alcoholics or Narcotics Anonymous (Recovery House), places that will maintain the rhetorical emphases of the training or treatment as much as possible. There is more, but these are central to both prescribed ideologies of "livings."

The main technique or method that attempts to induce new forms of consciousness and identity among the residents are regular ritual performances of "mutual witnessing" (mutual prayer and testimony at Redemption House and various therapy group sessions, including encounter, at Recovery House). Such rituals are common in the history of both utopian groups and conversionary sects in multiple forms (Goffman 1961; Kanter 1972). In these rituals, residents witness and enact (act as if) the new role of recovered addicts or discipled

Christians both verbally and behaviorally (McGuire 1987/1992). Both forms of mutual witness allow clients to practice new sober identities in the presence of fellow residents and staff, in part by actively de-legitimating (attacking, criticizing, regretting) verbal and behavioral "symptoms" of the old identity (addict or sinner) in fellow residents as well as in one's own behavior or biography. These performances in turn enable each man by trial and error to create a "new" recovering or redeemable persona that fits the House paradigm (Right living or Christian living). The "validity" of the paradigm is thus reinforced in the resident and the group as each resident projects it with increasing confidence in front of peers and staff over the course of months in residence. The new sense of a sober self that results from this artificial social feedback network is then immediately challenged when the new graduate finds himself back in his old neighborhood with the same social resources he had before treatment or training. Fortunate graduates have other resources to support the new persona.

Phenomenologically, i.e., in terms of what they actually do day in and day out, both Houses operate almost identical programs intended to rehabilitate their clients. The only place they significantly depart from one another is in the rhetorical systems they use to talk about what it is they are doing: drug treatment with scientific methods or discipleship training with religious methods.

Theory and Methods

The major thrust of both books is the comparison between the two programs much more than their successes or failures. Each chapter here, with the exception of Chapter 3 on religion in Recovery House, takes a directly comparative approach describing the actions and experiences of the residents and staff of the two Houses in the same contexts. This is of course a common and foundational method in sociology, although it is fairly unusual in individual ethnographic works. One reason for the latter may be the amount of material produced by fieldwork that must be processed. (This may also account for the necessity of a second book.) Comparison is typical of Weberian sociology in particular, which is one of the traditions that has influenced my fairly eclectic sociological approach to the world and to data.

Most introductory textbooks tell students that Weberian sociology is one of the foundations of "social interactionism." This approach is also peculiarly American, originally developed by George Herbert Mead at the University of Chicago where it then influenced many of the early sociology fieldwork projects among the various "underworld" sub-cultures of the city. Studies of drug use and users continue to be well represented in this tradition, not least by Howard Becker (1963/1964) and his studies of marijuana smokers, jazz musicians, and other "outsiders."

This approach to interactionism, however, was instrumental not only in continuing the Chicago School's dedication to participating in fieldwork, but also challenged its middle-class biases by defining the meaning of "outsider" (i.e., deviant) in a particularly comparative fashion. The meaning of deviance for Becker and much of modern social science depends on who has the ability to so label certain people and groups and enforce those labels via legal and other institutional means, including the medical professions. This perspective introduced another Weberian interest, power, into the study of deviance, but perhaps with a bit of a Marxian twist. While I do not claim to match these foundational studies, they are among my teachers, mentors, and role models.

Another Weberian who has been influential in my developing sociological imagination is Clifford Geertz, the cultural anthropologist (see e.g., Geertz 1973). In the previous book, I spent some twenty pages justifying my methodology and data collection via Geertz's explication of culture as text(s) that must be read and interpreted using "thick description" (i.e., contextualizing the utterances of informants as much as possible). This is essentially what I have tried to do and have used several recent drug and/or urban ethnographies (consciously Geertzian or not) as models. These include, but are not necessarily limited to, Mitchell Duneier's *Sidewalk*, Phillippe Bourgois' *In Search of Respect*, and *Cocaine Changes* by Dan Waldorf and his colleagues, Craig Reinarman and Sheigla Murphy, and Murphy and Marsha Rosenbaum's (e.g., 1994 and 1999) writings on women and drugs.

All of these writers and researchers understand in their bones the necessity of seeing the world from the perspective of the other, particularly their informants, if they want to get to the heart of the matter.[2] The heart of the matter for so-called "creative sociologies" (Morris 1977) is not the truth, certainly not in any sense of "objective reality" (religious or scientific). It is rather: what it is that our informants understand as true, regardless of what we may think we know. One of the central assumptions of this form of doing sociology (or what Benjamin Nelson [1981] somewhat awkwardly coined "anthroposociology") is that it is this "understanding of truth"—from the point of view of the "subject" (Weber called it *verstehen*)—that helps us understand why he and she do what they do. Actions, in the Weberian scheme, are motivated by "images of the world" and of the self that operate within the consciousness of the actor and, to add the Geertzian (and Bergerian) touch, within the intersubjectivity (shared understandings) of the group/s to which informants belong or orient themselves. It is this "heart of the matter" that I have taken to heart as a central direction (in the sense of stage direction) when observing and listening to the residents and staff members of Redemption House and Recovery House and when interpreting (trying to understand) their utterances, actions, and other cultural texts.

These cultural texts or—more traditionally—data were the result of four months I spent separately at each program observing and participating in what took place in various contexts (classes and seminars, chapel services and house meetings, prayer meetings and encounter sessions, meals and meal preparation, pickup basketball games and smoke breaks) and hours of interviews with several dozens of residents and staff members. The forms and formats of participation, observation, and interview are spelled out in more detail in the previous book, but should—with the assistance of this brief account—become obvious to a more or less degree as you read the various chapters, depending on your familiarity with the process of ethnography. If it is minimal and you are concerned with such "technical matters," you may want to consult Chapter 1 of the earlier book. Or, you may well find such "technical matters" tedious or unnecessary as you read through the accounts of life before, after, and during addiction treatment and discipleship training that follow in this volume. Nevertheless, it is considered appropriate for an author of a work like this to inform his readers—to some degree, at least—of his sources and uses of "the data." I hope this is helpful to those who have these concerns.

Why This Book?

It is also deemed appropriate for an author of a work like this to "situate" (or contextualize) her or his efforts in the larger scheme of similar academic work and/or issues and questions of import. In the introduction to the previous book I said that I saw this study positioned at the intersections of the sociology of deviance and the sociology of religion. More particularly, it has to do with issues of how both addiction treatment programs and certain religious organizations work to transform the behavior and consciousness of their clientele and what they have in common. This is often referred to as a form of "radical resocialization."

Conversion, including the practice of "brainwashing"—a widely misunderstood notion—was something of a "hot topic" in the wake of America's cultural revolution in the sixties. The period resulted in both increased drug-use problems and increased numbers and types of conversionary or proselytizing religious sects. The latter have been termed the New Religious Movements (NRMs) and attracted a relatively large and diverse literature in the seventies and eighties devoted to describing and understanding them from various academic perspectives (see Glock and Hammond 1973; Robbins 1988; Snow and Machelak 1984). Several authors and researchers found much in common between the proselytizing efforts of explicitly religious groups like the Unification Church of the Reverend Sun Myung Moon ("the Moonies") and ostensibly secular therapy groups like EST as well as the new drug treatment organization Synanon, the original therapeutic community. An interest in the similarities and differences among such groups continued at a lower temperature into the nineties. It was somewhat rekindled—for quite different reasons—when the "compassionate conservative" impulse of certain political interests began to tout the efficacy of "faith-based" social services.

Despite all the rhetorical flourishes by politicians and some interest and support from certain academics, the faith-based movement has not really convincingly demonstrated the superior effectiveness it has claimed for itself (Johnson 2002; Wineburg 2007). One fact recently noted by a relatively neutral academic provided some of the impetus for this (yes, and the earlier) book. Robert Wuthnow (2004, 174), the prolifically published and highly respected Director of the Center for the Study of Religion at Princeton, noted that "little research has [actually] been done to compare faith-based [treatment] organizations with nonsectarian organizations." In other words, there has been "a lotta" rhetoric and very little evidence.

Wuthnow's recent concern actually reflects comments made from other academic and professional sectors related to this study years ago. Two authors (Snow and Machelak 1984, 185), in a review of the NRM literatures, wrote

Can the transformative processes that comprise religious conversion be observed in other [non-religious] contexts? For example, can knowledge about religious conversion be generalized to explain radical transformation of political allegiances, life-style preferences and practices [such as substance abuse], or occupational commitments [such as drug-related criminal pursuits]?

A few years later, the Director of the Center for Therapeutic Community Research identified a related "need to clarify treatment process" (DeLeon 1990a, 130).

[The] interplay between treatment elements [e.g., therapy groups and peer surveillance] and client change ... defines [the treatment] process. Notwithstanding its importance, treatment process has been the *least investigated* problem in drug abuse treatment research.... [T]he process [of change] itself remains to be studied directly. [Emphasis added.]

This remains true today.

These concerns were central motives in the writing, researching, and analyzing that went into this book and its predecessor. My concern has been with how these two types of drug-free, residential programs for the transformation of people with drug-use problems affect changes in their residents. And what they have in common. What I found was that they have much more in common than almost anyone else has assumed (see G. Johnson 1976 for an example of one early exception from the treatment side of the issue). In fact, as a result of doing this research and analysis and writing, I have become convinced that the only significant difference between the faith-based programs and the science-based programs is the rhetorics and rationales they use to differentiate themselves from one another. More important, perhaps, I have come to believe—as Snow and Machelak implied—that we can learn more about this whole process from attending to the religious operation than to the scientific operation—although we learn most by watching both in comparative perspective. I do not mean by this that the religious programs have a better self-understanding of what happens in their trainings—I do not take their "side" against the secular. But, if we are to understand what is going on in both these settings from a sociological (decidedly secular) perspective, the metaphors of sin and redemption seem more revealing of what happens and how than the metaphors of illness and recovery or pathology and treatment, certainly better than disease and cure.

My purpose here (and there) is not to sell one program over the other. In fact, as readers of the conclusion of the previous book already know, my sympathies lie elsewhere—with more recent and "radical" alternatives to these more traditional and mainstream approaches, namely harm reduction. Needle exchange, drug substitution/maintenance programs (e.g., methadone and buprenorphine), decriminalization, and safe use/injection centers have proven themselves more humane and effective in saving lives and reducing the consequences of problematic drug use than either of the programs I write about here. And I trust they are the wave of the future in (public) health services for drug-use problems. My purpose here is rather to describe and understand the nature of the "use-reduction" programs without the cover of the rhetorics of either. Direct phenomenological comparison seemed the best way to accomplish this goal. However, this analysis does not shirk from conclusions where they are appropriate.

Recovery House, in particular, stands as a representative of the state of the current drug treatment industry that holds a virtual monopoly on services for addicts and others with drug problems, with Redemption House as its only quasi-legitimate alternative. This monopoly rests on the firm but seriously flawed belief in the necessity of perfection in abstinence as the sole means of sobriety for "diseased" or "disordered" drug (ab)users. It is imperative, in my view, that we understand clearly the operation and performance of organizations like Redemption House and Recovery House and the entire "drug-free" approach in all their flaws and subterfuges. Until we have a clear understanding of what happens in these programs, both religious and secular, we will not be able to release ourselves from our bondage to the ideology of abstinence. In fact, the broader cultural metaphor of addiction used for many of our social and personal ills also presents an impediment to more rational and humane approaches to these problems.

As Peter Cohen (2001/2003) suggests, we must rid ourselves of the "voodoo science of addiction treatment" before there will be adequate opportunity to treat all drug users as human beings with human failures rather than a different species of being to be shunned, condemned, imprisoned, and generally mis-treated and mis-trained by society in general and the drug treatment industry in particular. When that occurs, real redemption, so to speak, may become universally available for drug users and addicts, in the form of harm reduction services and other humane public policy approaches to not only recreational drug use(rs), but also to those conditions that tend to accompany misuse: poverty, unemployment, poor wages, inadequate education, and racism. If such a quasi-utopian situation is ever approached, I predict that both therapeutic community treatments and discipleship trainings will follow the latter's current approach of providing their services on a purely voluntary basis, neither "prescribed" by the medical/mental health community nor mandated by the criminal justice system. However, if that day ever arrives, the Redemption and Recovery Houses of the world may become few and far between because the vast majority of "addiction" problems will more likely take care of themselves.[3]

Notes

1. Redemption House refers to its process as a discipleship training and rejects the notion that it is a treatment program. I maintain the distinction between treatment and training when referring to these programs in particular. Part of Redemption House training was conducted by the Teen Challenge organization at its large facility in PA. This location is commonly referred to as "the Farm." Recovery House is a therapeutic community, the modality that claims to treat persons with the most serious addictions (see NIDA 1999).
2. And some, if not all, understand the necessity of getting close to their informants over time in order to accomplish this Weberian act of *verstehen*.
3. The irony of this claim/wish is that it strikingly echoes the claims of the early temperance and revivalist preachers like Billy Sunday, who once said that when alcohol is eliminated from American life, that event will be followed by the disappearance of all social problems, like crime, poverty, unemployment, and divorce (Shelden 2007).

1

Resident Demographics:
The Men of Redemption and Recovery

*I developed an interest in becoming an electri-
cian. I quit an $11 per hour job to make $6.35.
The training program was very racist. They let
African Americans in, but we ended doin' all the
busy work. They [regularly] sent me on a construction site and rather than [observing] and learning,
they had me sweeping and unloading light fixtures,
gettin' coffee, things of that nature. This is...the
time that I started druggin'.*

—Andrew, Recovery House

*[This executive] said, "All I wanna see your
black ass doin' is cuttin' grass or takin' out the
garbage." Right then and there, I snapped.
They had to call security to get me off the
property. So I lost that job. And he put the word
out, if I come back on the hospital grounds, they
supposed to arrest me. That's when I got frustrated.
I di'n' wanna go look for nothin' [no job]. I started
buyin' crack [again], drinkin' heavy. [Shortly
after,] I was wanderin' the streets, sleepin' in
abandoned buildin's.*

—Stan, Redemption House

*Not ideas, but material and ideal interests,
directly govern men's conduct. Yet very frequently
the 'world images' that have been created by
'ideas' have, like switchmen, determined the
tracks along which action has been pushed by the
dynamic of interest. "From what" and "for what"
one wished to be redeemed and, let us not forget,
"could be" redeemed, depended upon one's image
of the world.*

—Max Weber[1]

13

There are at least four central and specific ways in which the residents at Redemption House and those at Recovery House resemble each other. These are: (1) race and ethnicity; (2) occupational status; (3) family background and current family status or situation; and (4) drug-use history, including prior treatment experience. The first and most visible of the demographic variables they share is race and/or ethnicity. The residents at both programs are overwhelmingly men of color and/or of Hispanic descent. That is, they are not predominately white, which is the most common racial category of drug users in the general population. (They are also not young, by and large. Only one of my informants was under the age of thirty.)[2]

The men at both organizations are predominantly African American.[3] The second-most common group identity I observed at both Houses (that passes in the U.S. for a category of race or ethnicity) is Latino. White faces were conspicuous by their absence. It was not unusual at either location for my face to be one of the few, if not the only white one in a given room, meeting, or impromptu group conversation, unless, of course, the meeting was for staff, especially professional staff. At the management meetings I attended at both Houses, the lack of color in my face placed me in the majority. At Redemption House (except for the Director and House Manager), I interviewed two non-Latino white men, one staff member who was a graduate of a discipleship training program, and one resident. I recorded only two "white" interviews at Recovery House despite the fact that the total number of interviews there doubled that at Redemption House. I saw no one at either House whose physical appearance indicated Asian or Near Eastern ancestry; nor was I aware of any Native Americans in residence during the periods of my research.

A second important and related demographic factor shared by the men of both Houses is their previous economic situations and occupational histories. At both Houses there is a relatively wide range of economic and occupational experience. The spectrum runs from poor, homeless, and unemployed through intermittently employed at various low-skill occupations (construction worker, security guard) to moderate laboring skills (truck driving, building construction, factory work, operating earth moving equipment) to higher level and professional skills, some that require a college education (teaching in a business school, technical sales, accounting, drug counselor, independent businessman).

One trait that almost all of these men share is what human resource professionals call an uneven employment history. Some of the residents, like Bernard, never had a job; others, like Marvin who taught computer skills and programming at a local business college, had long histories of high-skilled, well-paying, and relatively prestigious positions. Most of the men worked at various levels of pay and skill in between these two extremes. Most of the men, however, tended to move from job to job at various rates and for various reasons. Those with more education and more marketable skills changed jobs less often and less dramatically. Those with less education and fewer specific skills recounted histories that included moving constantly in and out of jobs, both licit and illicit, and often being without occupational support of any kind. Sometimes, drug use was a factor in changing or leaving a job, but by no means was this always the case.

What is most striking in this respect is a certain kind of economic marginality and ethical or cultural duality that is shared by most of these men regardless of their level of economic, occupational, or familial success. One possible exception to this is those men whose social existence has remained at the very bottom of the economic barrel for some time, the chronically poor, alienated, alone, and homeless. I interviewed very few such men, one at one site, two at the other.

Although some of my informants gave dramatic accounts of periods of homelessness, joblessness, and loneliness, most who told such stories also had periods of relative success to recount, when they had work, love, and friendship as regular aspects of their lives. However, the majority of the men told me of their varied levels of skills and/or occupational successes in both licit and illicit businesses and of their varied successes and failures in building and maintaining familial and other social supports and resources. To demonstrate the general social and cultural background of the two similar groups of men I interviewed and observed, this chapter compares the tales of four men who appear representative.[4] They reflect both the most common levels of occupational careers represented within this sample and, more importantly, the complex pattern of successes and failures that most experience in their work, their family lives, and their daily quests for meaningfulness.[5] I have selected one man from Redemption House and three men from Recovery House whose accounts most epitomize this pattern. As I unfold their stories in this chapter, I also relate episodes from other residents in order to demonstrate the generality of their experiences, to highlight the nature of the cycles of drug involvement that are typical, and to indicate the similarities and differences between the populations of the two programs.

My attempt here is to comprehend these men as more than collections of variables that can be separated out and sifted for correlations, however helpful that may be. It is not just the elements of their lives that help us—and them—to understand who they are and the problems they face, but how all these elements, and more, fit together into complex webs of experience, into patterns of meaning and related actions. That one study such as this will be able to capture all the complexities of these lives is highly unlikely. Nevertheless, I hope to contribute to the comprehension of these complexities with the resources that I have been able to assemble.

Stanley

Stanley's life best epitomizes the dilemmas faced by most of the men I spoke with. As I see him, Stanley is situated amid conflicting directive systems or (sub)cultural systems of morality as well as structures of opportunity and exclusion.[6] His accounts display a cyclical pattern of "drifting" between extremes of seeking conventionality and seeking respite from or vengeance against it in contraventionality.[7] I try to interpret his actions as choices that to some degree always take some convention, some cultural directional system, as a point of departure. I assume that his choices typically involve cognition and are not simply impulsive, even if the cognition is ex post facto. My sociological rationale for this is considered below.

I use Stanley's account as illustration in this regard because the poles of desire that structure his life are so evident in his story and indications of this are well distributed across his biography. All my informants at both programs displayed variations on the themes of disparate directive systems and cycles of "success" and "failure" or "discipline" and "dereliction" with regard to their drug-using careers.[8] What is most interesting, from the point of this study about their commonalities in this regard, is how they all—almost to a man—tell tales about periods of considerable "control" over powerful psychoactive substances, tales which they disregard as meaningless. It is not surprising that the rhetoric of both programs also disregards any controlled use and sees only abstinence as beneficial. In the course of this chapter, I compare several other accounts, from both houses, to Stanley's ideal typical marginality and ambivalence.

At Redemption House, Stanley epitomizes the complex of life problems reported among men who are forced by circumstance to straddle several material and mental (sub)worlds. As he describes his career, Stanley has made significant efforts to attain the kinds of skill and experience necessary to fulfill the expectations of mainstream culture for legitimate success in work and family life. At least since he was fifteen, Stanley also has been attuned to the directions of another, somewhat less mainstream, cultural tradition, one that exists among young black men.[9] As he put it while sitting in the multipurpose chapel-classroom of Redemption House, Stanley was also constantly "tempted" by the excitement of the clubs, parties, and repeated romantic liaisons (that he seems to find everywhere he turns, including *inside* the church), as well as the added pleasures of recreational drug use and strict economic rationality of occasional drug dealing that are included in the tenets of this way of life.

When business and family life do not live up to his mainstream expectations, Stanley often resorts to the leadings of his alternative cultural muse: to heavier drug use, for example, to ease his psychic pain or to small-scale marketing of drugs to ease the strain on his pocket. Stanley also enjoys the "high life" that has always been an integral aspect of the post-slavery culture of African Americans (as well as other American immigrant "ethnic" working class groups), and this includes the recreational use of intoxicants.[10] The notion that some degree of participation in the "high life" is not only permissible but appropriate, if not "righteous" or "healthy" for all Americans, black, white, or otherwise, has been increasingly legitimated by, inter alia, the expansive growth of both the advertising and entertainment industries as we approached the current century.[11] Indulgence in intoxicants has little difficulty in finding "moral" support from several casuistries current in modern America.[12]

Stanley, and most of his compatriots are bombarded both from "above" (mainstream currents and institutions, including the media and other entertainment venues) and "below" (the popular cultures in the schools, the streets, and the clubs) with plenty of rationales and opportunities for resorting to illicit as well as licit use of intoxicants and little meaningful reason to distinguish between them. Thus, Stanley and the others live on a social and cultural boundary between worlds of varying constructions of reality, with different definitions (and values) for the same social situations, particularly with respect to work, leisure, and family responsibility. Included in these varying social definitions are the issues of the nature and appropriate use of intoxicants, both legal and illegal. Whether Stanley follows the directions of one view or the other often depends on the circumstances he is in when a decision is required. Whether he heeds the rationales of one or the other moral logics depends on what resources he has at hand and what consequences he can reasonably expect from his choices.[13]

In a tangle of familial/romantic and occupational ups and downs, where Stanley drifts between "fallin'" and "doin' good" (in his words), drug use and drug dealing become common, if intermittent, elements of his life. Drug sales are commonly a means of *supplementing* income for Stanley and many of the men he here represents. Occasional drug sales (and other financial windfalls) also enable him to lavish unexpected money on his "estranged" wives and children, which for Stanley is a way of proving to them (and himself) that he is responsible and "doin' good." (The latter phrase can be read in several ways, including financial and moral.) Despite a relatively unproblematic history of alcohol, marijuana and powder cocaine use, crack, once he encounters it, gives Stanley trouble. He becomes, he says, "hooked very heavy." However, its sale is also a means, at times, of pulling him out of a financial bind and putting him back in good standing with his family. Like all other elements of his experience, drug "use" seems a two-edged sword. In Stanley's account of his past, drug use as intoxicant, and drugs used as commodity for sale, (both of which he acknowledges as "fallen" behavior), appear to be as thoroughly integrated into his social and cognitive universe as are his definitions of the nature and meaning of legitimate work, family obligation, and appropriate "Christian living." How he uses and evaluates any of these elements, it appears, is largely situational. He seems to have thoroughly internalized the older conventional ethic of duty and responsibility, which he learned at school, church, and home. But he also finds direction in a more contraventional ethic that features self-indulgence and immediate gratification. Like all of us, he imbibed this from the media of advertising and entertainment. All of Stanley's "educations" and "socializations" have been filtered through his experience growing up black in America with its attendant sense of exclusion, its resentments and desire for vindication. This he acquired in the streets, in the clubs, and in other informal institutions of black youth, including his extended family.

Stanley is stretched thin across several social and cognitive-emotional universes. When he gets stretched too thin; one resort is to heavy drug use; another is to drug treatment. Redemption House is at least his third such resort, and he is here for what is technically a second stay, after having been expelled temporarily for threatening violence against a fellow resident. He was readmitted following a mandatory month-long hiatus. Although he has found relative success at Redemption House, earlier attempts at other programs ended after short stays of less than three months each.

Stanley epitomizes the residents at both houses in each of the elements portrayed here: occupational and family instability, racial minority status, drug use (which generally includes periods of problematic use interspersed with periods of unproblematic or controlled use), drug sales, a history of two or three treatment attempts. His story, which I compare below with residents at Recovery House, demonstrates the complex tangle of social, cultural, historical, and social–psychological elements that constitute the context common to many, probably most, of the men I have met and observed in residential and other programs of rehabilitation, both secular and religious. It is my contention that attention to this complex of sociocultural and historical elements can tell us more about the difficulties that bring these men to treatment or training than can the almost exclusive attention to their real or supposed psychological "complexes" they receive at places like Recovery House, or the statistical machinations that support its claims of success.[14]

Transition from School to Work

Stanley tells of being inaugurated into the world of work by his father at a relatively early age, similar to many working-class men.

My father got me after-school jobs in the garment district [where he worked]. The money started looking good and I dropped out of school [at sixteen] for a job in the shipping department. [Eventually] I realized my job was a nowhere job. I couldn't support myself if I left my mother's house. So I went back to school, to GED school in my neighborhood. I was nineteen. I got my GED on the second try. I missed by one point first time.[15] I was smart enough, but I was a class clown.

   I started working in the garment district, again. Excellent company. Beautiful people. I was the only black there with a bunch of Jews. I had no problem. I started in December and they gave me a $1000 Christmas bonus. I worked for them for five years, shipping piece goods out. I produced business for them [with] my speed and accuracy. I was the only one with my own shipping department, my own phone.

Introduction to the High Life

Stanley was also introduced to the traditions of the "high life" by a family member. It was to become his preferred style, but it clearly interfered with his aspirations for the more traditional style of family life. Ultimately, Stanley's relationships with work and women became, at best, a pattern of on-again–off-again attempts to juggle the directions from both mainstream and alternative ethical modes.

My cousin lived around the corner from my high school. His wife was still in school, at Seward Park. She would have girls come over and I took boys from my all-boys school over there to hang. That's where I was introduced to marijuana and beer. That also introduced me to women...and...partying. I would live for the weekend.

Family Circumstances

Stanley's attraction to and difficulties with women also began at an early age.

The summer I graduated I got involved with an older woman. She was 24, but looked older. My mother said she *was* older and we had a big fallout, because she didn't want me with her. So I moved out and moved in with this woman. She had my child, who is 14 now.[16] But I wasn't ready for responsibility. She couldn't tie me down.

So after one year she left with my child. I didn't hear from her for over five years. She went to Africa and married this guy from Africa. She didn't know this guy had several wives over there. She had a son by him, but came back bitter, trying to look for me to take her back.

But by this time I was with this girl I knew from the neighborhood since we was kids. But she would never sleep with me. She was from a Christian background family [*sic*]; but not that Christian. [Stanley means not evangelical.] Her father was from the South, that backbone South where [fathers believe] "these are my girls, you [be] in the house at a certain time, that's it." He was very strict.

She saw all the things I did; saw the women I was with, but still wanted to be with me. But she would not give herself to me until she was 18. She had my daughter at the age of 24. She lives now just down the street [from Redemption House] on Fordham Road. At that time I was moving into more heavy drugs, y'see. When my second daughter was born; we were about to be married. And I know I should have married her right then and there. To this day, I knew I should have married that woman, 'caus'a how much she loved me. She'd do anything for me. I was cheatin' on her; I had two other girlfriends in Brooklyn and Manhattan. I was telling her that I was sleeping in the clubs. She was a Christian and couldn't go to the clubs. She was not a Christian [i.e., not evangelical, born again] but she was strict and couldn't go to the clubs. She didn't get high with me. She stopped smoking cigarettes when she had the baby. God came into her life two years after my second daughter was born. [That is, she was born again and joined a Pentecostal church.]

Introduction to crack

I was sniffin' cocaine at first, when I was playin' [these] games with my daughter's mother. [Then] my cousin introduced me to crack. I started smoking and I got hooked very heavy. I lost my garment district job. They fired me from lack of comin' in and livin' up to the potential I was first givin' 'em. I became lackadaisical, and missed work and so forth.

Treatment

[Later] I was working in a church, cleaning the church. I was still using cocaine and crack. [Then] I got fired from the church; so I tried a program, The Half in Pennsylvania. It was supposed to be a Christian place, but they smoked cigarettes and cursed. Our work consisted of cutting down trees. We were 25 miles from the nearest town. These people were white. They put all the blacks in a group under a big black guy who had a $2000-a-day habit.[17] When this man had his moods, he would take them out on whoever was there. And I have a temper, so I couldn't deal with him. I told him, "We got all these saws and axes in this house, go ahead and go to sleep." They shipped me outta there. They hurried up and shipped me outta there, 'cause they thought I was gonna do damage to this guy.

Then about a year later, I went to a program up in Yonkers. There was too much favoritism there, for Puerto Ricans. I lasted there about a coupl'a months, too.

A Change in Circumstance

Drug treatment does not seem to help Stanley, perhaps for obvious reasons. However, a new tack in the world of work does seem to have some association with bringing his errant drug use under control. It may not be incidental that the new job situation includes relocation to a southern city where crack is not as readily available. But the move came only after six months of training in New York City. It may also be that the opportunity to realize, albeit in a diminished form, a childhood occupational dream redirects Stanley's attention to his latent conventional aspirations and vitiates, for a time, the urge to resort to abusive styles of drug use. When important aspects of his life seem to be moving in a more satisfying direction, more in tune with conventional career lines, Stanley seems to have little trouble keeping his substance use within recreational boundaries.

Then I went to Superior Training School, in home studies for heavy equipment. I studied for six months on front loaders, back loaders, tractor dozers, how to break them down, do oil change, change tires, etc. Then they sent me to Florida for another month's training on the machines. I got a student loan that I was suppose' to pay back when they got me a job. I said okay, maybe this is it. I [had] studied architecture at Manhattan Tech High School, so maybe I couldn't design the buildings, but now I could help build them.

So, on the construction job what we was doin' was building foundations and layin' terrain for the houses, beautiful houses, $200,000 houses down there where the cost of living is low. I was living in...[a place with] wall to wall carpeting....

I was makin' $13 an hour and sending money to my daughter to show her mother I was doin' good [i.e. being a legitimate success as bread winner].

Here is an indication of Stanley's continuing aspirations toward legitimate occupational success that are consonant with conventional values of the "work ethic." Stanley wants a decent, respectable, well-paying job. He wants the opportunity to be creative, to "do something" with his life. It is an aspiration that he traces back to high school and an interest in architecture that he let get away from him for the youthful pursuits of immediate cash and the excitement of the clubs. "Maybe this is it." Perhaps this is what will provide the meaningfulness he craves and the solution he has been seeking for his difficulties with cocaine and his family life.

Now Stanley has attained a position that qualifies him for acceptance according to conventional American values as well as the more stringent version of that ethic held by, as he describes her, "my daughter's mother, the desire of my heart." Unfortunately, just as Stanley is getting settled, temptation strikes from an unexpected quarter. It is the kind of temptation that threatens his hopes for reuniting with his wife. However, it is at the same time an offer that no self-respecting man of the streets can pass up and save face. Stanley's marginal social position and resultant dual structure of consciousness places him at a distinct disadvantage in the struggle to maintain his foothold in conventionality. Stanley, to change the metaphor, finds himself on the horns of a dilemma.

One day I was at the water fountain at the church and this lady says hello. She was 44 years old. She invited me to lunch. I didn' know this, but she had been followin' me on the bus. I didn' pay it no mind, but you get in the flesh.

Here Stanley means that he becomes overwhelmed by desires that are identified as "fleshly" or sinful. The term, taken from the King James Bible, is central to the American evangelical understanding of denial or rejection of bodily urges, especially sexual desires. From the perspective of young black manhood, however, it is precisely this sort of attractiveness to women that demonstrates one of the essences of true manliness (Oliver 1989). In retrospect, at least, Stanley is not altogether unaware of the contradiction in which he found himself entangled on this and other occasions, as his next comments indicate.

You trying to do the right thing, but then you got all these women around you, heh heh heh [Stanley lets go with a deep-throated chuckle in which can be read a combination of his delight at being the center of feminine romantic attentions, and at the same time a bit of nervousness, since he is uncertain whether I share the ascetic morality of the training program]. And down there it was much easier to pick up women, especially if they know you [are] from New York.... But I was trying to do the right thing in God's sight. I went to the church, right? But there was this woman and she wanted to be with me. This woman, she blew my mind, the things she was doin' to me, and all she wanted to do was that! So I kept fallin' and fallin'. I knew I wasn't growin' in Christ.

As Stanley begins to backslide, circumstances arrange themselves in such a way that more pressure is brought to bear on his resolve toward conventionality. Two fiscal events, one negative, one positive, contrive to incline him back toward the streets he left behind for a new career rather than toward the suites he was building as part of his new occupational direction (i.e., conventionality).

> Then I finally went to work for the construction company, but they close down at Christmas until May.[18] So I went to work for a clothing company (Miller & Rose). I worked there [over the Christmas season]. 'Bout that time the garment district company found me, 'cause they had another [! profit-sharing] check for me for $2000. I jumped on a plane for New York [to claim the money]. I went to visit my daughter and her mother to give them some money and she said, "Stan, I been praying for $500 and here you come with this money." So she figured I was doin' good down there. And I was. I wasn't into no drugs down there. I weighed 200 pounds because of that southern cooking.

Stanley was "doin' good" both financially and "spiritually." He was able to provide some financial assistance for his family just when they needed it, which makes him look good in his wife's eyes. He becomes an answer to her prayers, yet another evangelical indicator of divine operation, if not approval. But also he's "doin' good" by not "doin' bad." He was not into drugs during his stay in Virginia, at least not yet. However, this was about to change.

It is interesting how Stanley's simple change in geography and job situation (which, of course, includes a change in associates and opportunities) is accompanied by months of abstinence, or at least controlled use, something neither treatment program could accomplish in months of tree cutting or religious instruction.[19] Not surprisingly, precisely the same experience appears in resident accounts at Recovery House as well. Bud's account of his experience as a long distance ("over the road") truck driver provides an interesting parallel. In his case, whenever Bud is transferred to Georgia, he claims he stops using. But when he comes back to New York, he slips back into a pattern of bingeing that clearly interferes with his otherwise "responsible" work patterns.[20] Here he recounts one such experience.

> This one time I had stopped [using crack], y'know? I had stopped for about a year. When I'm down south in Georgia, down there with him [the boss, but working for the same company], y'know, I don't use. The thought [to use] comes, but it goes right away. As soon as I get in the TT [tractor-trailer] and I'm driving, everything's all right. We usually drive teams when we're running long distance. But coming back [to New York] my stomach starts flipping.[21] When it comes time to go to Georgia, I'm stable down there.

> Q: Do you think you'll be more successful in maintaining sobriety in Georgia?

> A: Yes. As long as I keep talking to people about my addiction; to people who understand. [There's a] lotta people who [are] naive about it. There's three people

down there I can talk to, my boss and three or four others. I'll probably be goin' to a lotta NA's and stuff between drivin' and whatever, NAs and AAs, to help keep my sobriety when I'm out there. Y'know?

For Bud, even more than for Stanley, it seems the change in geographic location is a key to controlling drug use. For both, however, a stable work situation is also part of the sobriety formula. As Stanley's story continues, his job situation is about to take another unfortunate turn.

Fallin' Again

It is interesting that this relapse occurred, as Stanley tells it, just as his circumstances involved an intersection of his two social worlds and their respective moral and ethical direction systems. Just as Stanley appeared to be making it in conventional terms, his new job laid him off. At about the same time, just as he had found the "church home" necessary to "growing in Christ," he encountered intense temptation from within the sanctuary. For a time he was able to maintain some equilibrium, but the appearance of a $2,000 windfall was more than his new-found stake in conventionality could take. He used the money according to the dictates of the street ethic, even when it gave the appearance—to his wife—that he was an answer to her prayers. Without yet a firm foothold (e.g., functioning family, secure job, steady income) on his climb up from the street toward the lower plateaus of conventionality, Stanley found the lure of the high life more enticing than the promised rewards of his new career and the passing pleasures of his equivocal experience in the church.

But Stanley has an excellent excuse for the choice he makes. He accounts for his "fallin'" in the midst of plenty, both of attention and financial assets, by resort to one of the common neutralizing techniques identified by Sykes and Matza (1957) and expanded upon by Scott and Lyman (1968). Stanley denies responsibility for his action, in this instance—even though he now "knows" he was in error—just as did the first human being to be caught in sin. In keeping with the biblical example, Stanley blames the Devil.[22] For good measure, he uses a variation on another neutralization, viz., appeal to a higher loyalty. He uses a good portion of the money he earns from his drug sales to help his cousin, who is a single mother in dire financial straits.

So I had about $1000 left and I bought $200 worth of crack to take back to Virginia with me. The Devil, he tempted me. I sold the nickel vials [$5 per] for $25 each. I made a killing. I made a killing! I spent the money on my cousin and her five kids, 'cause she had no husband to support her. We went to [a giant amusement park], and bought some school clothes. That's the way I am. I do something bad; then I do something good.

Stanley has, indeed, fallen from his precarious perch on the plateau of conventional approval. However, his fling (drift?) into criminality does not result immediately—or inevitably—in a life of depraved drug use and criminality. After sharing both windfalls, the profit-sharing and the profits from its investment in crack, Stanley returns to the world of conventional work.[23] There he encounters the one force that seems to push him over edge and plunge him headlong back into the street ethic of contraventionality. Racism pushes its way into the formula that shapes Stanley's negotiations with conventionality in a more direct, forceful, and fateful way than it has up to this point in his account.

Black spokespersons of various stripes: writers, ministers, social scientists, poets, novelists, dramatists, psychiatrists, have made it clear to us that all black Americans must cope daily with the constant din of institutional and institutionalized racism (discrimination) ringing in their ears, stinging like grains of sand in their eyes, and grinding like pebbles—or worse—in their mouths. Even when not directly confronted with the coarseness and indignity of open racial hostility—not to mention the threat and reality of its repeatedly associated violence or the costs of the personal rage that racism engenders in those who are targeted by it—black Americans (and other minorities) must negotiate a maze of bitterness and malice (some projected; much more real) for which they bear no responsibility beyond the color of their skin (or, for others, their country of origin, or their religious or political commitments or sexualities). This is a task, nay, a demand that makes life difficult enough to negotiate day in and day out without "fallin'" below the parameters of conventional ethical and moral conduct set by the dominant (white, Anglo-European) culture.

What Stanley encounters next, and perhaps the nature of his immediate response to it, must be appreciated as an integral part of the forces that impinge on him as he attempts to cope with the circumstances and options life presents to him.

Before the construction started, I [had] worked in my aunt's hospital, Richmond Memorial. She's a nurse. [Because it was still the off season, I began] working at the hospital again. I was cuttin' the grass durin' the day. Also, about the same time, I got a job with a contractor that [cleaned the operating rooms at night for the hospital] for $8 an hour. I can't remember the hours, but I think I worked from five [p.m.] to one [a.m.]. We would put on all white and go in there and spread bleach all over the OR [operating room] floor, 'cause they had to be spotless. So I was workin' during the day, cuttin' the grass and at night in the OR with the contractor. I lost both those [jobs] by one man. What you call those, a hospital administrator? But he was in charge of the kitchens, the laundry staff, housekeeping crew, grounds crew; and this man, he hated people. He definitely hated black people. I could see that from the way he treated people. He definitely hated black people. I'll never forget his name, its P____ A_____.

[One day] he came [at me] in his Jeep. A women asked me where was her son, because I was working with her son. He was picking up the grass. I told her where her son was. [Then, PA] pulled up to me, [with] all his other executives sittin' in the back seat. And he asked me what was I doin'? I said, "I told her where her son was." He said, "All I wanna see your black ass doin' is cuttin' grass or takin' out the garbage." Right then and there, like I told you, I had a bad temper. I snapped.

I snapped. I tried to kill that man. They had to call security to get me off the property. I said, "You don't call me on my character. You don't talk to me anyway you
want. I don't care how much money you payin' me, you don't call me on my
character."

Q: You attacked him physically?

A: I tried, but they stopped me before I could get to him. And I tried to kill this man.
And it was about time, because the way he was treatin' the people was very wrong.
The way he talked to them was very wrong.... So I lost that job. And he put the word
out, if I come back on the hospital grounds, they supposed to arrest me. So I said,
"Okay, well, I still got my night job, 'cause I still got [rent to pay on] my apartment
and all that," y'know. So I'm sittin' down eating my little snack before work, y'know.
Security comes up and says, "You know you not supposed to be here?" I said, "I'm
working for Ronnie [in the OR].... [Security:] "But you still on hospital grounds."
I said, "Oh no." So I lost that job.
   That's when I got frustrated. I di'n' wanna go look for nothin' [no job]. I started
buyin' crack, drinkin' heavy. I said, every time I try to do something I...[*pause*].
Instead of leaning on the Lord and going back to the church, I took it in my own
hands and started fallin'. I lost my apartment. Couldn't move back with my aunt.
(That's why we still apart today.) [Eventually] I was wanderin' the streets, sleepin' in
abandoned buildin's, and my cousin came and got me and called my mother in New
York and my mother and her boyfriend drove down and picked me up.... Then...I
fell back into the drug scene again, livin' in my mother's [hotel] in a six room apartment with my brothers.

It was only a few months after returning to the "people places and things" of
New York that Stanley received another financial windfall, which he also spent
on exorbitant gifts to members of his family and other forms of high living.
Soon after, distraught over continued rejection by his "daughter's mother," he
tried to commit suicide, failed, decided to "try Jesus" (again), and ended up at
Redemption House. This part of his story is told in the next chapter, "Resident
Accounts." Before discussing Stanley's situation, I want to compare it with that
of one of the men interviewed at Recovery House to attempt to demonstrate how
different men from different backgrounds can get caught in similar contradictions in pursuit of the American dream and how the influence of the high life
can both compensate for and complicate such aspirations.

Andrew

   Andrew began life with more opportunities than Stanley. Nevertheless, his
life and his aspirations became entangled by many of the same difficulties that
confounded Stanley. Andrew, too, experienced both occupational success and
failure. Like Stanley, he occasionally resorted to illegal drug sales to supplement
his income and drug use. Like Stanley, Andrew's drug use varied, generally
with the extent of the problems in his life. Even more than Stanley, his inabil-
ity to establish a stable and satisfying family life contributed significantly to

his difficulty with drugs. Andrew used drugs both as a means to cope with his psychic pain and sense of self-deficiency and, as things got worse, as a basis for relations with women. Although Andrew was not directly involved with the street culture in the way Stanley was, he fell under its influence through his wife and other family members. Andrew was not a stranger to the culture of street drug use, but he was not the "operator" that Stanley was.

Andrew, like Stanley and many of the men I interviewed, lived a social existence straddling two cognitive worlds that contrasted sharply with each other at certain points. Sooner or later, these points of contrast became horns of a dilemma for each of them. This dilemma appeared regularly in the accounts of the men of Redemption House and Recovery House, and in many cases included overt encounters with racism and/or other forms of exploitation or abuse. The elements in Andrew's dilemma vary, in some ways considerably, from those in Stanley's tale. As a whole, however, they both offer virtually the same set of contradictions and difficult choices that induce too many young men in their position into problematic involvement with illicit substances in ways that leave them little recourse but to seek help from the treatment industry, another choice that is far from ideal.

Transition from School to Work

Andrew, a resident of Recovery House, had a more circuitous route to the job market than Stanley. He landed on a somewhat higher rung of the socioeconomic ladder, but he also began with more advantages so that his landing was not all that auspicious.

As he tells his story, Andrew "came from a middle class family."[24]

> I went to public school with Hank Aaron's kids and kids of civil rights advocates, including the King family. My mother took my brother and I to church every Sunday and tried to get us involved in church activities. I was in the church choir for a while as a kid.
>
> During high school my parents were divorced. My father passed away in my mid-twenties. In high school I was pretty independent because my mother traveled a lot selling hair-care products and teaching courses in cosmetology at trade schools. My father lived in town, but I was very independent. I had a job, I was into track and field, and my mother trusted me. I was into T[ranscendental] M[editation] also. Those things kept me focused.

Like most middle-class kids, Andrew went to college. His prowess in sports provided a scholarship at a prestigious institution. He had high hopes, but fate dealt him an unexpected hand and he wound up selling burgers and going to school on the side. It was, as he says, "a period of frustrations." This is prime territory for induction into the high life even after decades of dedication to discipline and focus on the future. Andrew had just the right friends to show him the ropes.

After high school, I got a track scholarship to Tuskegee Institute. It didn't last too long. I got an injury to my leg...and I lost my scholarship [during my first year]. I had trouble with the stress of having to run faster and compete harder, learning how to study, and all that. [Also,] I had financial problems and lost 20 pounds in two months. So I came back home to Atlanta. I went back to get a job and go to community college. First I was a business major, then I switched to information systems. I ran into some roadblocks and got frustrated and let it go. I ended up managing some fast food chain stores.

Introduction to the High Life

Andrew's introduction to the traditions of the high life came a little later than Stanley's, but it followed similar paths.

This is the time that I started druggin' [because my running career was over]. I had a friend who did drugs at parties. He would sniff coke and have a beer. He [used to] call me names: health kid, sissy, pussy, because I didn't use anything [when I was running]. I used to drink beer watching football or playing chess, but that's all. [At this time,] I started off sniffing cocaine, and I was very much under control with sniffing on weekends [only].

Family and Work Circumstances

Andrew also found "strength" to control his drug use when his life took a turn for the better in both family and work situations. Like Stanley, he also reawakened (or rediscovered) aspirations that had lain dormant for some time, during a period of apparent aimlessness.

When I reached 25 I got a pretty good job and my attitude changed.... [I began] working for Atlanta Rapid Transit. I started as clerk typist in the maintenance facility. I saw a job with a future rather than a job you just do on a daily basis and then eventually quit [because it's going nowhere]. I worked in accounting and parts and maintenance. [Then,] I developed an interest in becoming an electrician. So I went to the [union] local and took a test. I passed and they offered me a program that took five years to become an electrician. I quit an $11 per hour job to make $6.35. I always wanted to do something where I could have my own business.
This is also at the time [when] I got married. I waited until I was almost thirty to get married because I wanted to be sure it was the right thing to do.

But like Stanley, not everything went according to plan for Andrew. In the course of training for the job that was going to allow him to obtain his piece of the American Dream, Andrew encountered the same form of discouragement Stanley faced on his hospital job.

The training program was very racist. They let African Americans in, but we ended doin' all the busy work. They [regularly] sent me on a construction site and rather than [observing] and learning, they had me sweeping and unloading light fixtures, gettin' coffee, things of that nature. I rode with it. I studied hard at the school, learned on my own, and eventually they realized it and gave me [some] job assignments.

Tragically, Andrew also faced family difficulties at about this same time. Not only was his childhood tainted by a divorce that left him on his own and lonely, but he suffered a divorce as an adult also.

Then the real cloud [appeared] in my life. I got divorced. When I got divorced I went through a lot.[25] We were married for three years and lived together for three years before that. The reason [for the divorce] was my wife was working and she would go off to work early in the morning and not come back until around one o'clock next morning. My son was one year old and he used to sit up to wait for her. This really bothered me, it tore me up. That led to fights, arguments. I was very much in love with her. It was like all my dreams and everything I worked hard for clouded up and, y'know, it was like a big nightmare. The biggest problem I had was the loneliness I felt when my wife divorced me. I was also concerned about being a father to my son.

Interestingly, the same family connections that proved so disappointing to Andrew were significantly implicated in his associations with the drug culture.

A: I started selling a little marijuana on the side to kick in a little extra cash.

Q: How did you get connected to do that?

A: From my wife. She smoked. I have to give her credit, she went to school, maintained a very good average, finished, and continued to smoke the whole period of time. She knew how to control it. She had a lotta friends who smoked also. I was supplied by her dealer, he was connected with Jamaicans. I dealt strictly to friends and associates.

Introduction to Crack

The discovery of crack was also an important element in Andrew's story.

Getting back to cocaine, I was [always] very much under control with sniffing. If I had to work some overtime, that's some extra money to blow away. In the beginning it was just weekends, a weekend type of deal... Then my best friend got introduced to crack around [eighteen months ago]. So I naturally picked up on it and I been doin' it from that time 'til [I came to Recovery House]. It seemed like I couldn' keep it under control [like the powder cocaine].[26] I moved in with my mom to see if I could get myself together. I was having problems on my job. I couldn' get along with folks. [I wasn't smoking on the job].

When his conventional world goes to hell, when those mainstream aspirations for family and career are dashed, can it be surprising that Andrew resorts to the gratifications that are touted by the ethic of contravention rather than the promise of the conventional ethos that has failed him yet again?

I had like a "stuff it" attitude [like Stanley's frustration] and I started doin' more and more and more [crack].... I continued to party with my friends and I became a functional addict. When I needed money, I did some sideline work [in the underground economy, non-licensed electrical work] and got some money. Or I'd buy enough [crack] where I could sell some and make a little profit, not spend so much on it. Somehow I got [along]. I was making $125 a day and in the afternoon I'd hustle $50 or $60 or, if I'd get lucky, get $200. I never stole or robbed anybody [like some other Recovery House residents had]. I always believed in working hard for what I get. Even when I was druggin', I was working, and used my money that I worked hard to get. So I was still a functional addict.[27]

Treatment

At this point, Andrew began a relationship with a woman who was also a user. For reasons he does not explain they decided to stop using and tried some local treatment programs to little avail. His experience in treatment is, in its results at least, not unlike Stanley's

Then I ran across a young lady who was active doing [crack] as well. We dated for a while. Once we both tried to quit. But rehab in Atlanta's not worth anything. It's so short term. We went to two or three different places. It didn't work out.

Shortly after these attempts, Andrew found himself locked out of his mother's house and sleeping in her car. This he calls "my bottom," using the twelve-step terminology that suffuses Recovery House discourse. ("Functional addict" is also part of that jargon.) At that point he called relatives in New York who worked in drug rehabilitation. An uncle, who works at another therapeutic community, is a graduate of Recovery House. Andrew was admitted within the week. Even here, contacts are all important to success.

One other interesting parallel between Andrew and Stanley's account involves their interest in religion. Stanley's (at Redemption House) interests are obvious throughout his account. Andrew's comments (at Recovery House) came late in our conversation and were unexpected and unprompted.

The only good thing that I was doin' durin' that time, the whole time I was druggin', was I was goin' to church every Sunday the whole time I was running, especially when I was on crack. I still had a small amount of faith. Something told me to start readin' the Bible, so I did. Then I started prayin' a little bit. I was still going from job to job, lose one get another.

I left everything in Atlanta. I left my girl. I left my son. I left my friends. I left some houses I had not completely finished wirin' up. I just dropped everything. I knew I was doin' the right thing. I knew nothing about a TC. When I started learnin' about what it was [after I got here], I just about left. But I also went through a thing called divine intervention. Like I felt I wanted to give my will over to God.

Discussion

The role of religion seems to have been instrumental in Andrew's entry into treatment at Recovery House—or at least he is trying to see it that way—just as it was for Stanley at Redemption House. Andrew was not alone in this regard. Although Andrew did not seem to be aware of it, there were at least three other men in my sample who understood their "process of recovery" in explicitly religious terms other than those typical of AA or NA recruits at Recovery House, i.e., twelve-step terms. I will have more to say about this in a later chapter.

Here, the central issue is the general tenor of the lives of these two men before they tried Redemption House and Recovery House, respectively, and how it illustrates what might be called the *contextualized* (or grounded) demographic profile that typified many of the men I interviewed at both programs.[28] Here, I am particularly concerned with how the experience of these two men illustrates the way demographic circumstances (especially race, education, family status, occupational skills) interweave to create scenarios of opportunity and impediment that they must negotiate in their attempts to carve out lives for themselves. Partly because of the nature of their demographic circumstances, the terms of negotiation proposed by these two men are the product of at least two different and often contradictory moral and ethical traditions. Each tradition has its own moral logic, and both have significant influence over the choices Stanley and Andrew have made and the directions their lives have taken.

As Matza (1964) would argue, Stanley and Andrew are neither totally free agents, nor totally determined subjects (of either biological or sociocultural circumstances). They stand, rather, at the intersection of freedom and determinism, capable of making choices, of exercising will, of acting as moral agents, but in ways that are bounded and limited by the opportunities and impediments they confront in their demographic and cultural circumstances. Certainly neither can choose to be white. But Stanley can choose to marry, if his proposed spouse will agree. By age thirty-five, the choice to be an architect is virtually beyond his reach, and he knows it. But he is able to choose to drive a bulldozer to help build the structures someone with more opportunity, or better choices, has architecturally designed.[29] But is he able to choose not to use drugs, highly reinforcing substances? Certainly under suitable circumstances! Is he *always* "free" to choose not to use drugs? It certainly appears to be a more difficult choice under different, less than suitable circumstances. Calculating the ratio between "doin' good" and "fallin'" is more difficult when you have to factor in disappointment, loss, humiliation, and repeated frustration.[30]

Andrew's account includes many of the same elements found in Stanley's: underemployment despite personal efforts, conventional occupational aspirations frustrated by various forces including overt racism, romantic and family difficulties that add to disappointments, encouragement in activities of the high life from using friends and family, and previous "failed" attempts at treatment. His calculus is much the same as Stanley's.

Does this logic include a biological or psychosocial impediment? There is certainly no consensus on this question—and little hard evidence. The problem I see with this form of the question (can they choose not to use?) is that it eliminates the elements of life that are highlighted by a sociological or anthropological approach. It sees the Andrews and Stanleys as, in essence, isolated individualities. The bio-psycho-social determinist (disease or disorder) view prized by the treatment community, a view shared at least in part by most medical and mental health personnel, sees the Andrews and Stanleys as singularities who are bounced around by the "forces" in their "environments" like so many billiard balls or lifeless planets. On the other hand, the moralist view typical of Redemption House also individualizes and isolates them from all context but moral demands (just say no).

Andrew and Stanley are thinking and acting beings, members of a species unique on this planet, because they create meanings and try, at least, to direct their behavior in accordance with those meanings. Certainly those attempts can be thwarted or impeded by biological and/or psychosocial hindrances. But that is just the point. Life is extremely complex and paradoxical. Many of the men I spoke to expressed the desire to act in a certain way, but also expressed serious doubt that outside of treatment they would be able to do so. And the high recidivism rates support those doubts. Are they lying to themselves and me and the staff? Are they morally weak? Are they diseased or disordered?

The question to ask, it seems to me, is what changes when they leave treatment or training? The most obvious change is their immediate social circumstance—their opportunity structure and their cultural surround, the chorus of individuals and groups who mediate the world of meanings and perception for them. There is a centuries-old philosophical principle known as Occam's razor. It suggests that when faced with many possible solutions to a dilemma, the simplest or most obvious is probably the best. To look for an explanation for this paradox of treatment or training and relapse, the simplest and most obvious answer is the varying contexts in which different choices are posed and made. When Stanley and Andrew are working and are relatively happy with their family circumstances, their drug use and other behavior is less dangerous and destructive. When their love lives are disappointing and their jobs are boring and humiliating, their recreational activities take on more significance and tilt in the direction of risk and harm to themselves and others.

As I read it, Stanley's life (or Andrew's) does not display an *inevitable* downward spiral of drug use, degradation, and despair. Rather, it appears to involve a cycle of ups and downs, (and in-betweens) with recreational or celebrational or moderate drug use (or abstinence) characteristic of those times when life is relatively good: when he is working, when his "daughter's mother" sees him "doin' good," when he seems to have a future that holds some promise of personal fulfillment in familial and/or occupational terms that approximate conventional definitions of success. During these periods, Stanley's celebration and recreation tend also to partake of the street ethic of masculinity, which causes him difficulty and perhaps some confusion about what his aims are in life. His attempts to maintain some semblance of both ethical directions, while a delicate balancing act between womanizer and family man, worker and schemer, do not inevitably lead into the kind of necessary failure that abstinence programs, both religious and secular, project in their rhetoric. As social control theorists predict, the closer Stanley stays to conventional others and activities, the more conventional his personal behavior remains (see Goode 1997; Hirschi 1969).

However, his marginal circumstance in life does provide Stanley with (supposed) coping mechanisms (alternative selves with attendant alternative meanings of success and failure) that he often resorts to when things go badly for him in conventional terms. When his dream job fails to materialize, when the woman he describes as "the desire of my heart" refuses to be his spouse for reasons that are more religious than romantic, Stanley has somewhere to turn for both the money he needs to pay his rent and the passion he desires/needs to feel good, also the escape he needs/desires to hide from feeling down.

Because Stanley resorts to these devices in periods of desperation and despair, that does not mean that he prefers them to his job as a heavy equipment operator (or, perhaps, even as a hospital grounds keeper) or life with his daughter's mother. His divided consciousness, between convention and contravention, his dual ways of viewing the world and the options with which it presents him, is, I contend, no less a habit than the crack use or womanizing that are condemned at Redemption (and Recovery) House. These habits are more than simple logical choices, obvious to everyone, but they are also less than fixed and immutable (biological or psychological) "traits" of character, or genetics. These patterns of life are better understood as wrapped up in the meanings that life events carry for Stanley (and Andrew and others in their circumstances) and how he *chooses* to respond to events and make his way in the wake of circumstances beyond his making or complete control.

What "being a man" or "being a success" means are not singularities for Stanley and Andrew or for other men (or women) in their "social location." The habits of mind, or better, the images of "(self-) interest" or, to use another, albeit, related language, (sub)cultural "logics of action" that direct or urge Stanley to follow one line of action over another are deep-set patterns (maybe even chemically inscribed somewhere in their brains) no more easily abrogated than is heavy cocaine or crack use.[31] But neither do they operate in a vacuum—again, just like a drug habit. They are part of intricate and complex social and social psychological dynamics that are all too often over-simplified by our attempts to

explicate them. I fear my attempt will be another oversimplification, nevertheless, I will take a crack at it.

In his "Economic Ethics of the World Religions" (translated as "Social
Psychology of..." in Gerth and Mills 1969) Weber writes:

> Not ideas, but material and ideal interests, directly govern men's conduct. Yet very
> frequently the 'world images' that have been created by 'ideas' have, like switchmen,
> determined the tracks along which action has been pushed by the dynamic of interest.
> "From what" and "for what" one wished to be redeemed and, let us not forget, "could be"
> redeemed, depended upon one's image of the world (Gerth and Mills 1969, 280).

I do not believe that I do any damage to Weber's point here when I suggest
that, as long as Stanley has concrete reasons to believe that following convention
holds promise *for him* (i.e., is in his [self-]interest), he is content (even anxious)
to follow his version of conventionality, adapted as it must be by his experience
in street culture and dark skin. When he can see, directly, that he, personally,
has something to gain from conventional action in the world, he generally
chooses that option, all other things being equal. But as a marginal man, Stanley
"carries" at least two images of the world, two of Weber's "switchmen," if you
will. One pushes in the direction of conventionality, delayed gratification, the
"good" life. The other urges Stanley in the direction of contravention, immediate gratification, the "high" life.[32]

When the promise of the "good" life dissipates, as it does so completely
for Stanley at the point of the racist attack by the hospital executive, it simply
reinforces the image of the world shaped by the street culture (the high life)
and the worst experiences of black people at the hands of white America. In
some instances it prompts what Stanley might call "riotous living," in the
language of the New Testament (KJV). In other instances it prompts what
Andrew, following Recovery House jargon, called a "stuff it attitude," which
tells the conventional world and its switchman to go to hell. Stanley might call
it a rebellious or "hardened" heart. In this light (in terms of the contraventional
view), Stanley's *logical* resort is pursuit of the high life. At the intersection of
job loss, continued family alienation, increased drug use and related criminal
activity, there occurs a switch from a pattern of life headed, more-or-less,
down the track of conventionality to a track more inclined in the direction of
contraventionality. "That's when I got frustrated. I didn' wanna go look for
nothin' [no job]. I started buyin' crack, drinkin' heavy." Likewise, Andrew,
who "started doin' more and more and more [crack and] continued to party...
[and] became a functional addict."

But this is not a one-way track. Stanley's life witnesses this because he came
back from this and other visits to the bottom end of the cycle (to return to a
previous metaphor), including resort to treatments that were unsuccessful. This
seems also true for Andrew, but it is less clear in his particular case, perhaps
because his career is at a relatively early stage. (Bud's different experiences

with drug use in Georgia and New York are also instructive here.) I suggest that Stanley's current visit to Redemption House is typical of this point in the cycle (or location on the track) and that had Stanley found—or been offered—another job similar to earth-moving equipment operator, his choices and activities would have "switched" in the direction of conventionality once again. At that point, he was morally exhausted by the impediments he had encountered in his negotiation with conventionality and lacked the social resources to protect him from choosing to opt out. When he was rescued from his despair, it was by his parents who returned him to New York and the social and familial context ("people, places, and things," as they say at Recovery House) that reinforced his high life choices all along. Stanley had not reached some ultimate moral or personal nadir. He simply ran up against the limits inherent in his contextual demographics, his socially constructed social location. He needed assistance, perhaps even "treatment." But, not necessarily the sort of abstinence-only program typical of our prohibitionist culture. What he needed, I contend, was to have his opportunities enhanced, e.g., another real job offer, preferably away from his current drug-using associates.[33]

Donald

There is good reason to maintain my skepticism about the unquestioning belief in the inevitable downward spiral to moral and physical ruin maintained in the rhetoric of the dominant recovery movement, including both the therapeutic community and faith community wings.[34] Several of my informants provide evidence for the more cyclical (vs. spiral) model of heavy drug use that I have indicated in the accounts of Stanley and Andrew.

Donald, a resident at Recovery House, whose contextual demographics are different in a variety of ways, nevertheless demonstrates a similar up and down struggle with hard drug use. Donald is more solidly conventional than most of the residents I met at either program. His contact with the street culture is minimal and mediated almost exclusively through his drug use and purchases. He was introduced to crack by a high school friend with whom he previously scored coke and played basketball.

> I started when I was 25, 26 smoking crack-cocaine. I was unmanageable behind that after a year or two. Meaning I couldn't support myself. I was a sales manager for a water heater company. As a result of smoking, I lost my job. I was laid off for calling in [sick too often]. After…that job, I went to Pergament's, still using while I worked there. I worked there until I got robbed. I was kinda "feeny." It's a kind'a slang term meaning wanting the drug bad. And I done something I'm payin' for now, I'm on parole. I committed a robbery myself and went upstate [to prison] for two and a half years.
>
> [When] I came back home [I] was substance free until June, [about six months]. Then I would get high and stop and then on and off for a while. I was not unmanageable. I was more or less a social [user,] getting high [occasionally, on

weekends and so forth]. But I knew more or less back in my mind that if I kept going I would [become] unmanageable. And I kept going. It lasted for four years.

That is, Donald continued to use crack in a relatively controlled fashion for four years while he maintained both his job and a reasonable family life. Based on details supplied throughout our two-hour conversation, Donald appears to have had occasional crack binges during this period. He reports that "two-thirds of that time my using was manageable; it wasn't a binge." Most of his drug use was what could only be described as recreational. Even the binges lasted only a day or two, most often on a weekend, and then he would not use again for at least several days, until the next weekend, and usually much later. Often he would "abstain" for weeks at a time.

This pattern of bingeing is a common one among crack users and is not the same as physical dependence on (i.e., addiction to) opiates, for example, which produces a very different pattern of use requiring daily or almost daily use (see Bourgeois 1996; Reinarman and Levine 1998; Waldorf, Reinarman, and Murphy 1996).[35] As near as I can tell from his description, Donald's use was not very serious as compared with many other crack users at these programs. Nevertheless, Donald displayed what the "peers" would call "serious guilt" over his use, which he obviously felt was out of character with the rest of his life.[36]

> I can remember getting high and coming home and I would always come home after my kids would leave [for school], if it was a weekday. Crying, "Why am I doin' this?" It was just terrible where everybody I talked to would say, "Oh you're such a smart guy!" That's what would make it worse. If I'm so fucking smart, why can't I stop using crack?

During these four post-prison years of crack use, Donald rebuilt his life with the help of family members. Despite all of his conventional successes, Donald's middleclass guilt continued to eat away at him. His only confessor during this time was, unfortunately, his parole officer. Although Donald was attending Narcotics Anonymous meetings as part of his parole requirements, he did not voluntarily disclose his use in the meetings or to any of its members.

> I started working with my uncle who has a construction company on Long Island. From there I started working for _____ Sales, then I went to _____Valve. I was teaching sales and engineering there. My company trained me. They were manufacturers of industrial valves for water, oil, and gas. So I stopped that [job] when I came here. I came here because my parole officer talked [me into it]. I'm not mandated here. But every time I would get high, I would tell him. I was seeing him every two months. He would say, "What are we gonna do about it?" I met a guy through going to AA and NA who told me about this place. It took me two months to get in this program.

Donald was not suicidal, like Stanley, or mandated to treatment, like many other Recovery House residents. From all appearances, his life, unlike Andrew's just prior to entry, was relatively in order. Donald claims that he did not treat his wife and children very well as a result of his crack use, and that seems to have bothered him greatly. However, his descriptions of his "mistreatment" were well within the parameters of typical, if not "enlightened," family behavior. He did not describe any physical abuse of his family. At worst, he often ignored, occasionally verbally misused, and, at times, humiliated his children. While he blames his crack use for this behavior, he also tried to protect them (and himself) from any knowledge of his drug use. I doubt that his drug use—and certainly not the drug use alone—is accountable in any significant way for how Donald related to his family. I suspect rather that this causal connection was made as a result of the time (four months) he had already spent at Recovery House.

As part of a new resident's assimilation into the therapeutic community, it is necessary that he or she "confess" to the ways that drug use has destroyed his or her life (see Hood 2011a, especially chap. 4). Given Donald's conventional existence, his stable job situation and current lack of criminal activity, it must have been difficult to discover indicators of moral decline beyond the drug use itself. (His earlier crime was truly an aberration that perhaps more than anything demonstrates the illusory nature of the idea of an inevitable downward spiral.) In order to display personal progress in treatment, however, Donald needed some way to "see" his recent crack use as debilitating. Emotional and verbal abuse of his children was perhaps the best he could come up with given the largely conventional reality of his life. It is quite likely that he, his peers, and counselors seized on this "sad tale" to legitimate his addict label and interpret his relatively benign drug habit as inevitably destructive of his relationships.[37]

The point is, Donald's account of his drug use provides very little detail to indicate that his life was in ruin, despite more than a decade of cocaine use and his own claims and fears to the contrary. In fact, the detail he does provide contradicts his own analysis. Donald had put his life back together following what for anyone not a member of the street culture had to be a terrifying and confusing (and statistically atypical) experience. He paid his debt and with help of family members had rebuilt a relatively stable family and occupational existence. All the while, he was maintaining a crack habit! He argues, and assuredly his peers and counselors at Recovery House reinforce this view, it was getting bad in the last few months. And perhaps it was. He claims to have lost one job previously to crack use. But I suggest the inevitability is more rhetorical than real in Donald's case. Donald seems to have believed the twelve-step prophecy of inevitable decline, and was expecting its fulfillment immanently. (In Donald's case, at least, the prophecy was working.) As he indicated, what he agonized about most was simply that he could not stop, not that he was in danger of losing his job or his family. The only real danger evident in his account was the danger of being "violated" by his parole officer and being sent back to prison.

This is not an insignificant consideration, but not an indicator of addiction so much as punitive prohibition.

Although there is real personal and familial devastation associated with crack use in many instances, it does not appear to be the case with Donald.[38] Nevertheless, the treatment system demands rhetorical purity (i.e., orthodoxy). Donald's guilt and fears were not enough; he was required to produce evidence of crack's devastation in order to be processed through the steps deemed necessary for treatment success. Donald's life has to be seen to conform to treatment rhetoric. Donald, conformist that he is, went along, I suspect, because he wanted to be free of his drug habit and, especially, the guilt associated with it. With the cooperation of his peers and counselors, he had constructed an image of his life as out of control in spite of evidence to the contrary. (Well, perhaps his children were out of *his* control, but that's another issue.)

In spite of his rhetorical correctness, like Stanley, Donald supplies clear evidence, that his crack use is not pharmacological enslavement and that, given the right opportunities, recreational crack use need not lead to inevitable decline of morals and behavior. Use often entails struggle and a cyclical pattern of "doin' good then fuckin' up," as one informant put it, which sometimes leads users to treatment at one or more of the low points in the cycle. But this is a rather different picture than is painted by the general discourse at Recovery House or Redemption House.

In Donald's case, certainly, he provides serious evidence of having put his one serious "fuck up" (the robbery for which he went to prison) behind him. And, except for dirty urines, there is little indication in his story that he is doing anything but "doin' good," despite certain personal shortcomings of the sort we all face. He was not on the road to moral, financial, or familial ruin, except that he was in danger of parole violation, and that alone could ruin his life. Perhaps it has already, since he is now in treatment and not at his job, with his family, or exercising his moral capacities "freely," because he is encapsulated at Recovery House, and when he leaves, will be forced to rebuild his life once again. The self-fulfilling prophecy of inevitable decline finds another victim via the criminal justice system. If this is not *criminal* justice, I do not know what is. The irony of this circumstance continues to be lost on the true believers at Recovery House and in the TC movement in general.

In contrasting different "ethical" aspects of and influences on the lives of my informants, I do not mean to contend that conventionality is somehow ontologically—or objectively—a better or more correct choice or set of goals than what I have been calling contraventionality. The preference for the former—as well as the latter—is itself a matter of social convention. Both ethical perspectives and the attendant structures of choice and action ("moralities of thought and logics of decision" *àla* Benjamin Nelson 1981, 99ff) and the values placed on them by various social groups are, of course, social constructions. As such, they can have no empirical priority. Their priority, that is, any preference for one over the other, stems from value positions not from empiricism. It is just that the perspective or ethic that I am calling conventionality happens to be shared by most of the population of the United States, including and particularly that segment that exercises and maintains economic and political power and control especially over those who prefer the contraventional view. As an expression of that power, one view and its attendant actions are labeled legitimate, and the other is labeled "deviant" and often "criminal." Thus, Stanley, Andrew, Bud, Donald, and hundreds like them also become "deviantized" or "criminalized" when they (get caught) engage (-ing) in essentially harmless, or at least victimless, activities. Their notions of themselves, their "identities," become stigmatized by these labels that are more "ascribed" by social forces beyond their control and understanding than they are "achieved" by any "evil" inherent in their deeds or intentions.[39]

Much of the official or formal labeling process with respect to drug use and sales is carried out by the criminal justice system. Increasingly, however, part of it is accomplished by the mental health care system where deviance is often "medicalized" and deviants become patients or "patient-like" in order to be cured of their "aberrant" world images and logics of action that do not correspond to the conventions of the age (Conrad and Schneider 1985). Stanley's deviance is seen in moral terms at Redemption House, a decidedly outdated motif for most of the treatment industry, although it continues a latent existence there as well. If Stanley resided at Recovery House, like Donald, he would be described more as patient than penitent. Whether this is actually the case or not, whether Recovery House and Redemption House are doing the same thing or two different things with their residents, remains the central issue of this book and its earlier companion volume (Hood 2011a). To continue along this comparative tack, I look at the account of Miguel, one more resident of Recovery House, in light of Stanley's experience.

Miguel

The account of Miguel at Recovery House provides a variation on the contextual demographics of drug users and the complex cycles they construct of their lives. It demonstrates the cultural and social marginalization typical of users from a somewhat different angle. Miguel's account differed in important ways from those already considered. Most immediately, Miguel was a heroin user rather than a crack user, like Donald, Stanley, and Andrew. This means that his patterns of use were different, in part because of the different pharmacological characteristics of the two drugs. Intensive crack use typically takes the form of bingeing. Users can spend prodigious amounts of time doing little else than pursuing a high, or their binges may last only days or hours. Heroin use, especially dependent use (or addiction), follows a more regular, long-term, daily pattern, wherein one injects two or three times a day, although this varies according to the size of habit, drug availability, and other factors (Johnson et al. 1985; Preble 1969).

As with Miguel, long-time heroin users develop alternating periods of use and abstinence, including treatment perhaps, but these cycles are rarely bounded by days or weeks. Heroin-use cycles are of longer duration, usually consisting of months or years. It takes weeks, if not months, to build a true physical dependency on heroin, and then often months of slowly increasing use before the habit becomes unmanageable and one begins to look for ways to back off, cut down, or quit.[40] The latter process may also take some time, and if a period of abstinence follows, it can be some time before the user starts up again, and yet more time to build another troublesome habit, and so on. At the worst point of their cycles of using, however, heroin and crack users often display similar chaotic and frenetic patterns of behavior. Nevertheless, the paths they have taken to these nadirs are often quite different.

Miguel was also different in another way. He was a man who displayed little of the split consciousness so evident in the accounts of Stanley and Andrew, but also shared little of the middle-class conventionality of Donald. Miguel told a story that had little sense of struggle, either moral or economic, yet he encountered many of the same demographic impediments the others had. The day I spoke with Miguel he had been a heroin addict for fifteen years. He had also been married for those fifteen years and had three daughters. His most regular source of income over that period was drug dealing. He spent two terms "upstate" in prison as a result of this activity. He had been in Recovery House for two weeks when we recorded this conversation. He was mandated to treatment because of a parole violation for dirty urine. His only alternative was to go back upstate to prison, which would take him away from his family. So Miguel opted for treatment.

Unlike the other men described above, Miguel is white. He was born in Puerto Rico to a family of eleven children. He was sixteen when he moved to New York with his wife and his father in 1979. Things looked good at first. He started working in a car wash, and a few years later became the manager. He went to school at night and learned to speak English by the time he was seventeen. However, the car wash was a double-edged sword.

Guys at the car wash smoked pot and drank beer. I started experimenting. Since I was working during the day and going to school at night, it was hard to stay awake. That's when someone introduced me to cocaine. This guy said, "Just take a few hits of this when you get up and you'll be awright." Sure enough, when I got up I took a few hits and it pepped me up. So I started using it every day to stay awake. I liked the little rush on it too.

Then I got to the point where I thought I was sniffing too much. I was messing up in school. I was missing days. In the morning I'd be sniffing and forget all about school. I was too lit up. So, I smoked pot to bring me down, but it didn' work too good. Then there was another guy in the car wash who used to use heroin. He used to mix cocaine and heroin and use the little needles. He used to go in this little room, and I had to [be a] lookout for him and I watched him. He would shoot up and he'd get all lit up one minute, I guess from the coke rush, and be all panicky and shit. Then the next minute he'd be all nice and relaxed and mellow [from the heroin].

One day I asked him could I try it and he said "Nah, you shouldn' mess with this." But I said, "Hey let me try it." I tried it out for the first time, and it was like Wow, a high I had never experienced before! At first I got this big rush even before the needle was out and I got like this tingling sensation in the top of my head and I just passed out for a couple of minutes. Then when I woke up I said, "Wow that was cool. Let's try it again." And a few hours later I tried it again. Then the next night, I said let me try the heroin by itself. So I did, and I liked that down little hit that it gave me, and I been with heroin ever since. I fell in love with heroin.

Miguel developed a heroin habit that escalated from $10-a-day to several times that over the next few months. To support his habit, he began embezzling money from the business and was eventually caught and fired. That is when he turned to dealing. He talks about this transition as if it were the most natural, untroubled progression imaginable. But then, this was the general tenor of his tale.

So, I was out of work for a while and one day, when I was a little short when I went to buy my drugs, the dealer said, "Listen, I can't give you a break, but if you hang out for a little bit here and watch out for the cops, I'll let you have a few dollars or a couple bags, whatever it is that you want." About a few weeks after that I started dealing drugs myself. I guess I wasn't that good of a dealer, 'cause about two weeks later I got arrested for selling. All I got was a DAT [desk appearance ticket].

Although the arrest was of little concern to Miguel, his heroin use had begun to intrude on his family life. He used the brief jail time he was given for dealing to "kick the habit," and thus began what was to become a fifteen-year dance with the on-again—off-again cycle typical of many heroin habitués.

My wife started noticing the difference in me. (She doesn't have anything to do with drugs, not alcohol, smoking, nothing, even to this day.) I wasn't that friendly any more. I woke up with an attitude, the shakes and what not. So we started having little problems between us. So I finally admitted I was using. Then, after I went to jail, it was just for a few days, I cold turkeyed there and kicked the habit and I said let me just chill for a little while and see if I can find me a job. My wife got me a job as a porter at the supermarket where she was working.

Miguel, apparently intended to try the straight life, but opportunity (to get high) was readily available to a man of his social and cultural location. Notice, however, that even though he returns to heroin and stealing from his employer rather quickly, he is able to maintain his job and not get caught pilfering for three years, an amazing example of controlled use. Following this, Miguel reports his return to the occupation that seems his true calling with no sense of remorse or hesitation, and without the need for any self-neutralization. He gives no indication of being divided between different systems of ethical direction. Working is working, "you gotta do it," whether it's selling groceries or street drugs, it's all the same. The risks are greater doing the latter, but he gives no hint of a sense of moral distinction.

One day I walked into the bathroom and the security guard was getting high; he was sniffing. I asked him where can I cop. We had moved. So I gave him some money and he came back with [some drugs]. Little by little, I started stealing from the supermarket. And I went back to heroin again. After about three years, they fired me for stealing, but because of my wife they didn't have me arrested. She was embarrassed, so she left too. After that I went back to the streets and sold drugs with the guys I worked for before.

Miguel prospers on the street and is promoted to supervisor of his own crew. Apparently, things are okay at home, too, because he has a new daughter. But soon Miguel experiences another down side of the user–dealer cycle.

One day a cop saw [a drug] transaction and arrested [me]. This was the first time I was really incarcerated. I got one to three [years] and that left my wife by herself with a new baby. We had this little basement apartment in [here he names the local neighborhood] Queens and the land lady was real nice. They took care of my daughter while my wife went to work. I did fifteen months. It was hard at Rikers [the New York City jail] because there was more drugs there than on the street. I was there for eight months. Upstate, where I did the last seven months, was even scarier than Rikers. So I came out of jail with a [heroin] habit.

Once again, the conventional horizons of his wife and family prompt Miguel to try to leave the street life and "settle down." In the process, he encounters the latest scourge of the drug-using community and two of the more promising and successful means of dealing with both the issue of AIDS and problems of substance use. Unfortunately, both programs Miguel encounters are limited in what they can do by archaic and irrational legal restrictions. Like all public support systems for the poor, these are not overly generous to or accepting of drug users, and going straight is more of a struggle for Miguel than dealing and using (though not more difficult than prison).

My wife told me it is either her or the drugs. So I cut down a little and then I detoxed myself over about two weeks. I started working again and I heard or saw people I used to get high with that had AIDS. One day I bumped into my wife's brother who was in a methadone program [and he] told me that he was sick and I went with him to get tested and he was positive. (He had helped me detox; when it got bad he would give me a few little pills to sleep and what not.) He got sick really fast and my wife helped me to take care of him. I was scared to get tested, but I was scared I had it, and it's really stupid, but I went and started getting high again [to help me deal with the emotional stress].

Then I got on the same methadone program as my brother-in-law. One of the counselors there told me about the underground needle exchange program. So I went one weekend [on their walkabout]. It was exciting; [we] had to look out for the police and whatnot. I got to know Allan Clear. He told me about the course I could take to be a volunteer, and I took that and [became a regular volunteer].

I was still on the meth program and I [occasionally] sold my weekend dose and bought drugs. Then I would pocket a few needles when I went around with the exchange and I would sell some of the needles and the whole *cycle started again*.[41] [Emphasis added.]

Miguel, himself, sees the cyclical character of his using and dealing career, at least as he tells this story in a semi-secluded storage room at Recovery House where this conversation took place. But he seems to indicate some sense of frustration with his cycle of seeming "eternal return" to the use of the needle. Given the experience of his brother-in-law and other fellow users, plus his training at the needle exchange that included extensive information on AIDS and its connection with injection drug use, Miguel appears to be looking for a way to end the cycle, or—perhaps more realistically—to find a safer way to continue. His account seems to indicate some uncertainty about how to deal with the new threats to his well-being. Also, he obviously still wants to please his wife, if possible. All of these pressures culminate in Miguel's next decision to stop using. Unfortunately, fate plays a hand that cannot be anticipated. And that hand, in turn, is only playable under the "table stakes" that are Miguel's contextual demography.

After a while I stopped messing with the heroin and I went back on the meth program again. I got me a regular job working for this little limo company, but had a bad accident. I was hit by a drunk driver. I got a lot of money.... I gave most of it to my Moms [and] my wife and I rented this little house, so the money went pretty quick. [Echoes of Stanley.]

The limo owner would drop me some money or drugs from time to time and I found myself going in that same direction again. I said if my wife finds out I'm messin' with drugs she's really gonna send me to hell this time. So I told the doc that I was using heroin and it was [blunting] the effect of the pills (Percodan). So he increased the dosage of the pills and I eased away from the heroin. But the fucked up thing was, now I was hooked on the pills. I had to go into detox to get off the pills.

But as all drug researchers and treatment professionals know, detox does not mean sobriety (Hood 2011a, chap. 1). The cycle is not over for Miguel, but its character is becoming more obvious to him. Even still, when the economic pinch comes to any of us, we turn to those resources with which we are most familiar and which are readiest at hand. Drug users like Miguel are no different from the rest of us in this regard.

Then I said [once again] let me try things straight for a while, but after awhile, with my little job and two kids at home, living in the same neighborhood, the money from the insurance was just about gone, I started selling drugs again. Then I start using again. So that whole cycle kept goin': use, slow down, stop, be okay for awhile, then gain my weight back, feel nice and healthy, whatever, and then start using again.

This is a fair capsulation of Miguel's using career, discounting the jail time and time in treatment, which to his mind are likely subsumed under the "stop" category. His account captures both major elements of this classic round of us-ing and abstaining and the typical extent of a using career, about fifteen years. As several researchers have shown, after about this period of riding the cycle, users begin to get the picture, as Miguel does, and either tire of it or find it too threatening to other valued aspects of their lives and leave their habits for good (though it often takes several tries, just like tobacco). In some cases, users simply cut back to more manageable levels of recreational use.[42] If anything, Miguel seems headed on this route, given the family pressures on him, the threat of HIV infection well fixed in his mind, and his numerous past detoxes. This cannot be a foregone conclusion, however, since the matter of making a living continues to confront him. Although Miguel had few skills, he was obviously intelligent. He was promoted to supervisor in a number of his jobs, both legal and illegal. And he did not seem to have the family and educational resources of Donald, nor the skilled training of Stanley or Andrew. Whether he would have taken this path or not cannot be known, since fate—or rather one of the contingencies typical of his contextual demography—once again took a hand in limiting Miguel's choices

Q: How did you end up at Recovery House?

A: I got busted selling drugs on 110th Street (we moved to Manhattan). I went away to jail and came back out last March. On parole, I gave a couple of dirty urines and they locked me up and they gave me the choice to finish my time upstate or come to this program.

One of the interesting things about Miguel's using career and its cycles is that he does not indicate any period when he is seriously "down and out." He was never homeless, and fortunately he avoided contracting HIV. Although he steals for drugs, it is always from an employer, i.e., he is employed at regular intervals and is always employable. The pressures to cut back or quit come from his "conventional" wife and his fear of jail and serious illness. His aspirations are relatively low by middle-class American standards. He lives day to day in a family-oriented existence rather than a future and career-oriented one. This ethos is common among first generation immigrants from "developing" areas. Although there are strong strictures against drug use in certain sectors of His-panic cultures, the traditional "peasant" approach to the cycles of work and play (good life and high life) fit comfortably with the street culture of drug use and petty crime that develops in the absence of regular opportunity for legitimate employment at a decent wage.[43]

The street drug culture is very adaptive for immigrant populations. This was as true for the Irish and Italians in the nineteenth century as it is for the Latinos and African Americans today. While Hispanic men and women are hard work-ers, they do not generally partake of a cultural ethos that puts ultimate meaning on work or occupation. Peasant (or quasi-peasant) cultures do not eat to work, but work to eat. Their ultimate meanings are found in family, religion, and community rather than in individual vocation, until they become assimilated to the dominant Anglo ethos, that is. Even the opposition of Miguel's wife to his drug use has more to do with the threat it poses to family stability, via his mood changes and the threat of prison, than it does with any sense of its inherent evil or threat to his "identity" or career.[44]

Miguel's drug use causes him very little in the way of a moral dilemma, especially when compared with Donald or Stanley. This is, I suggest, because it does little to violate the quasi-peasant canons of morality as they have been adapted to the street culture of inner city barrios. The "high" life for Miguel is not predominantly about partying and women or feats of masculine prowess. He loves heroin for the way it makes him feel. Except for the restrictions required by prohibition, his habit would likely create little interference in his desired style of life or aspirations. Were heroin readily available in legal, safe, FDA-controlled amounts and purity—at prices more in the range of alcohol or tobacco—his use would likely fit quite easily with his preferred manner of life and would certainly present no threat of disease or prison time. The fact that he finds himself in a treatment facility as an alternative to prison is purely contingent on the legal and not the pharmacological nature of the substance he chooses to ingest. So while the combined racial, educational, and population demographic "variables" play a role in "determining" his status as user and the choices he makes regarding use, the legal status of the drug seems a more relevant factor in understanding the personal *dilemma* or risk that Miguel faces regarding his drug use. His account does fit much of my contextual demographics profile, but he is decidedly not morally conflicted (or at least I could not detect it) about his use and that, I suggest, has more to do with his cultural background than with anything else.

Except for the color of his skin, Miguel's demographics parallel (or are "worse" than) the others in virtually every respect. Yet, his experience of his "addiction" is very different from theirs even while it follows many similar paths and patterns. Demographic data provide important variables in understanding the actions of individuals and groups. But as separate categories—or even combined in multivariate analyses—they often miss the context of meaning and purpose that ultimately give direction to user's lives and activities whatever their drug of choice (caffeine, nicotine, benzodiazepine, morphine, THC ...). Ideas about the world, its character and meaning, one's place in it, and one's relation to both "brothers" and "others" are what often, in the end, "determine" what track we take in the face of a given set of circumstances and its necessarily limited set of choices. Or so Max Weber saw it.

Meanings that are always socially constructed (both by and for us), and thereby deeply contextualized, are crucial to understanding why these men engage in the actions they do, both to use certain substances the ways they do and to seek to stop. It is those meanings that are buried in the stories they tell and how they tell them, and often to whom and under what circumstances they tell them. It is those meanings that I have attempted to uncover and understand in this investigation. Ultimately, it is only in the context of those meanings that the demographic data we gather so objectively can tell us—users, researchers, and user-researchers—what we want to know.[45]

Conclusion

In this chapter, I have argued for a more contextual view than is typical of much conventional treatment research about what sort of men come to treatment and training and why they have trouble with drug use. I have tried to see the lives of Stanley, Andrew, Donald, and Miguel as representative of the complexities and contradictions that my informants (mostly minority and poor users) encounter as they attempt to construct meaningful lives for themselves and their families. Given the impediments and limited opportunities they face, they use all means possible to negotiate a reasonable fate.

The means available to them for "making sense" and "making do" include at least two cultural systems of direction, two moral logics, which are often opposed to one another. This results in much ambivalence and often exacerbates their marginality. It results, as I have shown, in a "now they do, now they don't" pattern of adherence to what conventional institutions prescribe as appropriate conduct. The resultant attribution, however, is often unequivocal, especially when they encounter the criminal justice system. They are labeled deviants and drug addicts by society, its agencies of social control and correction, and, ultimately, by themselves. (They are also labeled sinners by the religious subcultures.) They then become candidates for redemption or recovery, both of which include a form of identity transformation or "re-labeling." Specifically how this happens in the context of religious and secular programs for rehabilitation was the subject of my earlier book (Hood 2011a).

As I have indicated, the overarching theme of the investigation in both volumes is the essential similarity of the two programs, how they process their "clients," and how the clients negotiate that processing. I argue for that similarity despite the claims of both programs to the contrary. More to the point of the present chapter, I have attempted to offer my view of who these men are and what their lives are about before treatment or training. Both programs are marked by the necessity of inducing "right thinking" in their residents. Right thinking means agreement with the program's ideology. In this chapter, I have tried to read between the lines of the residents' right thinking to see at least certain aspects of those previous lives still available in the their accounts.[46] I have used this evidence to argue a position that counters the similar ideological lines taken by both programs about the lives of my informants prior to treatment or training

Chart 1. Redemption House Residents[47]

Name	Occupation(s)	Education	Prev TX#	Prison	Ethnicity
Gordon	Drug counselor, US Marine	AA psychology	2	No	AfAm
Marvin	Bus schl faculty, systems consultant, US Marine	AA/BA computers	1	No	AfAm
George	Pimp, drug dealer, drug counselor	GED	2	Yes	AfAm
Slick	DJ, student, writer, drug dealer	HS graduate	2	Yes	H/A
AJ	College student, bootlegger/bartender	HS graduate	1	No	AfAm
Jake[a]	Cook, musician, stage hand	JHS dropout	2	Yes	W
Ervin	Building super, boiler cleaner	HS dropout	0	No	AfAm
Keith	Drug dealer, singer, songwriter	GED/1yr Com Coll	0	No	AfAm
Stanley	Heavy equipment. operator, hospital salesman	GED/trade school	2	No	AfAm
Martin[a]	Electrical repair, salesman	HS grad, some coll.	2	Yes	W
Alex	Clerk	Some HS	1	No	WI
Michael	Drug dealer	Seventh grade	0	Yes	AfAm
James	Unknown	HS	1	Yes	AfAm

[a]Redemption House staff.

Notes: Race/Ethnicity/Origin Key: AfAm, African American; W, White; H/A, Hispanic/African ancestry; H, Hispanic or Latino; WI, West Indian.

Education Key: HS, High school; JHS, Junior high school; GED, General education degree; AA, Associate of Arts; BA, Bachelor of Arts; CC, Community college; TX, Treatment.

Chart 2. Recovery House Residents[48]

Name	Occupation(s)	Education	Prev TX#	Prison	Ethnicity
Louie[a]	Cab driver, drug counselor	GED/three years college	2	No	W
Bud	Truck driver	JHS dropout (illiterate)	2	No	AfAm
Walter	Drug dealer, thief, owner security firm	GED/two years college (pre-law)	3+	Yes	AfAm
Rick	Construction, odd jobs	HS dropout	1	No	H
Jorge	Auto mechanic	Grade school	1	No	H/A
Roberto	Gang member, drug dealer, thief	JHS dropout	2	Yes	H/A
Donald	Construction, engineering sales	AA criminal justice	1	Yes	AfAm
Julio	Construction, accounting	HS and trade school	0	No	H/A
Tomaso	Construction, drug dealer, U.S. Army	HS dropout/ learning disabled	0	Yes	H
William	Security, stock clerk, sales, thief	Eleventh grade dropout	3	No	AfAm
Andrew	Apprentice electrician, restaurant manager, drug dealer	Two years college	1	No	AfAm
Miguel	Limo driver, thief, drug dealer	HS dropout	1	Yes	H
Robert	Delivery truck driver	HS dropout	2	No	AfAm
Nate	Drug dealer	GED in TX	0	No	AfAm
Forest	Bank account's clerk, drug dealer	Some college	3+	Yes	WI
Leonard	Key grip	HS grad	0	No	AfAm
Gary	U.S. Army, cook, jazz musician	HS grad	0	Yes	AfAm
Fred	Marijuana sales	Some college	0	No	W
Ricky	Hospital tech writer, union organizer	Some college	3	Yes	AfAm
Tommie[a]	Thief, drug counselor	HS dropout	1	Yes	H

(continued on next page)

Chart 2. (*continued*)

Artie	Gem counter, printer assistant, sales, manager	HS grad	1	No	W
Saul[a]	DJ, drug dealer, drug counselor	Some college	7	No	AfAm
Armando	Electrical repair	HS dropout	3	No	H
Barry	Homeless	JHS	2	Yes	AfAm

[a] Recovery House staff member

Notes: Race/Ethnicity/Origin Key: AfAm, African American; W, white; H/A, Hispanic/African ancestry; H, Hispanic or Latino; WI, West Indian.

Education Key: HS, high school; JHS, junior high school; GED, general education degree; AA, Associate of Arts; BA, Bachelor of Arts; CC, community college; TX, treatment

Notes

1. From "The Social Psychology of the World Religions," in Gerth and Mills (1969), 280.
2. Age is a crucial variable in the consideration of drug using and treatment populations. Most people who stay in treatment or training long enough to display what the literatures consider "positive effects," are over thirty. That the men I interviewed fit that category should be evident from the stories they tell. The "natural recovery" literature (see, for example, Biernacki 1986; Waldorf 1983; Waldorf et al. 1991; Winick 1962) also demonstrates the general "conventionalizing" effects of age on career drug users. My research only supports these findings. I do not focus on age per se, but only as it "folds into" the other categories, e.g., drug-use history.
3. There were a few men at both Houses whose ancestries included Caribbean cultures other than Hispanic.
4. This is, of course, a judgment call. Their representativeness is not statistical, but observational.
5. I.e., contentment or happiness. A more psychologically oriented observer might substitute the notion of "self-fulfillment" for meaningfulness. In our highly individualized society these may be considered interchangeable ideas.
6. The dramaturgic notion of cultural directive systems comes from Benjamin Nelson's work (1981). Also, much of the following argument is influenced by the theoretical traditions of strain and opportunity theory (e.g., Merton; Cloward and Ohlin) and subcultural theories from Walter Miller (1958) to Dick Hebdige (1979) all tempered by Matza's critical work on subcultural commitments in *Delinquency and Drift* (1964). There, for example, Matza (ibid., 28) writes that many juveniles are "in limbo between convention and crime." I suggest something similar for many, though not all, of my informants with regard to their involvement in the cultures of convention and contravention, as I characterize them. This, it seems to me, is what makes the most sense of the accounts of Stanley, Andrew, Donald, and Miguel, and by inference, the rest of the men at their programs.

   Reinarman (1994) has drawn a similar distinction between the "Protestant ethic" and the newer "consumer ethic." Elijah Anderson (1994) writes similarly about the mutual influences of the "code of decency" and the "code of the streets" on young people in African American communities in the inner city. In a similar vein, Phillipe Bourgois' (1996) ethnography of crack use and sales uses a distinction between "mainstream culture" and "inner-city street culture" to explain both why African American and Puerto Rican young men fail in their attempts to maintain low-level office and service sector jobs in the legal economy and why they then turn to crack and heroin use for psychic compensation and drug sales as an alternative means of livelihood. Bourgois' analysis is more systematically structural than mine, but cultural systems of meaning are nevertheless important to understanding why the minority men he writes about are unable to take his "structural" explanations of their (economic and ethnic) dilemmas to heart and, instead, interpret their own experience in the personal terms of honor and humiliation that seem so important to the men I am writing about as well.

From yet another academic front, Robert Wuthnow (1996), the Director of the Center for the Study of Religion at Princeton, likewise sees two opposing moral traditions traversing American life. He labels them "ascetic" and "expressive." Both models, he argues, evolved before the Civil War. However, as he demonstrates with numerous polls and interviews, both traditions remain powerful influences in American life today.

7.   I had three separate taped interviews with Stanley (not his real name). Two interviews occurred at Redemption House and one at the Teen Challenge Training Center in PA where residents went to complete the final months of their training during the period of my research (this transfer is no longer part of Redemption House training). The total time was more than four hours. I also had numerous informal conversations with Stanley during the four months I spent in this research.

8.   The terms in quotation marks are, of course, drawn from the mainstream notions of conventionality. Their meanings are in keeping with the directive systems currently dominant in American institutional realms and generally considered ideal among American cultural elite. They are similar to Anderson's (1994) notions of "decent" vs. "street" codes of ethics. He takes this terminology from his subjects and maintains their moral perspective in his own usage. I am uncomfortable, at best, with the moral implications of his categories. However, his descriptions of the struggles and ambivalences faced by all young people in these social settings are similar to what I observed in the accounts of the men I interviewed and observed.

9.   There are similar subcultures recognizable among other working-class ethnic groups, especially recent immigrants, most of which emphasize similar values of "manhood": drug use (especially alcohol), physical prowess (e.g., in work and sport), physical violence as a means of problem-solving, paternalism in general. See Oliver (1998).

10. I intend "high life" to mean not only the traditional illicit institutions (after hours clubs, speakeasies, brothels) and practices (what once was called promiscuous and more recently has been labeled liberated sexual practices) described (and generally condemned) in such portrayals of popular culture activities in African American communities as *The Color Purple, Autobiography of Malcolm X, Manchild in the Promised Land,* "The Great White Hope," *Cocaine Kids.* I intend here a broader meaning that would encompass these, but also include more licit leisure activities common today, such as, nightclubs or dance clubs, "discos," jazz spots, as well as the general trend toward "loosening up," "letting go," various forms of self-indulgence and sensual indulgence that find legitimation in such pop psychology notions as "healthy egotism," which may also be seen as self-improvement via self-indulgence.

This is an ethic that appears to have been popular within the entertainment and fashion industries and cultures for some time, but is now also being exploited by the advertising industry and widely "exported" from the entertainment subculture to a wider audience via the ubiquity of electronic media, initially television and the recording industry, and now the internet. Thus, I suggest, that those traditional "illicit" forms of the high life (drug use and "carousing") can now be seen as, in principle, drawing legitimation not only from their own "countercultural" notions of rebellion or nullification of the mainstream "responsibility" ethic, but also from the widespread expressions of the libertarian ethic in the entertainment and advertising media, as well as popular theories and systems of "self-actualization." For example, others have suggested that the Nike slogan "just do it" becomes not only a legitimation for indulgence in the purchase of high-priced sneakers, but more generally for subordinating any sense of duty or responsibility to the collective to the "responsibility" to indulge rather than invest. Thus, what may be a relatively "mainstream" justification for limited modes of behavior (shopping) becomes (unconsciously?) "engrossed" or expanded in other social contexts to include wider and wider forms of behavior. "Just do it" serves the perhaps unintended consequence of a neutralizing technique (Matza 1964) that "enables" individuals and groups in certain contexts to enlarge the ethic of liberation to justify otherwise illicit and illegitimate activities.

In this context, then, the term "high life" implies a wide spectrum of activities and approaches to "indulgence" from the more recreational (weekend warrior) to the more committed, burn-out rock star stereotype. The "high life" can be indulged in "dribs and drabs," or one can become immersed in "drugs, sex, or rock and roll" as an "escape" from, or "rejection" of, the every day world (Weber 1969, 323ff). Also, there are various points of entry along the spectrum that runs between these two extremes. The libertine culture is fed by many traditions and can be "resourced" in various ways, for various ends, by various groups and individuals. The affinity of black street culture and individuals for the broader libertine culture is a matter of historical contingency. I imply no necessary physiological, psychological, or cultural developmental connection here. Again, see Reinarman (1994); Waldorf et al. (1991, esp. 279ff); and Anderson (1994) for similar observations.

11. Some argue that:

> the ethic of the marketplace has always been to encourage consumers to choose among products that made them feel good; from there it was just a short step to choosing among life styles that made them feel good, whether that meant using drugs or freer sex.

(See a review of histories of the "sixties" by Patricia Cohen (1998), which claims "that the counterculture's hedonist impulses had their roots in consumer capitalism.")

12. A 1969 print ad for Love cosmetics reads: "Love today is different than it's ever been. It's freer, more natural, more honest—more out in the open." Quoted by Cohen (1998).

13. Matza (1964) refers to the juveniles he finds in similar equivocal circumstances as "in drift" between different sets of demands. The normative characteristics of the "subculture of delinquency"—something quite different from the "delinquent subcultures" posited by Walter Miller (1958) and others—he identifies are "techniques of neutralization" rather than positive moralities. Techniques of neutralization are rationales (or rationalizations) that permit situational release from conscience and

social norms and attempt to deflect the sanctions of social control agencies, but do not commit individuals to "oppositional values." Also, Anderson (1994, 103) argues that although there is only a small segment of the inner city population that is committed to (has internalized) the "code of the street," all inner city young people are intimately familiar with this code of conduct and demeanor and must, "on occasion…adopt street behavior. In fact, depending on the demands of the situation, many people *slip back and forth* between decent and street behavior." The situation of the population from which my informants are drawn is quite as marginal as Matza's delinquents or Anderson's inner city residents. Is it any wonder they are equally "double-minded"?

14. It will be my contention throughout this work that the "attention" paid to the problems faced by the men who come to Redemption House is relatively more realistic than that at Recovery House, while the promised solutions are essentially similar in all but certain elements of their respective legitimizing rationales and rhetorics. Problems are seen as spiritual (i.e., moral) issues at Redemption House rather than as "personality or character disorders" (i.e., pathologies). As such, these problems do not necessarily require the expertise of professional clinicians or sophisticated diagnoses from psychiatrists or psychologists. (Although some people with "addiction" problems may also have neuroses or even psychoses, I suggest this is less common than supposed by the interested treating or serving professions.)

What these men need and what they are offered at Redemption House is a change of life. To accomplish this they need to make some very hard choices, actually a series of choices over time. Each program attempts to "facilitate" these choices. These choices can be legitimated by either theological (at Redemption House) or psychological (at Recovery House) rhetoric. They can also be legitimated or "rationalized" (in both the Weberian and Freudian senses) by other rhetorical systems (e.g., existentialist, atheist, Buddhist). They are, regardless of the rhetoric, virtually the same choices regarding general style of life, often including social and perhaps geographic context of life, certainly of social milieux. Among the choices that people in treatment must make is one about the meaning of their lives.

Redemption House offers an explanation based on theology; Recovery House offers one based on psychology. In this respect, it is my sense that Redemption House actually clutters up the process with rhetoric *less* than does Recovery House. The issue of choice and change is more directly confronted in the theological language than the psychological, but perhaps only relatively so. Also, there is more of an "air" of acceptance or forgiveness (i.e., understanding of *common* human frailties) at Redemption House than at Recovery House, where these are not absent, but generally more difficult to come by amidst the harsh "mechanics of treatment" as described by Louie in Hood (2011a, chap. 4).

Certainly, the outcome studies, such as they are (seriously flawed on all sides) do not support the conclusion that one program is superior to the other in any practical way. Nevertheless, it has been my experience that discipleship training is *less* mystifying and decidedly more "user friendly" than the therapeutic community drug treatment programs I have visited and read about.

15. The "one point miss" seems to be a common experience among this population! At least it is a common *tale* among the accounts I heard during my work at Redemption and Recovery Houses; it turned up several times.

16. This piece of information, offered spontaneously and without taking time to calculate, provides a point at which Stanley's story can be evaluated for accuracy. The chronology does, in fact, check out. The *birth dates* he had been providing offhandedly as he recounted these events corresponded precisely with the *ages*

of his children as he described them *at different points*, with a similar lack of self-consciousness. These are minor points of fact, which have no central bearing on Stanley's story. Their accuracy does not insure that all the things he is telling me are truthful and accurate. They do provide a loose gauge, however, of the genuineness of his account, one that fits well with my own general perception of his basic sincerity—in the midst of his story-telling, at least.

Certainly there are points where the observer (reader and writer-interviewer) will be forced to be skeptical, such as, for example, Stanley's repeated claims of large sums of money serendipitously received. Nevertheless, it seems clear that his overall account weaves together real events portrayed accurately, though at times exaggerated, at times minimized or altered in other ways (e.g., altered chronology), in order to fit the meaning structure he has imbibed (or perceived as strategic) during his five-month stay at Redemption House (Hood 2011a, chap. 4).

He is telling the truth as seen through the prism of the Redemption House perspective. His selectivity is not likely to be a scam, unless it is one he plays on himself, as well as on me. His selectivity is part of becoming the Stanley of Redemption House rather than the Stanley of the streets. Both selves continue to "exist," more or less "available" to Stanley depending on the demands and opportunities of the immediate context. Like any other skill, he is currently more polished at being an evangelical Christian than at being a Lothario, because he has been working on the former set of skills for the past five months, twenty-four hours a day, seven days a week (more-or-less). But a reversion to Lothario requires only the appropriate change in social, and thus psychic, context, as would a re-reversion to evangelical Christian. This is a simple observation that can be made at any drug treatment program by observing relapses and readmissions, or at any conversionist religious group by paying attention to the "multiple conversions" of a significant number of initiates. Ultimately, the story that Stanley is telling is one about his "chameleonism" or, better, marginality.

17. Stanley means he used to have a habit. The price he attaches to this man's previous drug use pattern is almost certainly a gross exaggeration. As Johnson et al. (1985), have shown, users tend to overestimate the cost of their habits for various reasons, e.g., "discounting" days they do not purchase drugs when making estimates based on general or abstract, rather than specifically targeted recollections. Also, it is quite likely that Stanley increased the man's own exaggerated estimate of his drug-use proclivities as a means of dramatizing his threatening presence, which, in his account, Stanley overcomes by direct confrontation, thus establishing his own credentials as a powerful male figure in control of his own circumstances. This anecdote presents Stanley in a posture that violates the Redemption House ethic, but I am sure he would justify it by saying it was in the past, before his conversion. Nevertheless, this sort of "street rapping" (to use a TC phrase) is forbidden at both Houses. Stanley is posturing for me in terms of both the before and after ethics (directive systems) that are equally central to his perceptions of reality and crucial to negotiating whatever circumstances present themselves.

18. We should be skeptical here of Stanley's account of why he is not working for the construction company, clearly the highest paying and skill level he has attained in his on-again–off-again occupational career. He claims the work is seasonal, which it certainly is in the less temperate climate of New York. However, I am told that this is not typical of the milder climes of Virginia or even Washington, D.C. (personal communication with T. Hood, regional project manager of construction sites for Madison Homes, Inc. of McLean, VA). Whatever the reason, Stanley is not working for the construction company at this point. His story, nevertheless, continues its

theme of repeated changes and other disappointments in work situation that seem related to his use of drugs (as commodity or intoxicant) and vice versa.

19. We can give Stanley's account the benefit of several doubts here, but not total credibility. Although it is important to note that he does not hesitate to report heavy drug use, as well as no use.

20. Bingeing, of course, is not the same as addiction. It is, nevertheless a problematic pattern of use. See Reinarman and Levine (1998, 77–80, 142–47) on the difference between addiction and bingeing.

21. This is a common description among this group of users, as well as others in and out of treatment, of physical sensations they associate with the urge to use. The argot for this experience among the medical–pharmacological research and, increasingly, among treatment professionals is "craving." The adoption of this term to indicate a desire to use a psychoactive substance outside of medical context seems to me another attempt to medicalize (or medically stigmatize) what is a relatively normal response to very stimulating experiences. Andrew Weil (1986) argues that the desire to alter one's consciousness is a universal, and therefore, normal urge. The anti-drug forces that control much of the research and treatment industries appear intent on using the term "crave" as a means of deviantizing this experience. The appeal that the term has for these groups seems to be related to the implied intensity and supposed physiological origin of a "craving" as distinct from such common sense terms as "desire" or "urge" or even "need." Because the latter are more common in daily usage, they do not connote abnormality, but are too linked linguistically with normal interests in sex, food, elimination. Crave also may carry unconscious affinities with the word "craven" and perhaps with "craze." This linguistic usage serves a political end of continuing to portray drug users as deviant in the public consciousness as well as within the "scientific" community. This maintains their status as "subjects" for research and correction rather than fellow citizens in difficulty. It maintains the near-century-old notion of users as "enslaved" to abnormal desires beyond control, yet morally responsible for their condition (Acker, 2005). This position was reinforced by the much-acclaimed Bill Moyers' PBS special on addiction (1998). That series presented the claim, inter alia, that "addiction is a brain disease" for which people should not be held morally responsible, but addicts *are* morally responsible to seek treatment in order to become abstinent. See also, Leshner (1997, 1999).

22. In so doing, Stanley not only follows a time-honored tradition of "failed" biblical personages (e.g., King David and St. Peter, as well as Eve), but also one that has what Matza (1964, 62ff) would describe as a "subterranean convergence" with the legitimate conservative Christian tradition of accounting for behavior. According to the evangelical canon, it *is* the Devil who tempts Christians to betray their commitments to abstain from sinful activities. Interestingly, there is a precise parallel at Recovery House. At Recovery House, slips are constantly accounted for by attaching responsibility to one's "disease" or "junkie mentality." The material reality of this disease entity or psychic malfunction has about as much direct empirical support as does the personage upon whom Stanley and the brothers of Redemption House project blame for untoward behavior otherwise unaccountable except by taking moral responsibility upon oneself. Both Redemption House and Recovery House rhetorics provide residents with a(n unintended?) means of deflecting direct responsibility for individual slips in behavior that fairly mirror one another but draw on what are usually considered the ontologically opposed realms of faith (the Devil) and science (the disease or emotional disorder). Ironically, however, neither of the neutralizing techniques extends to excusing the overall "condition" of the

"brothers" (original sin) or the "peers" (addiction), a responsibility they must bear the full brunt of, in part by recognizing this distinction between the immediate and the general without it ever being made explicit in the rhetoric of either drug treatment or discipleship training. In other words, it is legitimate to blame the Devil, or the Disease, for a momentary lapse into a lustful thought or a sneer at a reprimand from a counselor. But one must take full responsibility for sin or addiction by surrendering to treatment (Recovery) or training (God) without excuse or justification. Both program ideologies mirror one another in this respect.

23. A more lucrative and more readily available entrepreneurial enterprise than the crack trade could hardly be imagined for a person in Stanley's circumstance. The irony, as Erich Goode (1996, 49f) points out, is that success in such business enterprises most often plunges the businessman deeper into the underworld rather than bringing him closer to the mainstream. See also Currie (1993); Bourgois (1996).

24. Andrew's account tends to skip back and forth in time without warning or chronological specification. This is not uncommon among my informants, but is particularly marked in Andrew's case. Therefore, some of his comments here have been rearranged to clarify the chronology of events. All comments remain in their original context and are in Andrew's own words and phrasing, except where brackets indicate otherwise. However, some "chunks" of dialogue, usually two or three sentences together, have been taken out of their original order for the purpose of clarification and readability. With each alteration, I made every effort to maintain Andrew's "story line."

25. "I went through a lot" is a therapeutic community mantra that points to a particular set of circumstances representing significant stress in the individual's life. It implies that so much stress is involved that drug use has become, if not an unavoidable consequence, at least a reasonable or understandable coping device. Like the Devil or the Disease (see note 22), the claim of "going through a lot" constitutes a technique of neutralization (Matza 1964). The phrase always receives knowing nods and looks from listening peers. The intent in repetition of the mantra and response is not to "legitimate" the resultant drug use, but to neutralize it. That is to shift responsibility for use from the individual to the uniquely stressful set of circumstances under which he/she was operating at the time. It is not to say that use in general is okay, or that use on that occasion was okay, but given the juxtaposition of user pathology and unusual amounts of stress, use is not surprising, it is understandable. That is, it makes "orthodox" sense in the TC and therefore helps establish the institutional identity necessary for success (i.e., peer acceptance) within the therapeutic community treatment process. A lot of stress plus pathology results in drug use. See Hood (2011a, chap. 4).

26. This pattern has not been unusual: moving from occasional, recreational use of powder cocaine to less controlled use of crack. It is a common story among this population and has an explanation that depends neither on "disease" nor on some uniquely dangerous pharmacological characteristic of crack, but on its method of preparation and administration. See Waldorf et al. (1991); Reinarman and Levine (1997, esp. chap 7).

27. This corresponds to the findings of B. Johnson et al. (1985) and Inciardi (1986) that the majority of users do not engage in violent crime as a means of paying for illicit drugs. Stanley also used his "windfalls" as means for binges. One such windfall included "misleading" an insurance company, a form of fraud not at all uncommon among otherwise conventional citizens (see Coleman 1998).

28. For the notion of grounded concepts, see Glaser and Strauss (1967).

29. Unquestionably, this is an ex post facto rationale. It nevertheless demonstrates Stanley's connection with or commitment to conventional career paths and

occupational pursuits, not to mention personal aspirations. These come to the fore when conventional opportunities are available and take a back seat when they fade. Should we expect anything different?

30. Anderson (1994, 103) writes, in a similar connection,

> These decent [inner city black] people are trying hard to be part of the mainstream culture, but the racism, real and perceived, that they encounter helps to legitimate the oppositional culture.... A vicious cycle has thus been formed. The hopelessness and alienation many young inner city black men and women feel, largely as a result of endemic joblessness and persistent racism, fuels the violence [and other street behavior, like drug use and sales] they engage in.

See Goode (1997, 149–51) for a similar perspective.

31. See Weber (1969, 280) for "images" and Nelson (1981) for "logics of action."

32. Here I intend "good" to mean moral as perceived by the dominant ethical perspective, especially its view of how "others" ought to live, and "behave." I intend "high" to carry the sense of happy, joyful, celebration. It does not necessarily include either the notion of illicit or drug use, although in the worlds of young American men these are not uncommonly joined, as Stanley's experience shows. Also, it should be obvious by now that I do not intend to suggest that these two worlds are mutually exclusive, nor are they singularities in themselves. People can and do indulge in both "lifes" in various ways, to various degrees, at various times, and with various successes and failures. Both "high" and "good" lives are intended as ideal types (Weber, 1969).

33. This is not to say that Stanley will "fail" at Redemption House, or Andrew at Recovery House. Obviously a certain, very small percentage of residents do succeed in the terms of either program. I am not suggesting that these programs do not offer alternative meaning structures that appeal to some people with problems of drug misuse. I mean, rather, that their successes are the exceptions, not the rule. And there may be better ways to solve these dilemmas, on both individual and societal levels. Better means more reliable and less coercive, among other things.

34. For obvious reasons, the secular wing places much greater emphasis than does the religious wing on the temporal consequences of this projected decline. It is clearly more prominent in their rhetoric. For the folks at Redemption House, the ultimate degradation that results from drug use does not have to be realized or demonstrated in the current life of the user, it can be projected onto the next life where the consequences of refusing redemption will be his ultimate (i.e., eternal) ruin.

35. Waldorf et al. (1991, 27ff) compare four types of cocaine users: coke hogs, nippers, ceremonial users, and bingers. At his worst, Donald seems to fit the last of these. According to Waldorf and friends, bingers are "weekend warriors." They are abstinent between binges and are able to "compartmentalize" their use, i.e., separate it from family, work, and other settings "where one has to be...'straight'."

36. Waldorf et al. (ibid.), consider this an important indicator of one requirement for quitting, viz., a stake in conventionality. This is a variation on Travis Hirschi's (1969) social control theory of deviance.

37. This process of cognitive assimilation is the subject of the following chapter and two central chapters in Hood (2001a). The term "sad tale" is Goffman's (1961, 67). It refers to the inmate's story of how he came to such an end, viz., incarceration. Goffman's inmates use their sad tales to deflect some of the stigma of their new label. Here, Donald uses it as a means of embracing and identifying with the label the therapeutic asylum thrusts upon him, as intended by the treatment process.

38. One of the truly interesting ironies of my "sample" is the fact that the "worst" guys I met at both Houses were among the few men who told me of their long-term ("successful") marriage and family arrangements. Both George at Redemption House and Nate at Recovery House were serious bad guys, yet both had long-standing marriages that continued over more than twenty years. This was the case in spite of the fact that both men were long-time drug dealers, pimps, and, perhaps hit men. Given the "family values" bent of both organizations, it is indeed ironic that these "bad guys" were among the most exemplary in this regard. Among my informants, this stands as one of the strongest arguments against the stereotypes of users and dealers widely accepted by the press and the public and perpetuated by programs like Recovery House and, to a lesser degree, Redemption House. The latter seems better able to accept such "atypical" realities when they occur and do not demand that they be forced to acknowledge and "construct" self-images and personal histories that protect treatment orthodoxy and deny actuality. Both Nate, after some initial hesitation, and, especially, George were very helpful informants regarding their respective programs. During hours of conversation over several days, neither man appeared to be the "bad guy" presented in their accounts. But I do not doubt they were such under other circumstances.

39. For another use of "achieved" addictions that more-or-less corresponds with mine, see Reinarman (2005).

40. The pattern I describe here is not a necessary or "natural" one. It is also quite common for heroin users to maintain a moderate, non-troublesome habit for years while also maintaining an otherwise relatively conventional lifestyle. Exemplars of this pattern include an elementary school teacher and a moderately successful neon sign maker, both of whom I know from interviews at a local needle exchange program. Each man works regularly and has lived for years in the same stable working-class neighborhood.

41. The walkabout was a scheduled excursion into inner city neighborhoods to distribute sterile syringes and other paraphernalia to injecting drug users (IDUs) in exchange for their used, contaminated syringes. This started as an illegal venture, but since has won New York State Department of Health sanction. (And just weeks before this text was copy-edited, the Obama administration recognized needle exchange as a legitimate form of drug addiction treatment.) The Lower East Side Needle Exchange program grew out of this venture. It now operates out of a large storefront setting in Chinatown, but continues the walkabout tradition twice a week. Other exchanges in New York are entirely mobile, distributing from vans at designated locations on designated days and times. Allan Clear is currently the Executive Director of the Harm Reduction Coalition, an umbrella organization for harm reduction services in the U.S.

42. Charles Winick (1962) was the first to document this process of diminution of use over time among heroin users, which he characterized as "maturing out." Patrick Biernicki's (1986) study of "heroin users who stopped" came to similar conclusions about the threat drug use posed to the "stakes" users had in other, more conventional, aspects of their lives, e.g., relationship to a spouse or child, occupation, education. A constant refrain at Recovery House, much more so than at Redemption House, was that men were "tired" of the hassles of using, just tired and wanted to quit. This seems to confirm another notion about eventual diminution of use after users reach their late twenties or thirties. In this respect, Waldorf (1970) suggests that the dynamic is not "growing up" so much as "burning out."

   Many of the men I spoke with at Recovery House talked about drug use as "a young man's game" that they were just too tired to continue. However, I did often get the impression that the refrain of tiredness was simply a mantra invoked as a readily acceptable means (a Goffmanian "sad tale") of explaining one's presence in treatment, one that certainly fit with program's pervasive rhetoric (see Hood 2011a, chap. 4). One thing that makes me skeptical about the use of this refrain in treatment is that most of the subjects of all these studies were *not* in treatment. Biernacki, in particular, was interested in what has been called "natural recovery" of users that were not in treatment. The process of natural recovery has been explored by a number of independent researchers (e.g., Fingarette 1988, 1988a; Peele 1989; Waldorf et al. 1991) and found to be common among users of all psychoactive substances.

Given the evidence regarding the cyclical character of using and abstaining careers in and out of dope, it may be that after so many cycles, it becomes obvious to those "addicts who survive" that, whatever the costs of abstinence or diminution, such a pattern is preferable to the hassles of heavier use under the conditions of prohibition in our temperance culture (see Levine 1992). As Miguel might put it, "I love dope, but I hate going to jail and my wife ain't happy." This sounds more like maturity than burn out to me. In support of their "burn out" thesis, Waldorf et al. (1991, 234f) suggest that the term "maturing out" is a poor choice, since it suggests a (perhaps unintended) "temperance-era moralism." However, all these authors agree, that a sort of "recovery wisdom" is not an uncommon consequence of long or heavy drug-using careers, albeit obtained "the hard way." Perhaps these theories need not be seen as entirely mutually exclusive. Each makes, ultimately, the same point. Intensive drug-use careers are self-limiting.

43. This discussion is based on my reading of, e.g., Scott (1976); Darnton (1984); Thompson (1971); LeRoy Ladurie (1978, 1979); Bourgois (1996); Steinberg (1989); Davis (1975); Hobsbawm (1959), and others.

44. If her opposition is religion-based, it likely includes the notion of inherent evil, but I doubt that it is. After all, she has not left Miguel. And this, I suspect, is because the family remains more or less functional over the course of the fifteen years. Prison was the only interruption until treatment. Miguel's wife may have an entirely different tale to tell, I can only speculate here.

45. Phillipe Bourgois (1996, 13) writes:

> The participant-observation ethnographic techniques developed primarily by anthropologists since the 1920s are better suited than exclusively quantitative methodologies for documenting the lives of people who live on the margins of a society that is hostile to them. Only by establishing long-term relationships based on trust can one begin to ask provocative personal questions, and expect thoughtful, serious answers.... In order to collect "accurate data," ethnographers violate the canons of positivist research; we become intimately involved with the people we study.

It was not possible for me to become as intimate with my fellow participants ("subjects") as Bourgois did with his over a three-year period while living in the same East Harlem neighborhood. However, my almost daily contact with them over four months created a modicum of trust with several of the men I interviewed and interacted with, in a way not possible (or necessary) via statistically oriented research.

46. Bourgois (1996, 184) also writes about the "terrors and anxieties (of a macho posturing central character) emerg[ing] *between the lines* of his *reconstructed* memories." [Emphasis added.]

47. This list consists of the thirteen individuals (about half of the total interviewed) whose records were most complete and/or whose accounts are widely used. It is reproduced from Hood (2011a).
48. This list consists of about half of the men interviewed. For this list, men were selected on the basis of the completeness of their information and extent of use made of their accounts. Accounts were selected throughout on the basis of representativeness or other distinction, usually noted or obvious in context. It is reproduced from Hood (2011a).

2

Resident Accounts:
Rationales for Treatment and Training

> I seen that I had to change sooner or later. I have
> to start doing things to help myself or I'm gonna
> die. At 37 I don't want to die. Today I want to live
> and enjoy myself. I don't want to die under the
> influence of drugs.
>
> —Roberto, Recovery House

> I ... spent three weeks in a hotel with three females ...
> I had crack, cocaine, and good Jamaican mari-
> juana, two bottles of Jack Daniel's. But I was un-
> happy because the woman I wanted to be with was
> a Christian.... After these women left, I took about
> 30 sleeping pills. I thought I was gonna die. I woke
> up without a hangover. The first thing I thought was
> to give my life to God. Deep inside I was too scared
> to kill myself, so I thought, let me try Jesus. Maybe
> he can help me.
>
> —Stanley, Redemption House

> [B]oth motives and actions very often originate not
> from within [individuals] but from the situation in
> which individuals find themselves.
>
> —Karl Mannheim[1]

One of the few descriptions of religious treatment programs to find its way
into the drug research literature is that of John Langrod and his associates (1972,
1981).[2] Much of what they have to say is empirically accurate, but certain of
their summations and conclusions are open to question on empirical and analytical grounds. Among these conclusions is the notion that the type of person
drawn to faith-based programs is likely to be different from that attracted by
secular programs, like the therapeutic communities (TCs). While this may be
true to some extent, I doubt it will hold up to extensive research. My research
strongly suggests that Recovery House and Redemption House draw clients

from the very same population(s) and include residents with essentially the same backgrounds. In effect, they are the same people.[3]

I met and interviewed men at Redemption House who had come there for help after spending time at one of several (secular) therapeutic communities, including Phoenix House, Odyssey House, Daytop, Pride Site, and Project Return. Some of the men had graduated from these programs. One man at Redemption House, George, had previously been a director of a therapeutic community on Manhattan's infamous Lower East Side for several years. Another, Gordon, was a graduate of Phoenix House, a classmate of Louie, one of the therapeutic community directors I interviewed, and a counselor at both Phoenix House and Odyssey House (both prominent TCs), before entering the Redemption House program. Yet another man, Keith, at Redemption House found his way there instead of meeting a scheduled appointment at Recovery House intake the very same day. As was true of several of the men I met there, none of these men had a strong religious background of any sort.

At Recovery House I met several men who had attended religious treatments previously. One of these men, Jorge, had graduated from Teen Challenge Training Center at Rehrersburg, PA, a large faith-based program affiliated with Redemption House. One other Recovery House resident, Roberto, had visited a private religious treatment before his induction, but could not afford its fees. In his interview, he lamented the lack of religious training available at his therapeutic community and expressed the wish to find an affordable place for treatment similar to the one he had visited. In addition to having direct experience with religious programs for drug users, several men at Recovery House had independently developed explicit religious aspects to their personal recovery programs. Many others at Recovery House claimed intense and meaningful religious involvement as a result of participation in Narcotics or Alcoholics Anonymous (NA or AA) programs, either inside or outside of their current program.

In addition to the similarities in treatment experience and religious inclinations, the biographies recounted by the men included numerous other factors that indicate a strong resemblance in the lives and experiences of the residents of the two programs. In this chapter, I explore the accounts, the stories, related in the conversations and interviews I had with the men of Redemption House and Recovery House (Orbuch 1997). One of the most prominent elements in these accounts are the tales of personal crisis the men experienced prior to entering their respective programs. The issue of personal crisis or the experience of tension or stress that predisposed them to recruitment to conversionist groups is one that has been central to the investigations of religious conversion over the past several decades.

Affiliation

The issue of how or why one affiliates with a communal conversionist group has typically been posed as an issue of motives. This focus on motivations assumes that the primary actor was the individual, as "joiner" or "seeker," and that the major causal factor was some personal, motivational "inner push" (perceived need or desire) to make a change of some sort in life, habits, or attitudes. This perspective was included in the influential Lofland-Stark processual, value-added model that has been tested, re-tested, and reevaluated numerous times since its conceptualization three decades ago (see Bainbridge 1997; Lofland 1966; Lofland and Stark 1965). The first stage in this model posits an experience of pre-membership tension that propels the individual toward the new group affiliation. Many later investigators also included (or found) this element of "relative deprivation" in their studies of conversionist groups. Spokespersons and the literature of both Redemption House and Recovery House include similar deprivations in their official explanations of the experience of addiction and consider them significant motivators in initiating individual affiliation with their treatment programs. From another perspective, some researchers have noted, especially in connection with recruitment to Alcoholics Anonymous, that organizational constraints pressure prospective members to *reinterpret* their past experiences as intolerably stressful because of alcohol use (Greil and Rudy 1983). This interpretation, obviously, calls the former into question.

It is also possible to frame the question of why one is in a program for drug users from the other side of the affiliative equation, as one of "recruitment" rather than seeking or joining a new organization or movement (see Bainbridge 1997; Robbins 1988). The questions then become: what are the methods that the organizations use to recruit new members or clients? How do they sell themselves and their programs to potential joiners? How do they entice or convince (influence) them to join? Or, in the language of "resource mobilization," how does the movement mobilize new recruits? These are questions not so much of motive as of organizational technique or mechanism, process, or procedure for growth or continuous full utilization of services. From this perspective, the affiliation results not from the individual's initiative so much as from "external" forces, particularly the recruitment systems of the organization, "pulling" on him to compel or perhaps cajole her into entering the program. The studies that have been done from this perspective have found two typically successful approaches to the "recruitment problem." The first is the "social network approach"; the second focuses on "structural availability" as the operative variable in recruitment of what have been called "loose cannons" (see Danzger 1986; Lofland 1966; Robbins 1988; Snow and Machelak 1984; Stark and Bainbridge 1980). In the social network case, recruits are introduced to a new movement by knowing or meeting socially someone who is already a member of the group in question. The instance of "loose cannons" has to do with the group's organized outreach to strangers, often so-called social isolates, who are approached in public places like parks or shopping malls. In another study, one sociologist (Bainbridge 1997, 168) suggested the obvious: "full analysis of recruitment should include the deprivations of recruits *plus* the resources and strategies employed by recruiters." Both of these approaches to the question of resident affiliation with a program seem to fit well with the information I collected at Redemption and Recovery Houses.

How is it then that the residents of Redemption House and Recovery House came to be at their respective programs? Most of the responses to this question at both programs had to do with what residents had to say about their own motives for entering treatment or training. When asked to account for their presence in drug treatment at Recovery House or in discipleship training at Redemption House, the men at both Houses recounted tales of deprivation associated with "drugging" lifestyles. These were easily ("naturally") categorized by type of deprivation or depravity and were, for all practical purposes, interchangeable between the religious and secular programs.[4]

The differences that appeared between the story lines of residents at the two houses had to do with issues of recruitment rather than motivations. Men at Recovery House, the secular program, talked of recruitment hardly at all. Even those who had been remanded by the criminal justice system did not see this as a form of recruitment, but rather as a result of the deprivation of drug-induced criminal behavior or, indeed, of arrest itself (see Hood 2011a). This is curious, since "mandation" has been a useful and common form of recruitment for rehabilitation programs in America at least since the invention of the asylum system more than a century ago (Empey and Stafford 1982; Rothman 1971). At Recovery House, clients focused almost exclusively on their predisposing motives, even when pressed—sometimes in very explicit terms—about the matter of organizational outreach. At Redemption House, on the other hand, only one man had been mandated to training. Instead, Redemption residents talked freely and passionately about the recruitment processes, both formal and informal, that were of special significance in "pulling" all of them into the discipleship program. For this reason, I considered the issue of organizational recruitment in separate chapters on each house in my previous book (Hood 2011a).

In this chapter, I explore a selection of typical accounts of the residents of both Redemption House and Recovery House regarding the *motives* they reported for being in a "drug program." Following the accounts, I address at more length the theoretical questions raised by these data: e.g., do they display comparability simply between groups of drug users drawn to treatment and training, or do they indicate some fundamental comparability between the two types of approaches (treatment and training) to individuals with drug problems? Also, are the data reliable or do they require explanation or analysis? For example, are the tensions or deprivations so consistently reported by all respondents actually "real," or are they somehow collectively imagined or "socially constructed"? That is, do they reflect the simple reality of illicit drug use, at least as it occurs under certain conditions? Or, do the stories reflect the ideologies of the two programs filtered through their acculturated residents? And, if the latter is the case, can the client accounts be useful at all in a social scientific understanding of resident experience? And finally, what exactly is the difference between these two programs? If the similarities are considerable, as I suggest, what does it say about the nature of drug treatment programs operated at least in part with public support?

Residents' Crisis Accounts

Despite the suggestions of earlier writers to the contrary (Langrod et al. 1972, 1981; Muffler et al. 1997), when I asked the men of Redemption House and Recovery House why they were in treatment or training, their accounts were amazingly similar and were easily organized into "grounded" categories of motive (for grounded categories, see Glazer and Strauss 1967; see also Kearney et al. 1994).[5] The categories were derived from both programs; i.e., they told the same kinds of stories at both places. The categories all entail a particular form of personal crisis or deprivation that reportedly influenced residents to decide to enter their programs and include accounts from residents of both Houses. The main categories are[6]:

1. the *fear* of AIDS
2. other forms of *death threats* associated with continued drug use
3. various forms of *self-degradation* such as stealing from one's family to secure drugs or wasting large sums of money on drugs and other profligate activities
4. difficulties with *sexual relationships.*

Several men suggested more than one motive for entering treatment or training. The fact of homelessness is included in several types of crisis tales, but residents rarely consider it their primary motive. Therefore, I do not treat it as a separate category here. The situation of being mandated, or coerced (i.e., recruited) into treatment or training by the criminal justice system in lieu of a prison sentence is treated similarly. Although it may appear to an outside observer to be the main reason for entering a program, it is rarely treated as such in the tales the men tell. (I have used pseudonyms for all these respondents.)

The Fear of AIDS

The *fear* of a life-threatening illness or circumstance was a common theme in many of the biographies related to me. Not surprisingly, a common source of such fears was the threat of infection with the human immunodeficiency virus (HIV). The men at both houses, as well as throughout other locations within the street drug cultures of New York, refer to it simply as "the virus." Everyone familiar with these and related cultures recognizes the reference. In too many cases the fear coincides with the reality of infection, but in other cases it does not. In the following cases, the *fear* of AIDS is reported to be a major source of personal crisis or anxiety and an impetus to seek treatment for continuing drug use.

"Slick" is a twenty-five-year-old man whose parents were born in the Dominican Republic. He had been in discipleship training at Redemption House for almost four months when I first interviewed him. According to his account, Slick was seven years old when his family settled in Brooklyn and joined a Pentecostal Church. Slick first talked about his early drug use:

> I began to use drugs when I was in junior high. [We would] smoke pot, huff glue, stuff like that. We were really wild kids. It was crazy. I liked to hang out, y'know? In high school I got introduced to cocaine at seventeen. I liked to do cocaine. Eventually I started to sell it. My sister went with this really big dealer and I asked him if I could sell it. He used to give me stuff free every weekend. It was just for me to make some get-high money so I could go to the clubs.

After high school, Slick developed interests in writing and radio work and had a part-time job as a disk jockey at a small FM radio station. He described how he enjoyed "the clubs" and spent his free time dancing and doing drugs. "Eventually," he seized the opportunity to sell drugs for his sister's boyfriend. After several years of escalating drug involvement that included increasingly regular days-long crack binges, Slick was arrested for "possession with intent" for the third time and opted for a shock program (boot camp-style therapy at an upstate facility) rather than prison. As he tells it, Slick did well in the program, but once back on the street resumed his clubbing and drugging lifestyle. Slick's particular crisis began after a four-day crack binge when he became distraught over the deterioration of his normally athletic body and general good looks. Frightened by the thought that he may be infected by "the virus," Slick soon decided it was time to enter the discipleship training program.

> It was January 1st. I was just home from a four day binge and I went to my parents' home and took a shower. Nobody was home. I just took a shower to try to wash myself. I felt real dirty. I was like, man, what am I doin'? I was, like, captive to it. I was smoking crack, y'know. I looked at myself in the mirror, and I had lost some weight and I used to work out. I said, Slick what are you doin' to yourself. I just couldn't look any more.... I was scared that I had HIV. 'Cause I was out there very promiscuous. [Sex] was one of the reasons that drove me back out there all the time.

At this point, Slick tried to stop using and "give [him]self to the Lord."

> [But] three days later, I was back doin' the same thing; back to my old self. Three days later I didn't feel [the Spirit] anymore.... The devil tricked me; he said, "you ain't got [HIV]." So I went back doin' what I wanted to do, what my flesh wanted to do.[7] Then my life reached a [de]crescendo. I lost my job. So I started selling again and got arrested. Then I did four months [in jail].
>
> Two weeks after I got out I went right back to getting high.... [One] night I went home...and was praying with my family. At that point the Holy Spirit was convicting me to take the HIV test, because I was still thinking I was sick.[8] I was holding

my niece...and I was crying because I wanted to have a child, a family, and I didn't think I could because I thought I was sick. I had no symptoms, but I thought I could be sick, because I got gonorrhea four or five times, y'know? My sister [the baby's mother] graduated from the [Christian discipleship] program [for women]. God delivered her. She had been out there in the street. I looked at my mother and tears was coming out of my eyes, and I said, "Mom I gotta serve the Lord."[9] Then my sister called Redemption House and got me in here. I slept the next two days and came here determined to serve the Lord.

Roberto at Recovery House was also concerned about his HIV status. Roberto is a thirty-five-year-old Nuyoricano from the South Bronx who had been in treatment for ten months at the time of this interview. As he tells his story, he grew up as a "little gangster."

Drugs got introduced to me when I first started affiliating myself with gangs. We had a gang by the name of Panthers. It was either be part of the gang or become a victim of the gang. Because I came from a dysfunctional family, I knew what it was to get beat down and I didn't want to get hurt on the streets, so I became part of [sic]. We started off drinking beer and little tabs of acid called "purple haze." At that time they had some kind of heroin they used to sell in $2 and $3 bags. It was almost pure, it was good, lotta people was ODin' behind it [overdosing on it].

Unlike Slick, Roberto's life was not characterized by the glitter of the clubs and prestige of deejaying on FM radio. Nevertheless, like Slick and other users, Roberto reports being afraid of dying as a reason for entering a program. However, he lived seven years with the virus before seeking treatment.

Well, between thirteen to fourteen [years of age] I was sniffing [heroin]. By fifteen I was skin poppin' it already. Before I got to 16, I was already mainlining it. By the time I was seventeen, I was doin' everything there was. I was poppin' pills, takin' tuinals, seconal, peaches, Christmas trees.

Q: How did you pay for all this?

A: Well, I sold drugs also. After the gangs, we got involved in the marketing of drugs. Also I made money by stickin' people up. There came a time I got so involved with the heroin, right, that I got addicted. And some mornings I would get up with no drugs to sell because I would do it all. So I would go out and stick up people. That same attitude I used in the gangs to establish my reputation. I would use that same attitude, that gangster [attitude], to go get my money. I would stick anybody up.

I spent about 20 years of my life in and out of jails. My longest term was 37 months. But I spent eight months here, a year there, 24 months, 27 months. Out of that 20 years I spent fifteen in prison. I threw away fifteen years. That was behind drugs. What made it comf't'rble in jail is that drugs follow you there. All I had to do was project that gangster attitude. We used to make our own wine in jail. But you can get what you want if you have the attitude and heart.

I came here [because] at the end it was something that said listen, it's either or—either you gonna do it [go into treatment] or you gonna get killed.

Q: Was there anything in particular that brought that to your attention?

A: Yeah, I caught the virus, HIV virus. Right? And what I was looking at was: if I don't stop using drugs it's gonna kill me. Or I'm gonna end up in jail and I'm gonna die in there. So I told myself, listen, either get yourself together or you gonna die. I tried everything else. After I caught the virus seven years ago, I tried getting killed. I was too much of a punk to jump off a roof or in front of a car or to pull a trigger on my head. So I decided, if I'm gonna live, let me live the right way. I seen that I had to change sooner or later. I have to start doing things to help myself or I'm gonna die. At 37 I don't want to die. Today I want to live and enjoy myself. I don't want to die under the influence of drugs.

Other Death Threats

The accounts of Slick and Robert reveal commonalities in the lives of street drug users. But AIDS is only one form of death threat that was presumed inherent in the drugging life. The notion that death is an almost inevitable alternative to recovery or redemption pervades the rhetoric of the two programs and is typical of every similar residential treatment my informants had contact with.

Robert, an eight-month resident of Recovery House, told me a story that exemplifies the general sense of a death threat that applies more universally to street users than does the virus. Like Slick, Robert looked in a mirror of sorts and saw what he believed to be his fate without Recovery.

I used to get off in the portable toilet at a construction site in the Hunts Point area. One morning I went in there to shoot my drugs, and I seen this black kid in there. He was all twisted down and the belt was tied up around his arm, the needle all hanging out and the blood was dry. And I tapped him on the shoulder, I seen his pants were down, and I felt that stiffness. I said, "Oh shit," he was cold.

The first thing I thought was to go in his pocket. I pulled out an empty pocket. Then for some strange reason I caught myself and I backed off. I told somebody working in the site, and they called the cops. This was at nine o'clock. At four PM was when they were ready to remove his body. This was after they pulled him outta that portable toilet. They had him on the floor with his pants down his ass and one sheet of paper covering him up. I told myself, that's the last way I want to go is like that. I don't never want to go out like that. All fucked up, dead, stiff, people not carin' about me, people walkin' by me. I told myself he could be a splittee from a program. I keep that in mind, 'cause I don't want to do that.

This happened about a week before I came to Recovery House. I decided to go to St. Barnabas Hospital and detox on methadone. They gave me methadone for five days and then two days of cold turkey. When they released me I went and got high again because I couldn't deal with the pain of the methadone withdrawal. The following day I came into Recovery House. I saw my reality; I saw my future. Every day I would get like a vision. I would visualize where I was gonna be at.... I refuse to go out like that.

The next story comes from Gordon at Redemption House. It shows how graphically death threats can be "revealed" in the daily life of users on the street.

Gordon was a three-month resident when he told this tale of a life-threatening occurrence that influenced his decision to seek discipleship training.

One particular night I was sitting in the park getting high [on crack] when a guy tapped me on the shoulder. I was paranoid. I jumped up and took a [martial arts] stance. This guy looked at me and said, "Calm down. My name is Dave. I was in my bed sleeping and God spoke to me and said, 'Get up, there's someone who needs you.' God sent me to you. Are you saved?" I said, "No." He said, "Can I sit down? God loves you." He read John 3:16. I accepted Jesus Christ right there. But I did it to get rid of him. I wanted to be alone to get high. He gave me $20 and said it was God's money. "Go get yourself together, because God has something wonderful for you."

Three days later, I went to get my unemployment check. As I was coming out two guys stuck me up with guns. I jumped them and had both on the ground beating on them. A girl came up behind me and slashed me in the face, right here. When she cut me, I heard a gushing sound. I said, "Oh, my God, I'm dead." I thought my jugular was cut. I was running away and took my shirt off to stop the blood. I ran to a hospital. It took about 66 stitches to close me up.

A week later, I was in the same park getting high again. The [same] guy came up to me. As I was walking he said, "Gordon, God is an *avenging* God. He will *take your life*, if you continue to disobey him. You don't have many more chances." He gave me $40 and again he said, "this is God's money. If you don't use it right, something is going to happen to you. He's going to let you know." He told me that the devil had a hold of me. "You don't see it, but he has you." I was getting high that night, but I threw away everything [the drugs] I had on the spot. I went to the Upper Room [outreach center] and they sent me to a discipleship program. [Emphasis added.]

Saul, a supervising counselor at Recovery House, tells a story that might be considered paradigmatic with respect to the experience of physical danger associated with the world of illicit drugs.

I've been in treatment seven times, all TCs, over a period of maybe fifteen years. [Getting serious about treatment] had a lot to do with what happened to me prior to coming into treatment the last time around. I was almost killed. I really saw that as a sign.

Briefly, a guy pointed a big 357 magnum at my face and pulled the trigger three times, no twice, and the gun didn't discharge. At that instant it was like time had slowed down.... I heard the first click. And it was like this loud slow motion click and my whole life is flashing before me. I said. "Oh God, he's gonna kill me." And I remember thinking: your family is gonna come and see you dead in this abandoned building in this crack spot. And I remember saying to myself, you can't die like this. And then I remember saying, "Damn, if you're gonna die like this, you gotta do something. You can't just stand here." That's when I heard the second click. Like in the movies, after the second click, everything came back and I jumped at the guy and the rest is history.

I managed to come out of that okay, I didn't kill him or anything of that nature, but...[sigh] I didn't go straight home that night. I continued to get high. Then the next morning about six, six-thirty, I remember going home. I remember saying to myself, "Damn, you [were] almost killed." That's the first time in all the years that I been on the street that I came face to face with death.

A couple of weeks later, I ended up in Phoenix House. I called them and had to wait two or three weeks for a bed. I haven't looked back since. That was eight years ago.

Life-threatening violence involving the use of firearms was not limited to the men at the secular program. AJ, a thirty-five year-old black man, had been at Redemption for three months when he told me his story. He recounted a tale that took place in his home town of San Francisco, in the house of the uncle who raised him after his parents split up and abandoned him at nine years of age.[10]

When I went to my uncle's house, I guess he was upset about something. When I came in he was throwing papers all around and had spray-painted our $500 stereo set. Stuff was, like, ransacked. He told me the police came up there and they tore up everything. They cut up every piece of furniture that was cutable. But he never told me what they was looking for. I kept askin' what the search warrant was for, but he wouldn't tell me. I found out two days later they was looking for cocaine. Supposedly, someone had tipped them off about my uncle hiding over a million dollars of cocaine in the house. They never found it.

I became afraid that if they came back and saw me there, they would hold me and try to get some information outta me. I told my uncle to pack up and close the house and go live with some friends for awhile. But he didn't want to go. So I had to force him out.... So I took the 32 [caliber pistol] and forced him outta the house. About two days later, my uncle's ex-wife came to the house while I was cleaning it up. Supposedly, she was the one that told the police. Me and her got into a big fight, fist fight. And I wound up shooting her in the back. Then I got so scared that she would identify me for the police that I packed my bags and left for Washington. I had some relatives who lived there.

They called my uncle to check on the situation, and he said his ex-wife was shot, but she never told the police. So I went back to San Francisco and resumed cleaning up the house. My uncle came in with three other guys and we got in a serious fight. They wanted to do some serious damage to me. We got into a gun fight. I had two 32s that I always carried with me and luckily only three shots were fired. I got hit in the leg, which I still have the scar. [At this point AJ showed me a jaggedly circular scar about the size of a nickel on his right shin.] I ran outta the house as fast as I could, went to an old girlfriend's house, got some money from her and came here to New York. [Shortly after arriving in New York, AJ was recruited by a Redemption House outreach team (see Hood 2011a, chap. 3).]

Physical threats to life and limb that reportedly stem from involvement with illicit drugs are not limited to firearms. Bud, a tall, bespectacled black man of thirty-six, was a two-month resident at Recovery House when he recounted this tale of a dangerous truck accident that he attributed to his use of drugs. This, he explained, is one of the elements that led to a previous ten-month stay at Phoenix House.

It was like this: I was driving for almost eighteen years, trucks, small or big, whatever. I was getting into driving tractor-trailers now, from state to state. If you get busted with drugs on you that's inter-drug trafficking [sic]. But I wasn't looking at it that way 'cause I was using. But who knows how they gonna look at it. So basically, I couldn't see myself destroying [my boss's] life. Any kind of accident I get into I gotta take a urine test. If I got drugs, he can get sued by the other people in the accident.

Q: Was there any particular event that occurred around this time that led you to this decision?

A: Yeah. I had an accident on the Manhattan Bridge. I was using drugs at that time, but not that day. It was just that my mind was clouded. My boss had just gone down to Georgia and was trying to build up his (interstate) business and he left me up here in charge. He had a 24-foot Mercedes truck, beautiful truck. I picked up a load that was too heavy.

So coming up the bridge on the outside lane, I had to speed up because of the heavy load. Then when I got to the top, traffic is all backed up from some guy had a flat down there. And here I am, my mind is wandering, I'm like, yeah he left me in charge; he got a lot of confidence in me…. And then I saw the backed up traffic, and I got all this speed built up and I can't stop. The brakes wouldn't grab. I tried downshifting, that didn't work. So I thought: I can't kill nobody. So I thought of throwing the truck off the bridge, jumped up on the rail. It wouldn't go over. It rode the rail for a while, then it bounced back on the road. Next thing you know, it was a six car pile up, y'know? Nobody died. They say a guy lost a finger, all this and that. Thank God nobody was in the back seat in the first car I hit, because the trunk ended up in the guy's back seat, y'know?

That really scared me. It made me think a lot. I can't see myself taking nobody else's life. [So] after that accident, I started thinking a lot. It got my wheels to rolling, man what am I doing out here using drugs? But at that time I couldn't stop.

Q: What was the outcome of the accident? Did you get arrested?

A: No. They used my truck to pull some of the other cars apart and they gave me a ticket. I told them the brakes failed, they didn't grab, so they gave me a ticket. But I saw life pass before my eyes. I thought I was going to jail. But then nothing happened and I didn't go to jail. I went to the rest of my stops, finished the day, went home. I told my boss about the accident, he said not to worry. Then what brought it to light, there was some guy taking pictures and [they] ended up in the Daily News. I was standing at the front of the truck looking down as if saying, Damn! I wish I still had that clip now.

Self-Degradation

In addition to the fear of AIDS and the generalized violence that lie in wait out in "the world"[11] for those who resist treatment or training, another common theme of life crisis that predisposes to treatment or training is the general degradation and degeneration of one's life and sense of self that is considered an inevitable consequence of illicit drug use. This particular type of deprivation tale is not about the possibility of physical death, but rather a kind of death of self. It is about a sense of disparity between an ideal self or desired way of life and the current situation of the respondent prior to entering treatment or training. Labeling theorists refer to this as a kind of self-labeling (Davis 1980).

In the cases detailed here, it reportedly led to treatment rather than continuing deviant careers.[12]

Keith, a four-month resident of Redemption House, told the following story about his loss of status and the consequent personal decline into a form of activity that carries a unique stigma among both treatment and training clients.[13]

I wind up leaving the state and going to Baltimore to sell drugs. Did pretty well. Made a lot of money selling drugs. We were…buying cars, jewelry, living good. I was still getting high, sniffing coke, smoking' crack. Even though people thought I was some big time drug dealer, I would sneak off to the crack houses at night smoking…getting everybody high. I started sniffing dope then. [That's when] a woman there introduced me to it. They have this terminology there, you know, women like the DD. That's the dope dick. A guy high on dope, it stays hard longer or something. We were making a killing…really doin' well.

Q: How did you get from that situation to here?

A: I came back, you know, my friends wind up getting killed. Everything went away. God took everything away. We had [trouble with] some guys out there and [had to] come back to New York. I wind up from co-op apartments with terraces to living in the streets. After that I wasn't working for two years…. My life was not going anywhere, and there was nothing I could do about it…. [If] I got back with my wife, maybe that would help me. I loved her and my daughter madly. I would do anything for them, only I couldn't. We lived in a shelter for seven, eight months. We finally got money to get an apartment. I spent the money getting high. Pshewwww! [This seems to indicate not merely frustration, but resignation, as if this is some sort of final, absolute indication, even confirmation, of his hopeless condition.]

Man that's it, my mother breaking, my wife flipping, I said I just want to die. Lord kill me, take me outta here. I don't want to live no more. I can't take it. Next thing you know, my wife don't want anything to do with me no more. She ain't got no place to stay, [because] they threw us out the shelter. (I had been getting high with people in the shelter and stealing from people in the shelter…)

My wife is [now] in Jersey with her mother. I just really felt like crap, man. Felt like nothing. There wasn't no hope for me nowhere, no how. One night, it was four o'clock in the morning, I couldn't get in the shelter, so I went uptown to my mother's house. Took the train from Brooklyn to her house. I told them they threw me outta the shelter, so they let me in the house, but they watching me, y'know? They know I came here to steal something. When I was in the closet getting my clothes, I saw my mother's suede jacket, so I stuffed it in the bag to sell the jacket. I just wanted to get high. So I went back out on the street, four, five o'clock in the morning, walking around all morning trying to sell this jacket that's worth $400. I could not sell this jacket. I went down to, "Yo, gimme five dollars bro. All I want is five dollars." Even the guys at the crack spot were not interested.

In the process of peddling his mother's jacket, Keith meets the person who becomes his conduit to Redemption, and in a week he is in the training program (see Hood 2011a). The reason Keith offers for seeking help is the downward spiral of his fortunes from "ma[king] a lot of money…buying cars and jewelry" to "Yo, gimme five dollars" for the $400 suede jacket stolen from his mother. This downward spiral, which Keith sees as the inevitable consequence of his involvement with illicit drugs, is considered a common symptom of sinfulness among the men at Redemption House.

The story of falling so low in the course of the drugging life that you stoop to stealing from your own family is a common one among my interviewees at both programs. Consider the account of Larry, a two-month resident of Recovery House, regarding his motives for entry.

> Yeah, I started selling drugs, but I got caught up in the mix, as they say. Got busted, went through the system. Then I was mandated. They sent me to [a program] down on 100 Street. I had to stay there for six months. That was only a six month program. After awhile, I started running wild. Using every day, not just occasional using, on the weekends. You use just on the weekends, can't nobody say he's using crack again. But then after a while you don't care who knows, and it starts to show, losing weight and this and that.

> Q: What was it that brought you to the realization that you needed to get back into a program?

> A: I was stayin' at my cousin's house. Had a little room fixed up in the basement. You start by stealing little things when you was using. I didn't go out and rob from other people, but I take from my family. Then things started getting out of hand. I took an air conditioner that was stored in the basement; Nintendo cartridges. I was only working at odd jobs at this time. Then it got to the point where he said, "You got to go. You can't be doin' that here." After I got here, I wrote a letter thanking him for that. I told him that he saved my life. He seen that I couldn't manage my life at that time. I went back and stayed with my Moms and this and that. But I found myself doin' the same things wherever I go. So I know I needed help. So I went to an agency trying to get back into Phoenix House, but they sent me here.

Armando, who was a Level III resident back for his second time at Recovery House, related a similar experience:

> Q: Tell me about your first treatment experience.

> A: I was here in 1990. Here for fifteen months.

> Q: How did you come to be here on that occasion?

> A: Due to the crack. It got me to the place where I stole everything from my mother's house and sold it. Sold my mother's stuff! Anything I could find to sell, I sold. To the point where I couldn't take it no more, Moms couldn't take it no more. I was too paranoid to go out and do a robbery or something like that. I had a car and I used to go around here [Recovery House] and see the people in the [yard out] back [where residents take cigarette breaks]. One day I said I better go get some help.

I came here and they sent me to [the induction center]. I bought a quart of beer and went [there]. The following week I was in here for treatment. It was hard; it was weird. I didn't know anything about treatment. Little by little, I learned how this place runs. After a couple of months, I was able to talk about my issues and how I started my addiction.

Alex, who said he was born in the "British West Indies, but raised in Brooklyn since I was four," still spoke with a lovely, rhythmic, back-beat island accent. At Redemption House only two weeks, he seemed resigned to the fact that he was unable to control his behavior without outside "gui-DANCE." He also seemed bewildered by the fact that some in his family were not supportive in the wake of his "fetchin'" activities.

When I was down dere [Miami], [I] started get-tin' into drug life more serious. But I would come to New York for coupl' a days. You know, see my Moms. I go back and forth on vacations. Sometime I go to islands for vacations. I go to Barbados, Trinidad, Antigua.

But as life goes on, you know, my drug life began to get more serious. I start takin' t'ings from outta my house, you know? Coupl'a years back, I came here to New York and my Moms leavin' da house. And I fetched lotta t'ings up outta da house. When I fetched dese t'ings up out da house, it happens my family didn't want ta see me no more. Start fetchin' all deir little valuables, TV and everyt'ing. Dat's how far I went. De only t'ings I leave in de house, de furniture, a little bit a' ornaments. I even took de microwave. It was friends from New York who had turned me on to da high, influenced me. My Moms, she on a job. She works nurse's aide work. They had a big floor model TV that I couldn't move out, but I was about to.

My brother in Florida has a mechanic's shop, a restaurant, some stores.... I used to work for him. But when I live with him, I got to follow his rules. He don't do no drugs, no cigarettes, nut'ing. He drink occasionally.

After I came outta the [28 day NA residential] program, I stayed with my brother t'ree years. He be my gui-dance. Everywhere that I would go, he be dere or have someone dere to watch over me. If I'm out dere by myself, I'm quick to pick up on drugs or bad company. [After NA,] I stayed clean for t'ree years. Then after t'ree years, he got me a condo by myself. After a month, he leave me and go home. I went and picked up a hooker. The hooker was smokin' [crack] and I started smokin' too. We end up smokin' $500 that evening just to have some pleasure and some fun. It end up leadin' back to da street.

Shortly after this, Alex found his way to New York and, like AJ and others, encountered an outreach team that introduced him to the discipleship program at Redemption House (see Hood 2011a).

The careers of Larry and Alex in drug sales did not parallel the success that Keith claims for his business; and Armando did odd jobs before his downfall. However, in the end, which is the focus of all accounts, all of the men told of stealing from their own families to pay for their drug use.

Bud, who went to Phoenix House after the accident with his truck on the Manhattan Bridge, later added another element to his drug-induced decline into depravity. His story of stealing from his company probably does not bear quite the same degree of stigma as stealing from family. However, Bud seemed particularly attached to his boss, who he said had treated him "like a son." As a result, he reports strong feelings of guilt and self-recrimination as a result of betraying this trust.

Q: So your using didn't disrupt your work?

A: At times it did. At times it didn't. It was a time that I was staying up here [NYC], driving a straight truck that I did something that really hurt me. They gave me a truck with a load on it to deliver. I sold the whole load. It was a load of scouring pads; the big ones for doin' floors. You can find anybody to buy that; hardware stores, places that rent floor cleaning equipment. I went from store to store until I sold almost the whole load.

[The next day, when] I told [my company] the whole story what I was doin'.... they replaced the merchandise I stole and told me to go out there and deliver it. They didn't fire me. They told me, "We gonna take this outta your pay." They never did. That messed me up right there. Because I'm hurtin' all these people and they still love me like a son, treatin' me better than I should be treated. I didn't know how to deal with it. That was one of the overall reasons that made me go into a program.

Julio had been at Recovery House for six months when I interviewed him. His story is yet another variation on the degradation theme so prevalent in residential programs. He is a powerfully built young man, perfect to play muscle for petty schemers.

Q: So you stopped using powdered cocaine on a regular basis and started using crack regularly?

A: Right. See, the coke I would use [only] when I got paid, when I had money. Then the crack got me to a point where I didn't really care if I didn't have any money, I would go look for the money. You see? When it was the cocaine, I was able to maintain and hold on and do it whenever I had money. But I guess the crack was so intense that I would have to go and sell things, pawn things, steal things, whatever, just to do it. Then I would see myself doing the same thing over and over and I didn't want to do that anymore.

Q: Then what happened?

A: Then I came into treatment.

Q: How did you get into treatment?

A: The last month before getting in here, I was with some young ladies and a friend of mine that lived in the same block. They would go out in the streets and sell themselves, and I would be the lookout and so forth. And I would get money and it would go to drugs. I had just started doin' that. So that right there, me going home late mornings, having to deal with different situations in the street, putting my life up for a hit of crack, I told myself, this is not me. Today I am worth more than this. That's [what] made me go into treatment.

Q: How long did you work at this activity?

A: 'Bout a month. I had been hangin' out with them longer, but wasn't part of the [business]. They would tell me, all you gotta do is just watch what car I get in and make sure I'm okay, and twenty minutes I'll be back and get you high. So I did it just for the get high part. I didn't have to go steal anything or borrow or anything else, its just there.

Female Troubles

In the era of crack, the most commonly told tales of sexual obsession were stories about women[14] giving themselves away for payment in crack (see Mc-Coy et al. 1995; Williams 1992).[15] Therefore, I found it particularly interesting when several of the men I spoke with also reported troubling obsessions with women that they believed were related to their own drug use. Some of these men considered their relations with women or their desire for sexual gratification in general as troublesome as their drug use. Nevertheless, they all viewed their use of drugs as an integral part of these "troubles."

Stanley, a six-month resident of Redemption House, is a tall, deep-voiced, handsome, fun-loving black man in his mid-thirties. His sexual proficiency and the dilemmas it created for him are among the central themes of his biography spelled out in the previous chapter. In the following—only one of the half-dozen or so similar exploits he recounted—Stanley decides yet again to seek help.

I was always girl crazy. When I got introduced to drugs at seventeen that also introduced me to the women, to the partying. I would live for the weekend.... I was always at clubs and partying. All the women that I was with were always older than me. I was always the youngest in the crowd, but I was big for my age. I was getting into the [night] spots because of my height...

When I was seeing my second daughter's mother, I was [also] messing with an Italian woman and a Chinese woman, and they would all come to visit me at different times, at lunch time or, or, I'd get so confused. The Lord blessed me, because doin' all these women, I can say I slept with 150 women, since I started from fourteen [years old] 'til now. The Lord blessed me. I never had to go to the hospital for a rupture or any kind of [venereal disease] or whatnot. God really had his hand on me, 'cause I did some really wild things. I know God had his hand on me. I never used rubbers, even to this day, never.

I lost my garment [district] job for one thing.... [T]hey had gave me a profit-sharing check for $10,000. I took that money, gave my mother some of it, gave my daughter some of it, $1000 for herself. I gave her mother $1000 to spend for herself. The rest of it I blew in three weeks. I took that profit-sharing check and spent three weeks in a hotel with three females. I had crack, cocaine, and good Jamaican marijuana, two bottles of Jack Daniel's. But I was unhappy, because the woman I wanted to be with was a [born again] Christian.

After God came into her life, two years after my second daughter was born, God had touched her...she accepted the Lord. All three of those sisters are saved, filled [with the Holy Spirit], and work for Social Security. They all [are] administrators. They go to Pastor Gray's Pentecostal Church in Brooklyn. I was the only person she ever slept with. But ever since then, I couldn't touch her. She wouldn't see me. She tried to bring me to the Lord. She tried to study [the Bible] with me. But every time we study, I'd get into the flesh.

These women [in the hotel] satisfied my flesh, but that inner heart desire that I wanted, she wouldn't go with me. After these women left, I took about 30 sleeping pills, I smoked up everything I had and slept for two days. I thought I was gonna die. I woke up without a hangover, no sickness or nothing. The first thing I thought was to give my life to God. I [had] tried to kill myself, but I couldn't even do that right. Deep inside I was too scared to kill myself, so I thought, let me try Jesus. Maybe He can help me.

Stanley's "troubles" relating to women are matched at Recovery House by Barry, as well as is his inclination to seek a religious solution.[16] Barry, a three-month resident, is also African American, but there his physical resemblance to Stanley ends. Barry is short and a bit stocky, with a prison-honed musculature. Moreover, he seems moody, quiet, and a loner, quite unlike the gregarious, good-time Stanley.[17]

My girl said I had a problem 'cause I would stay away from home like two days at a time getting high with this guy who lived upstairs from me.... I just continued to get high. Then I went to Star House program up in Borough Park, part of the shelter program. It's a six-month (residential) program. I left after six months, but I didn't graduate. Then I went home. Three days later I started getting high again. I went on a run with the money I accumulated in there. And then I stayed sober from March 'til September. Then I started getting high again. Then I stayed sober for few months and started again. Then I went to Daytop for about four months, came home and started getting high again.

Q: Why did you leave Daytop?

A: They put a lotta pressure on me. I started liking this Italian girl. And most Italian people don't like it when you trying to get into they kinda little sect there. I started catching problems. We was always looking at each other and smiling and it started going too far. I tried to slow it down, but she always followed me around and talked to me. She's a real nice person. But they started putting me through a lotta contracts.[18] I think it was a racial thing, to tell the truth—from both sides. I got black pressure and Italian pressure on me. I left.

Q: How did you get here?

A: Well, I started getting high again, and one day I was at a friend's house, and he was a drug dealer, but he got mad at me for smoking crack in his house. We got into an argument, and he stabbed me in my leg. I was staying at the shelter program. A guy that works in the reachout program there asked, "Who got a problem?" I said, "I do. I have a drug problem." He said, "I'll get you in a program." I said, "No I'll do it myself." Then I went out and sold everything I had left and went on a sixteen-day run. I went back, and he sent me here.

Q: What do you think you're problem is?

A: My problem? I don't know. I been getting high for ten years. It's like I don't even know myself no more. Whenever I get in a relationship with a girl, it only lasts [a couple of] months. That's one reason I'm here. All my life, I always like beautiful woman. I just feel like I can't give 'em up. I tried, you know, but...

Q: Doesn't the Quran allow you to have more than one wife?

A: Wives!? But women, heh heh heh, that's different. I think that's why I fell a lot. 'Cause God...wants you to be morally totally [*sic*]. Like looking at women, y'know, with little dresses on, half naked. Not supposed to look at women; that's a little sin. You get sins on top of sins, then He put a rap on you, y'know? And that's why I always fell, because I did little stupid things.

Q: What things?

A: Women. Start getting crazy about them. Start playing, go to extreme with [them].

Q: What will you do when you leave here to avoid doing that?

A: Nah, it's gonna be very hard. I was hoping that this time I get a wife. I almost had a wife before, but I start getting high. Oh, you know how I fell again? I got this girl an abortion. I think I caused myself some compunctions from guilt and I started getting high again. I went to extreme. I had girlfriends....

Q: Didn't you tell me when we were talking before [a few days prior to the recorded interview] about an elder in a mosque praying with you for several days?

A: Once I went to stay at a mosque to do my [religious obligation] and the brother saw my face and knew something was wrong. So they kept me around them. I used to spend the night at the mosque and all that. They used to keep me around because they said they were trying to keep Satan and his demons away from me. That lasted for about a month. It worked too. It did a miracle. I was really out there at one time. I started praying, and, like I said, I start getting money from all kinds of places. And things started coming, just like being a human being again. It was like a marvel. Then I started drifting off; started putting women in my life. You know, clothes and stuff like that. They [the elders] let me go 'cause they thought "God must be with him." Eventually I fell real bad, women, sex; started having sex with lotta women, getting high, losing my possessions, real bad.

In the course of our conversations, Stanley and Barry cited identical scriptural promises that they felt were important to their spiritual quests. Stanley's was from the Bible, of course: "Trust in the Lord...and he will give you the desires of your heart" (Psalms 37:3-4 RSV).[19] Barry paraphrased the Quran:

I believe that if I kept more to the religious norms, I would be more successful in life. 'Cause God, He just wants us to do right...and love Him. So if you love people, you show love for Him. Stay away from drugs, gambling, fornication, and He said He'll give you everything back that you want.

Q: It says that in the Quran?

A: Yeah.

Q: Says that in the Bible too.

A: Yeah?!

Forest, at Recovery House for a second tour, recounted yet another common variation on the theme of sexually oriented crisis.

I was in that relationship four and half years. In that time, I was in treatment three times. I relapsed; she relapsed. Now [I'm] back in the fourth time. She's active [still using drugs]. I decided to stop. The cycle has to stop somewhere.

I was in two other programs, one a three-month and the other a TC in Pennsylvania. I finished December eighteen. January first I relapsed, and March eighteenth I came back to treatment here. I left the Pennsylvania TC after eleven months, because of the relationship with the same woman. I'm no longer in that relationship and my focus is now on my treatment. Before I was doing what I had to do in the relationship, but now I'm doin what I have to do for my treatment. I knew she was dippin' and dabbin' and lyin' to me. I guess we both were in denial and that's why I relapsed.

After I left here the first time, I stayed clean about four months. We would drink beer from time to time. Then one night, after drinking, we decided to get some crack. We thought things would be different this time. First thing I felt after I first picked up was I felt really rotten. Because after working so hard for fifteen months…I went on a run…umm, actually I didn't go on a run. We kept dippin' and dabbin' for awhile. We lived together, so every time we got money we got high. It continued like that until I'd go into treatment and she would stay at home. She told me she was gonna change, she never changed. It went like that for four and a half years; it was madness. She never went back to treatment.

Even among residents for whom difficulties with women were not seen as a major source of program entry, sexual proclivities were nevertheless interpreted as continually problematic. "Slick" is a prime example at Redemption House.

One of the biggest struggles here as I go out on visits and everything is women. I know that's a weak area in my life and I'm glad the Lord has opened my eyes to that. So I can "above all else guard my heart, for it is the wellspring of life" [biblical quote]. So I focus on the Lord, and I pray a lot. And whenever I'm in a situation where I can be tempted, I run from it. For it says in James 4:7&8 "Resist the Devil. Submit yourselves to God. Resist the Devil and he will flee from you. Come near to God and he will come near to you. Wash your hands you sinners and purify your hearts you double minded." And when I'm in a situation where I think I'm gonna be tempted, if she's very pretty, I just walk away. Because I know that will draw me near to the Lord. I know that's always gonna be with me, that desire for a companion. But I don' wanna be in a situation where I'm gonna look at a woman and she's so beautiful that I'll remember the things I used to do and undress her [in my mind]. Lotta people get caught up in that area and end up submitting. I wanna stand strong. I wanna be like Daniel. I'm reading the book of Daniel right now. He said "I will not defile myself with the king's food." That's how I wanna be.

In each category, the parallels between the perceived problems that account for what induced or led residents of both houses to seek organized assistance could not be clearer. The stories are the same stories; the "sad tales" that they relate to account for their presence in a drug program are the same sad tales.[20] In addition to accounts of "why we are here," the two programs share rationales regarding "who succeeds."

Success Stories

As I indicated, I do not intend that my description of residents' accounts be taken as exhaustive, but only illustrative and indicative of the program parallels, especially at the level of program rhetoric and residents' consciousness. I chose to focus on the problem of entry because it became clear to me that "why we are here" is a primary concern for the residents, reflected in their daily conversation as well as the accounts reported here. It is also reflected in the rationales developed by staff members to deal with that question at both programs.

A similar parallel is evident in accounts concerned with the other "end" of treatment and training, that is, why some people succeed (in program terms) and many do not. The agreement on the explanation for this quandary was almost unanimous across the two Houses.

Forest and Walter offered comments on this question that were typical of virtually all Recovery House respondents.

Forest: Recovery House is like shock treatment, especially since we have to get up at 5:30, but without the physical exercises, 45 minutes of physical training and a five mile run. I kind of miss that. When I left shock, I was in pretty good shape. Recovery House is okay. I see there can be a lotta treatment here, *if you really want it.* But whatever program you're in, *you have to really want this.* You have to have a sincere desire to put your life together to stop using. [Previously,] I just complied; I never really applied! [Emphasis added.]

Walter: My honest belief, programs, they're good, but it *all depends on the individual.* I've seen peers of mine who have split programs after three and four months and never picked up again. They're sitting on six and seven years [abstinent]. They never picked up; they never graduated that program. Here I've graduated programs, split programs, and still picked up. What's wrong with this picture? What's wrong with the picture is me. I still wanted to get high. I didn't listen to the messages of staying away from those people, those places, and those things, because I'm that individual who does those things and goes to those places.

Q: Are there any particular techniques that you can use now to avoid those people, places, and things?

A: There are no techniques. *You* just have to *be determined.* There again, *you* have to want to get clean. [Emphasis added.]

At Redemption House, AJ and Marvin see things in much the same terms.

Q: Why do some people who come here get their lives turned around…and others don't?

AJ: Umm. [After a long moment's reflection:] For me, I would say it's the way I identified myself with the program. It's something inside of me, a desire that *I really wanted* and did my best to obtain that desire. Some guys come in and spend the same four months, and they want to [improve], too, but something happens and they don't. The best that I can say is *they didn't really want it*. It's like the Apostle Paul said, y'know? We run the race to finish. Some don't have that desire and that's what stops them, that desire *not* to finish. They might not want to admit it, but that's the underlying problem. You'll get it *if you really want it*. I was told that when I first came in here. If you really want…a better life for yourself, *it's up to you*, you make that decision. Harry mentions that a lot. [Emphasis added.]

Marvin: I got into Redemption House not understanding it wasn't just a Christian program, but a drug rehab. As I mentioned before, if I had known it was a drug rehab, I wouldn't have walked through the door. I wouldn't be here today. I wasn't interested in a drug program. I was working in a drug program for the government. As far as I'm concerned, they don't work. I sat in that program for four years. I conducted some of the N[arcotics] A[nonymous] classes, then I would walk out and get high. So would everyone else, the staff and so forth. But this program, this program works, *for those who want it to work.* [Emphasis added.]

Is this a curious claim to find at either program: one that asserts the community is the therapist, the other that the Holy Spirit accomplishes the change? Obviously it serves a legitimation function for the organizations. If some (or most) do not get saved or get well, whose fault is it? The "gotta want it" claim exonerates the program for any individual's failure: Why didn't it work? Well it didn't get a fair trial. That this is also a program rationale is indicated in AJ's comments about being "told that when I first came" to Redemption House and "Harry (the Director) mentions it a lot." This "gotta want it" mantra is extremely common at both programs, among both residents and staff members.

But what cognitive benefit do the residents gain by adopting this adaptation? For one thing, overt attacks on the program are not allowed. They are immediately "cooled out." Or if they persist, the source (the resident) is eliminated from the residence. The "want it" claim is a necessary complement to the program ideology. But more than that, perhaps, it allows residents some (illusion of?) cognitive space in the midst of massive conformity demands. Is this their way of finding room for some sense of autonomy? "I may be conforming, but I'm choosing to do so, since it wouldn't be happening, if I didn't do it, if I wasn't cooperating, using what's available here, via my own volition." Here perhaps is a means for clients like Walter or AJ to believe they *are* in control of their destiny, and to take pride in their accomplishment. Also, it is a way to differentiate themselves from those who failed to turn around. AJ suggests that "finishing the race" is "something to be proud of" something he could "look back on and say, 'I made it'."

What is left out of this bit of program rhetoric is the evidence from "natural recovery" studies, which show that to "want it" users need a *reason*, i.e., a **stake** in the conventionality they are seeking. Recovery or sobriety is rarely an end in itself. This is implied in the crisis stories described previously. More often, sobriety is seen as a means to salvage or regain some other conventional value, like a career, family connections, "self-esteem," or to avoid an early death (Waldorf et al. 1991). Recovery and redemption, from this perspective, are not about "wanting *it*," but about wanting *something else*, something important, something of value that drug misuse tends to interfere with. This particular notion is exemplified by the following story of several years ago from a less-deviant American subculture[21]:

> ...the biopsy and the chilling diagnosis [dysplasia...the stage before malignancy] was convincing enough to make [Philadelphia Phillies' pitcher, Curt] Schilling stop [chewing tobacco after sixteen years of ten times a day]. "I want to be a great husband and father, with a full face," said Schilling, who is married with two children.... "The thought of losing my family almost made it easy...to quit." He had tried to stop before and endured headaches and insomnia.... He used a six-week nicotine patch [and] an organized support group.

Several years later, I spotted Shilling in the Red Sox dugout with a large bulge in his cheek! Sometimes, at least, wanting something else is not even enough.

Discussion

This comparison of accounts of previous lives and motives for entering treatment and training recounts widely shared experiences of deprivation and depravity across the two programs and seems on the face of it to indicate a strong similarity, if not identity, between the client populations at Redemption House and Recovery House. These stories of motives and previous life experiences confirm the demographic data discussed in the previous chapter and book (Hood 2011a) that the two populations are really one, that, contrary to the claims of earlier studies, both types of programs, secular and religious, draw their clientele from the same population.

However, there are important reasons not to rush to this conclusion alone. There may be other reasons why these accounts are reproducible across the two program settings. The demographic similarities are real, of course. However, accounts of moral failings can be read in various ways. Since this is an investigation in the sociology of conversion as well as the sociology of drug treatment, it seems pertinent to look at what the former perspective has to offer on this subject. For example, the New Religious Movement (NRM) literature discussed by Snow and Machelak (1984, 175ff) contains a significant number of observations regarding the *suspect* character of convert accounts. This includes reports of pre-recruitment distress by clients in drug treatment programs (Greil and

Rudy 1983). Moreover, Heirich (1977) has offered evidence that preconversion "deprivations," like those of the residents' accounts above, do not adequately explain conversion experiences, nor does earlier socialization such as religious training, as the Langrod studies suggest (see also Danzger 1989a).

Although numerous empirical studies of conversionist groups have found that clients tell typically similar deprivation stories, other works conclude that these "self-reports" are formulated in conjunction with the programs' conversion rhetorics. McGuire (1991, 73) summarizes the methodological problem:

> The main difficulty in distinguishing the degree of change that occurs in any given conversion is that the individual who converts reinterprets past experiences in relationship to the new meaning system. Therefore, it becomes difficult to determine what amount of the convert's description of the changes…represents the objective process of conversion and how much expresses the convert's subjective reinterpretation of those events. The convert [typically] constructs the story of [his] conversion, drawing on a socially available set of plausible explanations or "rhetoric."…Rhetorics of change [often] emphasize the dramatic nature of personal change [and] compare the evil or unhappiness of their previous way of life with how wonderful their new way is. Rhetorics of choice emphasize how much the change resulted from personal, often agonizing, decision, [since] our society places [so] much value on individual decision.

As McGuire summarizes the NRM conclusions, she suggests a different possible, or at least a more complete, explanation for the similar stories at the two programs. The two groups of residents create similar stories to present to their programs (and any researcher who happens along in the meantime) because they discover that these kinds of stories are expected of them. They are expected because they fit the treatment program's ideology, its image of what a "drug addict" is, and the training program's belief about what a "sinner" is. And, it is common knowledge that an integral and constant part of treatment (and training) is admission of these fundamental "facts." Almost any American adult can quote the first of AA's twelve steps: first, I have to acknowledge that I have a problem. "I am an addict/sinner or we are all sinners/addicts in here," were constant refrains included in my conversations and observations at the two Houses. From this perspective, since these client tales of "before" are constructed "after," they must be considered the products of the social context (including the individual consciousness) in and by which they are produced, that is, the treatment or training program. They are retrospectively constructed accounts that in all likelihood reflect the (ideological and rhetorical) viewpoints of the treatment or training program as much as the "actual facts" of the client's biography.[22]

In addition, from the sociological perspective, the issue of motives is never treated in an abstract, individualistic fashion. In the tradition of the classical sociologists, motives are not merely the "property" of individuals, but can be readily seen to vary by social group and or category (see e.g., Danzger 1989; Douglas 1978; Mills 1940; Wuthnow et al. 1984). Both the NRM conclusions regarding self-reports in highly ideological settings and the "sociology of motives" suggest that the similarities in the accounts of the clients at Redemption and Recovery Houses may be more appropriately understood as indicating similarities between the two programs at least as well as similarities among the individual clients or their backgrounds.

Danzger (1989, 223f) has developed a "constructionist" perspective on motives and accounts regarding conversions to Orthodox Judaism that incorporates insights from an intriguing variety of sociological and social psychological sources. Among the theories and studies Danzger has synthesized are Weber's notion of "adequacy" and C. Wright Mills' observations that "vocabularies of motive" vary over time and across social locations and cultural settings. He combines this insight with similar ideas from more psychologically oriented observers (e.g., Festinger, Asch, Milgram) to conclude that "we will not find a motive...to explain why a person [converts]" simply by listening to his description of converting. For social science, the explanation lies rather in one's "group affiliations," and other social structural variables. Thus, if two groups tell similar tales, they are likely to be similar in ways worth exploring, *especially if they claim to be very different.*

Therefore, it seems prudent to investigate further the issues of clients' previous lives, their reported motives for entering treatment or training, the reconstructed nature and general status of their accounts as data sources for this research. Are the similarities really just the result of similar backgrounds of the clients? Or does this similarity of understood motives indicate more about the nature of the programs themselves and their view of world, self, drug addiction, treatment, and training? Do the stories that clients tell have any validity with regard to their experience before, during or after treatment and training? Can they be trusted as data, or must they be dismissed as mere rhetoric? Is there evidence available to indicate whether or not these stories are reliable or mere rhetoric? Or, is there some, as yet undiscovered, middle ground?

My investigations lead me to believe that both explanations have validity at Redemption House and Recovery House. (Perhaps because of the special population they serve as compared to other conversionist groups.) Most of the stories the men tell, I believe, are essentially true (i.e., they represent real events), but are not necessarily accurate. The events recounted probably did happen to somebody, perhaps even to the story tellers themselves in most cases, but probably not all. Certainly, most, if not all of the men embellish their accounts. They exaggerate, conflate, imitate, vary, create; they borrow and adapt stories in ways that meet the expectations (rhetorical paradigms) of the treatment or training setting in which they find themselves at any given moment. Goffman (1961, 150f) writes:

> Given the stage that any person has reached in a career, one typically finds that he constructs an image of his life course—past, present, and future—which selects, abstracts, and distorts in such a way as to provide him with a view of himself that

he can usefully expound in current situations. Quite generally, the person's line concerning self...defensively brings him into appropriate alignment with the basic values of his society.

It is also likely that residents utilize real events of their own lives where they are applicable, but in selective and "distorted" fashion. This process has been typical of all cultures (perhaps oral cultures especially) everywhere and, I submit, continues to be true of this one, but is decidedly intensified in these highly ideological movement settings.

Above all, the men of Redemption House and Recovery House are selective in their storytelling. They select the stories they tell according to the largely informal directions they have received from other members of their program, both staff counselors and more experienced residents. The selection process is learned, beginning with the very first day in treatment or training by listening to others and eventually trying out "drafts" of tales on "peers" or "brothers" until they get the desired response. The selection process appears typical of all conversionist movements and total institutions (see Danzger 1989, 224ff; Goffman 1961). It is generally done in good faith, at least without conscious fabrication. It is part of learning "the (appropriate) truth" about one's self, one's world, and one's fellows (Orbuch 1997). But it can be done cynically as well; more commonly called "playing a role." All the residents, I submit, are to some degree playing a role—as are we all. The only difference is the degree of self-consciousness (i.e., cynicism) with which we play (see Berger 1961; Cuzzort 1989).

This form of storytelling is not limited to treatment floors; it occurs as well on street corners, in sports bars, or "police" bars, private business clubs, suburban "ladies teas." Wherever people (whatever their drug of choice) gather and promote camaraderie through discussion of their own "exploits," this type of "tale-spinning" goes on. These tales are plentiful and meaningful; they are integral to the experience of being human.[23] The world of the street drug addict, like any other social world, has its mythologies and lore, its "stocks of knowledge" about what the experience of drug addiction is or is expected to be in various contexts. The stories of degradation and deprivation that residents tell, for example, bring them status and acceptance among their peers and overseers—sometimes it is the same story for both audiences, sometimes not. For residents in general, and newer residents in particular, the stories help them orient themselves in the new cognitive universe, once they learn which ones told with which emphases are meaningful in the new setting and which are deemed inappropriate.[24] But drug addicts in treatment and training are far from the only population that selectively alters its biographies according to social setting. After all, we have all written resumes and had job interviews, or testified in court—even those of us who happen to be police, prosecutors, psychiatrists, social workers, or other protectors of the public order.

The general process of selective recollection is well recognized, especially under conditions of intense ideological "bombardment" in a closed or protected organizational or cultural setting (see Berger and Luckmann 1966; Lofland 1966, 1977; Ofshe and Watters 1996). It is fundamental to any resocialization process, especially in formal settings like Redemption and Recovery Houses. The similarity of the life stories that I heard at the two communities is a reflection of the similarity of the real experiences and associations shared by both groups of men *over the years* prior to entering treatment (i.e., of belonging to the same sub-population) *as well as* to the similarity of the expectations about the residents' previous lives shared by the two program ideologies, despite their sharp differences with regard to other realities.

The programs direct their clients not only to be selective, but how to select the elements of the stories they tell from their own memories as well as from the collective stock of knowledge provided in the treatment and training processes. Each program provides its own interpretive paradigm that directs what sort of story elements are acceptable and which are not. As Danzger (1989, 224) writes, "the account is thus a reflection of the group's values and self-perception, *as well as* the individual's." [Emphasis added.] And, as the accounts of degradation and graduation (i.e., who "makes it") exhibit amazing parallels in both Houses, it stands to reason that the residents and programs are likely to be similar in other ways as well. Indeed, phenomenologically, science-based drug treatment at Recovery House and faith-based discipleship training at Redemption House are one and the same in more ways than are generally recognized.

As I have suggested, one of the things that the two paradigms share with one another is a rhetoric of change. This expresses the "fact" that before the residents of the two houses entered their respective programs, their lives were filled with danger, depravity, degradation, and distress, but now they have seen the error of their ways and are ready to change (McGuire 1992). Carefully attended to, and viewed in this comparative framework, resident autobiographies, like those explored in this chapter, can point to the process of selective recollection at both programs and give indications of the nature of the paradigms that shape it.

To discover the ways in which resident tales are shaped by the separate (but equal?) program rhetorics, including important ways they are similar and important ways they differ see Hood (2011a). There, two chapters look at the evidence of these separate but similar selective processes. One chapter analyzes resident accounts of conversion at Redemption House, the self-admitted and indisputably ideological movement organization whose view of the world of drugs and the world in general is grounded in religious faith rather than in clinical science or mental hygiene. Then, a subsequent chapter looks at similar procedures at Recovery House, how its treatment processes can be illuminated by comparison and contrast with discipleship training, and what the results imply about the claims for a scientific and rational basis of the therapeutic community form of treatment.

Notes

1. Quoted by Mills (1939/1974, 442).
2. See also Muffler et al. (1997), which includes Langrod as a coauthor.
3. Considerable research on religious conversion does in fact suggest that "previous disposition" is an important contributing factor in religious conversion (see extensive literature cited in Greil and Rudy 1983, 12). However, I intend to argue here that the apparent differences in ideology between the religious and secular organizations are in fact less significant than their similarities. As a result, we should not expect previous dispositions regarding the nature of "addiction" or religious outlook (with the exception of converts to Islam, perhaps) to play a major role in recruitment. This claim is supported by the important work of Heirich (1977) and Danzger (1989).
4. On the face of it, this would seem to indicate that the experience of illicit drug use was the same for both sets of residents regardless of the ideological character of the program in which they participated. However, things are not always what they seem (Berger 1963, 23). The precise nature of the similarities in resident accounts, and the methodological status of those accounts and the information they entail, I address in the course of this chapter (see also Hood 2011a). Also, the extent of these similarities appears to belie the conclusions of the Langrod studies, which suggest that the two types of programs draw from separate populations.
5. A Note on Method:

    Whether the new resident is seen as a joiner (seeker) or a recruit, it seems, may depend largely on who is doing the investigating and how the question of affiliation is posed (see Robbins 1988). My research at Redemption House and Recovery House attempted to avoid biasing the issue from the outset by posing the question to interviewees in language that was as neutral as possible in this regard. This generally meant asking: "Why are you here?" or "How did you get here?"

    In addition to asking "neutral" questions, I probed residents in both directions at various times during the interviews. If a resident talked about motives and deprivations, I asked, at appropriate moments and in different ways, whether specific recruitment networks or procedures influenced his decision. Likewise, if a resident talked about recruitment, I asked about decisions and deprivations. In general, this meant being alert to comments that suggested the de-emphasized side of the equation and asking, "Can you tell me more about that?"

    All interviews included deprivation tales. At Redemption House, the men also talked about recruitment, so very little conscious interview "technique" was necessary there, in this regard. At Recovery House, except for those men who had been remanded to treatment by the criminal justice system, almost no one talked of formal recruitment systems. And when I probed in this direction, it proved almost entirely fruitless. According to their accounts, residents are there because they chose to be, and they chose to be because of the privations they experienced related to their drug use. Very few men (only three or four) mentioned informal recruitment networks consisting of kin or acquaintances; the latter included, for the most part, AA or NA associates. Those men who alluded to informal recruitment downplayed this aspect of their experience, unlike the men at Redemption House who made it central to their accounts (see Hood 2011a).
6. I do not intend to suggest that these categories of motive exhaust the reasons men had or gave for entering treatment or training. They are simply the most prominent; they are the most typical among the men I interviewed. Other individual motives were identified; some of these will be considered as they relate to other contexts and issues.

7. "Flesh" is a familiar expression in evangelical and Pentecostal circles. It refers to one's carnal or sinful (often, though not always, sexual) desires or activities as opposed to spiritual (Godly or righteous) desires and activities.

8. "Convicting" is another evangelical term that refers to a sense of guilt that is believed to be the result of God or the Holy Spirit communicating directly with the individual "Christian's" soul or "heart." This is the ultimate meaning of a "personal relationship" with Christ: God is in constant and direct communication with those who have "accepted him into their heart and been saved." In essence, the Holy Spirit becomes the individual's moral conscience. "Conviction" is that conscience "reminding" one of what he or she "ought" to do or not to do. In this case, Slick believes the Holy Spirit is the source of his fear about the virus.

9. This refers not simply to being saved, but to following "God's will," i.e., His individualized life plan for each "Christian."

10. AJ's point is the violence and danger that surrounds drug use and dealing, but it is also interesting to note how the various categories of drug tales overlap and intermix in real life. This story could also easily fit in the degradation category (see below), since AJ's depravity leads him to do serious damage, both morally and physically, to his own family. In addition, as a result of this encounter with his family, AJ ends up homeless on the streets of New York where he eventually makes contact with an outreach team from Redemption House (see Hood 2011a).

11. In this context, "world" is a term of decidedly religious origins that is used identically at both Redemption House and Recovery House. Nelson (1981, 220) writes that it is "from the cloister that we receive...the dualism of 'Religion' and 'World.'" Max Weber adapted the term from the ascetic groups he studied and paired it with the term "religion" to demonstrate the sectarian consciousness of a strict boundary or "tension" between the realm of the sacred group of brothers and the realm of all others, the outsiders, the uninitiated, the enemy, the rest of mankind that is not saved, that does not belong to the elect or the enlightened.

> The 'world'...is a realm of temptations...not only because of...sensual pleasure...but because it fosters...complacent self-sufficiency ...at the expense of the uniquely necessary...active achievements leading to salvation." (Weber 1922/1964, 165)

It is indicative of the approximation or affinity between the ascetic life at the therapeutic community and in a Protestant sectarian organization like Redemption House that both groups use this reference to indicate the chasm and tension between themselves, the righteous, and the culture beyond their walls, the unrighteous—or merely complaisant.

12. From another angle, this could be seen as part and parcel of the career of a drug addict. This is so because treatment, more often than not, serves to attach (or reinforce) the label and, thereby, the identity of "addict" upon those who enter such programs. This is especially true of the majority who split the programs, some of whom will return time and again until they find some accommodation with this socially imposed identity. See Skoll (1992).

13. In this connection, it is interesting to note the solid agreement across programs about the depravity of violating certain aspects of "family values," despite the differences between the two programs regarding other items on the conservative agenda, such as, e.g., abortion or single parenthood.

14. The sexual obsessions discussed in this section may just as well be categorized as a variation on the general degradation and degeneration theme, since they, too, contribute to a self-recognition that accounts for entering treatment or training.

However, due to its formally "victimless" character, I decided the issue of relations with the opposite sex was better treated as a separate, though obviously related, motif. Additionally, the choice of title for this section has received some criticism for its *apparent* insensitivity to issues of patriarchal bias and discrimination against women that continue to afflict both formal and informal relations between the sexes in our society. The initial use of the title, "Female Troubles," was prompted primarily by my sense of how this matter was *experienced by the informants*. Despite the criticism, which may have validity regarding possible misperceptions of my intentions, I have chosen to keep the title precisely because it *reflects the perspective of the main speakers* in this document, the men who told me their stories. I believe this to be consistent with an ethnographic approach to social research. I also enjoy the play on words that, I believe, ultimately tweaks the nose of yet another icon of male domination, i.e., the marketing of sex for drugs that exploits women in ways conventionally considered beyond the pale of all civilized behavior. On the contrary, I suggest that such behavior simply extends and reflects the "normal" patterns of sexual and market relations in this society, including the traditional patterns of the market for sexual relations, i.e., prostitution. See Erich Goode (1997).

15. For a different perspective on this phenomenon, see Kearney et al. (1994); Murphy and Rosenbaum (1999); Rosenbaum et al. (1990).
16. Note that Stanley's inclination toward a religious solution led him to Redemption House, a religious program, while Barry's led him to the (ostensibly) secular program at Recovery House.
17. Incidentally, Barry's is the only story at Recovery House that includes a reference to formal recruitment other than through the criminal justice system.
18. I.e., official program sanctions that include additional work and/or loss of privileges.
19. The staff at Redemption House might have pointed out to Stanley that his ellipsis includes the phrase "and do good."
20. Goffman (1961, 67) refers to the inmate's sad tale as an "apologia...for his present low status."
21. *New York Times*, April 26, 1998.
22. Snow and Machelak (1984, 176) write:

   the social construction of conversion accounts may thus be regarded as a kind of 'alignment process' involving the linkage of individual biographies with group goals, ideology, and rituals. Converts' constructed accounts do vary, but the variation is around a central theme.

23. Orbuch (1997, 455) writes:

   Humans are inexorably driven to search for order and meaning in their own and other's lives; accounts are a major avenue for sociologists to depict and understand the way individuals experience and *identify with that meaning and their social world*. The concept [of accounts] is useful for gaining insight into the human experience and arriving at meanings and *culturally embedded normative explanations*. [Emphasis added.]

24. Danzger (1989, 226) writes, regarding converts or "returnees" to Orthodox Judaism,

   The repetition of [inappropriate] stories [of their conversion] is discouraged, and a different account...of return is constructed, with *neither the community nor the returnee aware* of this process. [Emphasis added.]

3

Religion at Recovery House: Nihilation and Orthodoxy

*There are two ways to respond to differences in
[people's] religion or view of God. One: "mine is
right, yours is wrong," leads to hurt feelings,
arguments, dissension, and disunity. The other:
"you believe what you believe and I believe what
I do," that's spirituality. It emphasizes what we
have in common, the experience of comfort and
support we all get from our Higher Power. It
emphasizes the positivity of the experience, not the
negativity.*
                              —A Recovery House Counselor

*Well, I know now it's not about religion. I kinda,
y'know, rebel against religion. To me religion is
like a set of rituals, y'know, practice. But to me,
I realized that religion and spirituality are really
two different things. Y'know, 'cause I don't want to
get caught up in the politics of religion. But
spirituality, it's like, that's a good feeling... a feeling of contentment. Spiritually, I felt pretty ... safe.*
                              —A Recovery House Resident

    Although the early Synanon philosophy still informs therapeutic community practice in many ways, some things are different at Recovery House today. At Recovery House these days, elements of the Alcoholics Anonymous (AA) twelve-step philosophy mix freely with traditional therapeutic community notions and practices. People at Daytop Village, Phoenix House, Odyssey House, and other contemporary treatment centers, report that they have experienced similar changes as well. One important deviation from early treatment practices is the "return" of religion to the therapeutic community. The form that this return takes is the emergence of Higher Power spirituality within the therapeutic community treatment process. The degree to which this system of religious thought and practice has been integrated into therapeutic community treatment is the subject of this chapter. Here, I describe how thoroughly Higher Power spirituality has been assimilated at Recovery House. In particular, I detail how this religious system serves the program's ideological functions of commitment creation and maintenance as well as the more mundane task of population control and systems maintenance. Above all, I analyze how the system of Higher Power spirituality is used at Recovery House to suppress the potential of other religious ideas and organizations to represent to clients' alternative worldviews that may compete with the treatment process. As a result, I suggest that the treatment process at Recovery House (and most therapeutic communities) is ideologically bound to this particular religious perspective and thereby limits, to varying degrees, freedom of religious practice and thought among the people who reside there. In this respect, therapeutic community treatment at Recovery House is better understood through sociological models of religion and conversion than through medical or psychiatric models of treatment.

The Denial and Recovery of Religion

As a religious notion, Higher Power spirituality is something of a hybrid. It combines a partially secularized and highly subjectivist image of the supernatural. This image, however, is not foreign to American religious consciousness. The notion of a Higher Power evolved directly out of evangelical Protestant images of God that were current in nineteenth and early twentieth centuries. Higher Power spirituality was the brainchild of Bill Wilson and Bob Smith, the co-founders of AA. (Their ideas continue to inform most so-called twelve-step programs.) Wilson and Smith adapted this and many of their theological ideas from the Oxford Group movement. Ernest Kurtz (1991, 176), the historian of AA, describes the Oxford Group as an "ardently non-denominational, although specifically Christian movement."

Charles Dederich, the charismatic founder of Synanon (the original therapeutic community) was a long-time member of AA. Many members of Synanon's original circle were also AA members, and the group was initially conceived as an adjunct or alterative to AA (Dederich seemed not always clear which). But Dederich was decidedly not a proponent of Higher Power spirituality. As he put it (Yablonsky 1965, 65):

> Although I'll always be grateful to AA for helping me personally, synanon [*sic*] has nothing to do with AA. We emphasize self-reliance rather than dependence on a higher being.

Thus, in the earliest days of the concept therapeutic community movement, religion, in any traditional sense (McGuire 1992, 9f), was not an important consideration. Everyone was too busy with what is today called his or her recovery.

Dederich's original models for "cured" ex-addicts had been inner-directed individuals like Emerson and Thoreau, whose independence he interpreted as a product of their typically nineteenth-century authoritarian family structure. Ultimately, Dederich decided that the addict's supposed characteristic personality flaw was constitutional; it could never be corrected. As a result, he declared that the only solution to addiction was lifetime membership in Synanon's closed community which meant complete encapsulation in his *total institution* and isolation from the threats and temptations of the outside world.[1] From this position, it was not difficult for Synanon to morph into an explicitly religious community (some would say cult), but one that had more to do with ideas about tax evasion than Higher Power spirituality (Janzen 2001; Mitchell et al. 1980). Whatever Dederich took from AA in his shaping of Synanon, twelve-step religion was *not* part of it.

Major therapeutic community movement organizations, like Phoenix House, Daytop Village, Odyssey House, Project Return, and Samaritan Village, currently dominate the long-term residential drug treatment field. They are Synanon's stepchildren. They were not begun by charismatic lay personalities like Dederich and Wilson. These "second generation" therapeutic communities were for the most part organized under the direction of medically trained psychiatrists who emphasized the profession's reigning behaviorist notions of rehabilitation and resocialization of social deviants (see Kennard 1986). The psychiatrists' programs were developed as secular treatment organizations grounded in scientific research and clinical practice. For the most part, their "treatments" had nothing to do with religion, even though some people involved recognized the similarities between what they were doing and ancient notions about religious communities.[2] The idea of a transcendent Higher Power apparently found even less room among the second-generation "scientific" shapers of therapeutic community treatment than it did in Dederich's charismatic, creative era.

The new research-based therapeutic community organizations were founded mostly in large metropolitan areas of the northeastern U.S., where the post-war "heroin epidemic" was considered most rampant. This area of the country was also not quite so enthralled with the growing cultural development known as the "human potential movement," which flowered much earlier in California and provided some of the cultural soil for Synanon. The eastern treatment organizations showed no interest in spirituality, Higher Power or otherwise. They developed a strictly utilitarian and decidedly non-religious notion of rehabilitation based in part on psychological theories about personality development and in part on the work of similar "group therapy" treatments in England for long-term "battle fatigue" among British soldiers following WWII. They also drew on the "empirical" knowledge of former Synanon members.[3]

Under the influence of the psychiatrists, including Daniel Casriel, Mitchell Rosenthal, Judith Densen-Gerber, and David Deitch,[4] the therapeutic community became a temporary residential instrumentality (like a mental hospital) for the rehabilitation of drug addicts, not a permanent placement (like Synanon). In this revised treatment scheme, the addict's rehabilitation was to be affected by up to eighteen months of encounter groups, role-modeling ("acting-as-if"), and other specialized therapies that were supposed to resolve the internal conflicts and childhood crises believed to be at the root of addiction. Once the "treatment" was completed, when the addict was no longer subject to ("enslaved by") his cravings, then the temporary treatment community became superfluous for him. He was then an *ex*-addict and deemed ready to return to the normal world outside the healing community (see Carroll 1992; White 1998).

At this point, according to this psychiatric viewpoint, the treatment community had the potential to become a crutch, a dependency, almost as dangerous to the new ex-addict as the chemical addiction itself. The new psychiatric therapeutic communities, like the Marines, intended to build men—individuals who would take on the world on their own, once the treatment had rehabilitated them.[5] Whole, mature personalities, the psychiatrists believed, should stand on their own feet and face the world confident of their ability to cope with no crutch whatsoever, chemical or communal.[6] Although Dederich and Synanon eventually jettisoned the goal of Emersonian individualism for addicts, many such first-generation ideas resonated well with the psychiatric theories that were prominent during the movement's second generation. For example, the therapeutic community's social organization (often referred to as "the TC Family") is authoritarian and hierarchical (like Dederich's image of the nineteenth-century family). This structure, which submerges all independence under the rule of the whole, is intended to produce fiercely independent, strong-willed individuals who will "graduate" back into the real world outside the community's cocoon. The inherent logical contradictions seem obvious.

One of the concepts that the second-generation therapeutic communities substituted for the scuttled notion of the transcendent was that of the "heroic" *self*-reformed junkie, not someone who submits to a transcendent power (greater than one*self*), but who frees him*self* from all non-rational controls, internal and external (Johnson 1976). This image of the rehabilitated addict as a quasi-superman, tempered by the fires of intensive encounter therapy, may be partly responsible for the typical antagonism of the early therapeutic communities for the "softer" Alcoholics Anonymous approach that included dependence on the supernatural figure of a higher power (Nash 1974). George DeLeon (1990–91, 1232), the Director of the Center for Therapeutic Community Research, refers to this antipathy somewhat obliquely when he writes:

> Historically, TC drug abuse graduates were not easily integrated into AA meetings for a variety of reasons [including] style differences in interactions (e.g., encounter

vs. discussion or testimony) as well as…approach to recovery (e.g., many TC gradu-ates who are former opiate addicts are not comfortable with the 12-step emphasis on disease and higher power…).

This oppositional posture remained characteristic of the two treatment options at least into the mid-eighties, and lingers in certain local organizations still.

Although it has not been noted in the literature of the therapeutic community, the return of religion to its treatment process constitutes a radical departure from the early "heroic" days. The recovery of twelve-step religion by the therapeutic communities most likely occurred as a partial response to independent crit-ics' findings regarding the lack of follow-up care for therapeutic community graduates.[7] Because graduates were relapsing into drug use at very high rates, critics argued that follow-up (or after-care) programs were necessary to help graduates maintain the "prosocial" treatment goals of abstinence, employment, and non-criminality (see, e.g., Hoffman 1987; Nash 1974; Winick 1980). As a result, apparently, the treatment regimes determined that AA and Narcotics Anonymous (NA) were appropriate and cost-effective means of responding to this critique. During the 1980s, according to several field informants, the therapeutic communities began allowing clients to attend AA and NA fellowship meetings off-site and, in some cases, encouraged such attendance as a means of continuing post-treatment support. Eventually, the therapeutic communities introduced regular, on-site AA and NA meetings. Not surprisingly, along with AA and NA fellowship came their religious and spiritual concepts, at the center of which was the Higher Power.

Treatment "retreads" constitute another likely conduit for the return of Higher Power religion to therapeutic community treatment. As described in earlier chapters and Hood (2011a), drug users who resort to formal treatment to cope with the untoward consequences of addiction in a prohibitionist society often do so more than once during their using careers. Several men at Recovery House, including some counselors, reported they had been in treatment two, three, even four times. Some of these men had used AA or NA fellowships as a means of support between leaving Recovery House and "picking up again," i.e., relapsing into drug use. Some of the counselors continue to use NA or AA fellowships as supports for maintaining their "sobriety." One counselor told me that at least one of his instructors for the CASAC (Chemical and Substance Abuse Counselor) training that certified him for his position at Recovery House advocated the use of AA religious concepts as an integral part of addiction counseling. Not infrequently, "retreads" become leaders during their subsequent stays in treatment. Naturally, they pass their "wisdom" on to others whom they counsel about the "tools" for sobriety, which for many includes seeking support from one's Higher Power.

Whatever the actual motivation or mode of access, there is no question that Recovery House has "picked up again" the religion of the therapeutic community's immediate predecessor, Alcoholics Anonymous, where Charles Dederich dumped it and the psychiatrists let it lay. The present Recovery House regime has reshaped this religious system somewhat for its own purposes and incorporated it into its treatment process in ways that serve its particular ends. Recovery House is not, however, an AA fellowship. Nevertheless, given its extensive and exclusive use of Higher Power religion, Recovery House is—also—a faith-based treatment.

Nihilation: The Function of Orthodoxy

In his ethnography of a therapeutic community, Skoll (1992) argues that therapeutic communities maintain their regime by means of persuasion rather than force or coercion, i.e., control is maintained by ideological means. The result, according to Skoll, is not the creation of new identities (or "character"), but the reproduction of addict identities. What therapeutic communities produce best, he claims, are individuals reinforced as passive consumers in the face of both the illegal drug market and the drug treatment market. The 85 percent of clients who do not finish the program become drug consumers again, in both senses of the word. The 10–15 percent who do graduate switch products and become consumers of (i.e., they convert to) the treatment view of self and world. It is this segment of clients that therapeutic communities base their success claims on and depend on as a major source of their paraprofessional counseling staff, the real workhorses of—and true converts to—this treatment process and ideology. In this light, it is tempting to interpret therapeutic communities as nothing more than self-recruiting grounds for the front line troops necessary to keep the movement alive and professional organizational careers intact. That is, the treatment process is simply a self-perpetuating process. Its main product is its own institutional existence. Skoll comes to essentially this conclusion.

In Skoll's view, the therapeutic community programs are repressive because they disallow public discourse on alternative meanings of addiction, and, I would add, alternative meanings and means of recovery. He further demonstrates how therapeutic communities delegitimate potential alternative views of person and world based on gender, race, or ethnicity by disallowing public discourse on these issues as well. In the terminology of the therapeutic community, such formations constitute "negative contracts," alternative social formations (i.e., friendships and formal or informal, internal, subgroup affiliations) that threaten therapeutic community solidarity or control. Since such "external" attachments are disallowed in the therapeutic community, clients are compelled to cooperate in their own repression. Their "voluntary" cooperation is insured by the *lack of alternative explanation or association*.[8]

Skoll uses Gramsci's notion of hegemony to describe and account for this coercion at the therapeutic communities. However, in Peter Berger's language of social construction, the notion of *nihilation*, or negative legitimation, is perhaps more appropriate to describe the day-to-day establishment and maintenance of the hegemonic "regime" on the floor of the treatment facility (Berger 1966, 133f; Wuthnow et al. 1984, 52). What Berger has reference to specifically are "universe maintaining mechanisms" or, in more common terminology, therapies. Therapy, in Berger's terms, includes anything from pastoral counseling to psychoanalysis to exorcism. It is the application of the legitimating apparatus (the philosophical, theological, or psychological justifications or rationales for normative prescriptions) to *individual cases*. Nihilation or negative legitimation plays a role complementary to that of therapy. Nihilation, too, prevents deviation from, and promotes adherence to, official worldviews and behavioral requirements. Unlike therapy, however, which constructs the *new* reality for clients, nihilation actively *de*legitimates any threatening alternative views; it negates the client's previous or current beliefs that run counter to therapeutic community ideology.[9] As an active process of "desocialization" or "disculturation," nihilation occurs at both individual and collective levels and is typical of all "carcereal" organizations (Goffman 1961; see also, Giddens 1991, 369–70). Since Skoll did his research, the return of religion to the floor of the therapeutic community adds yet another element to the potential alternative identities the treatment must repress. It is difficult to know what role the religious sentiments of therapeutic community residents played in the process as Skoll and others observed it, since they did not address this issue. In fact, from reading the literature in general, one could easily assume that religion was entirely absent from this treatment modality.

When I began this research, I did not expect to find religion in the therapeutic community. I anticipated neither the widespread use of religious practice nor a discourse about religious issues in various didactic and other group sessions. Even less did I expect to find a dominant religious orthodoxy supported by and supporting the treatment process. However, my research at Recovery House demonstrates that a particular religious view has become a prominent factor in the treatment process of the therapeutic community as well as in the lives and sentiments of the residents and staff. Religious sentiments, I suspect, were always a factor in the lives of the treatment clientele; however, the treatment staff did not recognize them in any systematic way until recently. This is no longer true at Recovery House itself, and I found numerous indications that similar changes have occurred at other therapeutic communities as well.

Whatever else Higher Power religion is at Recovery House, it is also an ideological tool the staff uses to help secure the commitment of clients to the "recovery process." Put differently, Recovery House advocates a religious orthodoxy to which all residents must adhere, or at least appear to adhere (i.e., submit), if they are to complete the treatment successfully. The para-professional counselors, who are therapeutic community graduates, are the primary agents of this orthodoxy in the day-to-day discourse of the house. In the face of this orthodoxy, religious heterodoxy is not only discouraged but also suppressed (nihilated) in a fashion and to a degree that approaches, but may not (yet?)

entirely coincide with, the internal religious intolerance typical of faith-based treatments such as Redemption House. Starting at the Orientation Level, in the very first days and weeks of treatment, the staff members at Recovery House openly and directly advocate the adoption, by all residents, of the twelve-step approach to religion, and oppose any public consideration of another particular historical religion by any client.[10] There appears to be more unanimity among the staff on the latter than on the former issue. But there is wide tacit agreement about advocacy as well. Although Higher Power religious doctrine is nowhere systematically codified in the literature of Recovery House or therapeutic communities in general, it is evident in the discourse on religion that occurs daily on the treatment floor.[11]

Religious Discourse at Recovery House

I attended numerous orientation group meetings during my first weeks at Recovery House. Para-professional counselors led each session, and religion often became an important topic of discussion. Leroy led the first such meeting, a regular 9:00 a.m. session especially for new residents.[12] Leroy is a tough, wary ex-addict who has been clean for eight years ("after 30 months in treatment") and a counselor for most of that time. A fifty-year-old black man of moderate height and wiry build, Leroy strikes me as one of the angriest men I have ever met. Always friendly towards me and quite helpful, Leroy often seemed ready to explode at the least provocation, though he never did. Like many of the counselors at Recovery House and other therapeutic communities, Leroy reported that he was "enrolled in a college degree program, although I'm HIV positive."[13]

Leroy's comments on religion were brief and to the point. He opened the group session by saying that he wanted to "respond to something that had occurred in Morning Focus." The Morning Focus meeting takes place each day right after breakfast, before the 9:00-a.m. orientation session. It is attended by the entire resident population, which in therapeutic community argot is the Family or Community.[14] This first group meeting of the day is one of the forums where new residents must "present" something (song, biography, poem, reading) to the collected body of the house by way of public introduction. On the morning in question, Juan, a new resident, had presented a Bible reading (a brief chapter from the book of Psalms) to the meeting. In the orientation meeting that immediately followed, Leroy began by stating that he did not want to say "anything against the Bible, you can read the Bible if you want to while you're here," but, he went on to indicate, reading in public like that was inappropriate.

> What you need to do in here is to work on your recovery. When you were on the street you weren't reading your Bible; you weren't worried about God. It's all right if you want to do that in your room, in your private time, but keep it to yourself. In these groups and meetings we should be concentrating on our recovery, *not on God*. What's most important in here is your recovery. That's first. You gotta keep that in mind. Okay, now we're gonna talk about change.[15] [Emphasis added.]

Leroy referred to no alternative approach on "spiritual matters," but other speakers, in other meetings had much to say on this topic.

A week later in another orientation group, the discussion topic was the structure and purpose of Morning Focus. Saul, the leader for that day, asked the group for suggestions for starting the day off on an "up beat." One recent inductee offered: "we should think about God and talk about him." Saul seemed unprepared for this response and tried to discourage the idea. He was only partially successful when he asked the group: "why isn't this a good idea?" The rest of the answers received from the group seemed to please Saul, because they hewed more closely to what I soon learned was a central aspect of the ideological line at Recovery House. Most responses focused on the plurality of belief found in such a large group and the resultant potential for offense and conflict. One commenter drew the doctrinaire Alcoholics Anonymous distinction between "religion and spirituality," and reiterated the necessity of the latter to recovery. Saul quickly picked up the thread and launched a ten-minute homily about the difference between "religion and treatment."

> The therapeutic community doesn't directly include spirituality [*sic*] as part of treatment. That's because we are here to get in touch with our self *before* we can get in touch with God. The therapeutic community is about finding yourself, then you can develop or find spirituality or religion as it applies to you, in a way that's meaningful to you. Therapeutics is not religion. [Emphasis added.]

Well over six feet tall and slightly overweight, Saul nevertheless speaks with a natural gentleness, and is deliberate—almost sermonizing—in his delivery. He followed this statement with some personal biography, a typical source of evidence for creedal claims among staff and residents alike.

> Spirituality is very important to me in my recovery. My Higher Power is important. And for me it's internal. *After* I got myself together—straightened out in treatment— I discovered that spirituality or God was inside me. My spirituality comes from within. But I needed to clear up the drug induced fog before I could discover that spiritual part inside me.

After this personal account, Saul returned to the organizational line:

> But that's my thing; it's not for everybody. [E]ach person has to find their own spirituality. At a therapeutic community we cannot force religion or God or spirituality on people. Many addicts, when they first get off the street, don't want to hear about religion or God.

At this point, Juan, the resident who had read the Bible in the earlier Focus meeting, added that "we shouldn't get religious [in here] because we weren't [religious] on the street. I read the Bible in Focus and Leroy put me down. He's right." Saul responded, echoing Leroy's earlier comments:

If you want to read the Bible and pray, that's fine, but you should do it on your own. Or some people get with friends and share religion, but it's not part of therapeutic community treatment. Religion is very individual. Therapeutics is about discovering yourself, getting straight. After [that] is the time to focus on religion or spirituality.

This discussion, a side issue for Saul, went on for at least half an hour, despite his attempts to shut it down. Many of the people present were anxious to ask questions or offer comments. Religion was obviously a hot topic. Saul finally ended this "sidebar" by resorting to the claim that "most arguments are over religion or politics." The group agreed with this old saw, and Saul moved on to his planned subject for the session.

At an afternoon orientation group soon afterward, Maria, a young (mid-thirties?) Latina counselor introduced her topic for the day: Higher Power. She started by explaining that one's Higher Power is not necessarily the same as God, nor was spirituality the same as religion. "Your Higher Power can be anything you want it to be," she said, echoing AA doctrine. She then announced that "we are going to go around the room, so that everyone can share their thoughts on their Higher Power." As usual, some forty to fifty residents encircled the living room in folding chairs. Personal observations started a bit hesitantly, but quickly began to come readily with feeling and seriousness. The majority of remarks referred to God, Jesus, or the Lord as "my Higher Power." A few African American men identified themselves as Muslims and claimed Allah as their Higher Power. Two other men said they had no Higher Power or God; another said that he was confused about the issue. One of the group's avowed atheists, a tall and slender muscular man, was quite candid about his experience. After briefly and cogently describing his hitch in Viet Nam, Gary said, "I lost lots of friends in Nam, and I lost God along with them."

At the end of the period, Andres, who came in late, avidly attempted to dissuade the group of any belief in God or religion as simply irrational. Maria cut him short and restated her distinction between God and a Higher Power: "Higher Power is not about any particular religion, it's whatever it means to you." This began her concluding discourse on the subject as Maria went on to reiterate some of the "conclusions" she had drawn during the "sharing" process. Her emphasis was clearly on the phenomenological, the experiential, and mystical, rather than the theological, analytical, or historical.

> For *everybody* Higher Power includes support, comfort, inspiration, guidance as feelings or emotions…how you feel *inside* about this experience of Higher Power. We stay away from trying to analyze or explain it. That's when we get into trouble, arguments. [Note her agreement with Saul.] We are not going to hurt anyone's feelings. If you say your God is the right one or the only one, then you step on the toes of someone else who has a different idea of Higher Power or spirituality. You know, as junkies, we're always stuck in the black or white. When you're in the black, that's all you see. When you're stuck in the white, that's all you see. We need to be in the gray more. When you stay in the gray, you can see both the black and

white, and we need more of that. As junkies, we need to stay in the gray more often.
[Emphasis added.]

Juan (the Bible reader) also tried to set everyone straight from a somewhat different perspective: "Lots of you have misconceptions about the Higher Power." But Maria would not tolerate that either. Maria was fair in shutting off debate about the nature of the Higher Power from various sides, theist and atheist alike. But in her reconstruction of the gist of the group discussion she cleverly (and, I believe, genuinely) hewed to the Recovery House perspective. For example, one respondent had expressed a profound sense of injustice. He complained angrily that God let him suffer "so much pain" following a gunshot wound (four bullets) and then let him get re-addicted to opiates as a result of prescribed medication. Maria gently cooled out his sense of injustice (even calling it by name) by "sharing" her own experience.

I always had a problem with: Why does God let children die? I don't know. Maybe I'm not meant to know. But other good things happen, too. I focus on that and don't try to understand what I can't.

Maria encouraged the residents to "use these tools" in pursuit of recovery: the feelings of comfort, support, inspiration, and guidance that come from the Higher Power. "Don't worry," she said, "about where it [specifically] comes from or what the source looks like." Then Maria summarized:

There are two ways to respond to differences in [people's] religion or view of God. One: mine is right, yours is wrong, leads to hurt feelings, arguments, dissension, and disunity. The other: you believe what you believe and I believe what I do, that's spirituality. It emphasizes what we have in common, the experience of comfort and support we all get from our Higher Power. It [spirituality as opposed to religion] emphasizes the positivity of the experience, not the negativity.

Orthodoxy and Its Discontents

Through their actions and comments, Maria, Saul, Leroy, and the residents attending their groups suggest that Recovery House (and perhaps therapeutic communities in general) holds and advocates a single, sanctioned religious perspective. Moreover, I suggest that the therapeutic community movement (at Recovery House and most likely elsewhere) has adapted Higher Power spirituality to serve the typical functions of commitment formation and maintenance. The regime at Recovery House has shaped its particular religious orthodoxy into an agent of the treatment process and uses it actively to suppress (nihilate, delegitimate) other religious concepts and organizations within the treatment facility. The therapeutic communities repress alternative religions because they may present to residents alternative views of self and world that compete with, rather than complement, the treatment process. As a result, the treatment process at Recovery House has become ideologically bound to a particular religious perspective and thereby limits both freedom of religious practice and thought to varying degrees. Nevertheless, Higher Power spirituality has not taken over the treatment process. Rather, it has been subordinated to the "true" higher powers at Recovery House, the treatment (or recovery) process itself, and especially the institution that operates it.

It is clear from the above comments and conversations, as well as numerous others, that the religion of Recovery House is a variation on the AA system of religious ideas and practices. The AA system, commonly known as the Twelve Steps, is itself an adaptation of classic sectarian Protestantism, the nineteenth-century religion that shaped important aspects of the culture and consciousness of Middle Americans of the twentieth century (Kurtz 1991). (Throughout this book I refer to the Recovery House version of its religious perspective as Higher Power spirituality, because this terminology replicates the everyday language among its residents and staff.)[16] This religious perspective stresses an inner-oriented, individually defined, mystical sense of "spirituality" or religion. Subjectivism is all, objectivism is highly suspect. The Recovery House counselors, as the instructors in spiritual correctness, actively discourage religious analysis, intellectualization, development of doctrine, and especially proselytizing among the residents. In contrast, staff members openly encourage residents to "experience" the Higher Power, to "feel" or "sense" its presence internally and individually. Moreover, the daily discourse among treatment staff and the senior residents takes for granted the reality of the Higher Power *as* inner feeling. The constant flow of their conversation in both formal groups and informal discussions repeatedly emphasizes "spirituality" as inner feeling (e.g., comfort, support, and encouragement) and openly delegitimates publicly expressed ideas or reflection about religion (e.g., doctrine, ethics, or political claims) as "negativity." The treatment discourse at Recovery House earnestly disallows any religious element among the residents that has a potential for group affiliation or the foundation of a personal identity other than "disordered addict."

Higher Power spirituality as defined at Recovery House resembles nothing so much as the "feel good" spirituality typical of the "recovery movement." Wendy Kaminer (1992) has characterized this general current in modern American culture as "packag[ing] authority, encouraging conformity, surrender of the will, and submission to a higher power." According to her analysis, the Higher Power never makes demands or sets obligations; it only "advises" conformity, adjustment, and adaptation. Similarly, the Higher Power adept at Recovery House only encounters demands from the outside, from the treatment process, never from the inside, the locus of his Higher Power. This way residents experience neither (inner) tension nor create (outer) conflict between (his) religion and (the treatment) regime. And, as Saul explains, facility with Higher Power spirituality seems to depend on attaining a degree of bourgeois conventionality that is generally considered impossible for active addicts:

> The self-esteem has to be built up, the self-worth, the self-value, the belief in oneself to do the right thing has to be built *before* addicts can successfully look at spirituality as *another* agency of dealing with their recovery. [Emphasis added.]

According to some, at least, the comfort and advice supplied by Higher Power works only for already recovering individuals, those at the higher levels of treatment. Higher Power spirituality seems to require, as a prerequisite, a certain degree of attainment in the direction of bourgeois adaptability and conformity. As I describe elsewhere (Hood 2011a), that attainment, by definition, begins only with a resident's identification with the therapeutic community perspective, including personal "surrender" to all the "higher powers" therein.

Spirituality as Religion

The staff members and the men of Recovery House who practice and preach Higher Power spirituality claim that this individualist, inner experience is quite distinct from religion. As one resident put it:

> Well, I know now it's not about religion. I kinda, you know, rebel against religion. To me religion is like a set of rituals, y'know, practice. But to me, I realized that religion and spirituality are really two different things. Y'know, 'cause I don't want to get caught up in the politics of religion. But spirituality, it's like, that's a good feeling…a feeling of contentment. Spiritually, I felt pretty…safe.

This claim is objectively mistaken in at least three ways. First, the generic "religion" that he rejects as "not us" is not generic at all. It is, rather, a specific, historically identifiable form of sectarian Protestantism. This supposedly "generic" religion approximates the varieties of Baptist and Holiness sects that are familiar in minority neighborhoods, from which most of the men of Recovery House originate. Saul characterizes it as "fire and brimstone religion." Thus, Higher Power spirituality at Recovery House is not "something" distinct from religion per se. It is distinct in some significant ways from the historical form of religion familiar to most Recovery House denizens as (that fire and brimstone) "religion," but that remains only one (other) form of religion, not religion per se. Second, Higher Power spirituality itself, as developed in AA, is a direct descendant of American Protestantism and therefore sociologically a first cousin to the "fire and brimstone" movements. A number of scholars have demonstrated this family connection, among them Ernest Kurtz (1991) and Paul Antze (1979). Thus, the Recovery House version of "spirituality but not religion" is in fact close kin to the very religious formation it mistakenly considers "religion and not us." Recovery House spirituality is not only *not* something other than religion, it is historically and doctrinally related to the very form of religion it chooses to pose as its antithesis.

The Recovery House notion of spirituality *instead* of religion is quite limited in yet a third sense. The spirituality of Higher Power is easily categorized with other, similar historical forms of religion, including recognized forms of Christianity. Harold Bloom (1992), echoing William James, summarizes an entire strain of religious criticism that views American religion as essentially experiential rather than theological. Sydney Ahlstrom (1975), perhaps a dean of historians of American religion, concurs. Whether in the form of Baptism, Methodism, or Mormonism, Bloom (1992, 45ff) finds the American religion profoundly "post Christian," "creedless," and "gnostic." It is a religion of the self, lonely, and "absolutely personal." But, he claims, it has descended directly from the Protestantism of the nineteenth century. Much the same observations have been made by sociologists of religion like Thomas Luckmann (1967), with whom Bloom seems unfamiliar, and Robert Bellah (Bellah et al. 1985), whose analysis Bloom likes, but whose *evaluation* of American religion he criticizes as not a "religious insight"![17]

Although Bloom does not directly consider the issue of (twelve-step) Higher Power spirituality, his description of the gnostic character of the American Religion fits this particular outlook quite well. A more traditional student of religion makes this point a bit more directly. In her analysis of ancient Christian gnosticism, the historian Elaine Pagels (1981, 148) unambiguously identifies gnostic religion with modern forms of "self-discovery."

> For gnostics, exploring the psyche became explicitly what it is for many people today implicitly—a *religious* quest. Some who seek their own interior direction, like the radical gnostics, reject religious institutions as a hindrance to their progress. Others...willingly participate in them, although...they regard the church more as an instrument of their own self-discovery than as a necessary "ark of salvation." [Emphasis added.]

In this light, it seems clear that what the Higher Power spiritualists of Recovery House have in mind when they reject "religion" is what Pagels refers to as *religious institutions*. Kurtz (1991, 176f) makes much the same point:

> The Oxford Group, AA's proximate parent, was ardently non-denominational although specifically Christian.... The [AA] fellowship perceived its problem as two sided: to remain attractive to the temperamentally non-religious while avoiding giving offense to the personally religious.... [It] solve[d] this dual concern by projecting itself as "spiritual rather than religious...." [Many] detected in the newborn Alcoholics Anonymous...the "primitive Christianity" that characterized the Oxford Group's self-image...[and] the understanding of AA's own...program [w]as fundamentally religious.... Over the years, other careful students...intuited the key to the program...to be "religion."...[S]uch diverse unanimity cannot be ignored simply because of AA's own insistence that it is "a spiritual rather than a religious program."...But...the more proper distinction lies between "spiritual" *or* "religious" [on the one hand] and "churchy" [on the other].

Pagels (1981, 149) identifies another of the central differences between orthodox [institutional] Christianity and gnostic Christian forms as the disagreement about the source of suffering and its alleviation.

> Many Gnostics…insisted that ignorance, not sin, is what involves a person in suffering. The Gnostic movement shared certain affinities with contemporary methods of exploring the self through psychotherapeutic techniques. Both gnosticism and psychotherapy value, above all, knowledge—the self-knowledge that is insight. They agree that, lacking this, a person experiences *a sense of being driven by impulses he does not understand.* [Emphasis added.]

(Could there be a better description of the stereotype of the addict in modern America?)

As Pagels continues her analysis, she could easily also be describing the therapeutic community form of treatment.

> Many Gnostics share with psychotherapy a second major premise: both agree—against orthodox Christianity—that the psyche bears within itself the potential for liberation or destruction.

Thus, I suggest once again, that Recovery House Higher Power spirituality, the inner source of feeling and comfort, may be a form of religion different in some ways from that found at Redemption House and many a resident's home church, but it is *not* not-religion.

Using Bloom's distinction, the major point of difference between Redemption House religion and Recovery House religion marks both a serious divergence between nineteenth and twenty-first-century American religion and the re-emergence of one of the earliest roots of the Christian tradition: gnosticism. In the history of western Christianity, strains of inner-light or spiritualist religion similar to that manifest in the notion of the Higher Power have often broken through the "repressions" of orthodox institutions, especially at points of the latter's decline and restructuring. The mystically oriented movements of the late Middle Ages, such as the Friends of God and the Brethren of the Common Life, and those of the Reformation period, like the Quakers, Ranters, and Spiritual Anabaptists are examples of such historic eruptions. The New Religious Movements of the late twentieth century, such as the Unification Church ("Moonies"), the Catholic Charismatic Movement, Hare Krishna, and others also reflect the reemergence of inner-light religions in a period of considerable cultural ambiguity in "the Occident." In many instances, these mystical religions have been truly disruptive, even revolutionary, from the perspective of established religious institutions, and, on occasion, they have challenged the general status quo. It is interesting to note that Higher Power spirituality, at both Alcoholics Anonymous and the therapeutic community, operates in service to the ethical and legal status quo. Recovery House spirituality teaches men to find inner resources for conformity and assimilation to the status quo rather than to challenge or question it. Recall the *Serenity* Prayer, which asks for the *"Serenity* to accept the things I cannot change" (see Hood 2011a, 50ff).

As Pagel's analysis suggests, the emphasis of Higher Power spirituality on internal resources corresponds more with the tenor of modern psychotherapeutics and ancient mysticisms than the authoritarian emphasis in the evangelical and fundamentalist religion at Redemption House. However, that is not to say that authoritarianism is lacking at Recovery House, or spiritual inspiration and comfort at Redemption House. Rather, these religious resources are organized differently, with differing balances and emphases at the two programs. One thing both programs not only emphasize, but insist on is the thorough rejection of the past—past activities, past morals (or supposed lack thereof), past comforts, past identities, past associations—and an equally thorough adoption of the new outlook on self and world, central to which is the notion and practice of abstinence (see Hood 2011a).

In his classic analysis, Nock (1972/1933, 14) called attention to this character of Christian conversion with the phrase "renunciation and new start." A somewhat different (forensic!) analysis of religious experience describes conversion similarly as a three-stage process: (1) a turning away from an unsatisfactory situation; (2) a state of suspension; and (3) a turning toward a newly integrated sense of self and world (Flinn 1987). It is belief in and adherence to this practical dictum of personal transformation, as *both* recovery and redemption, that is central to my analysis, regardless of the purported source of inspiration or strength of will believed necessary to carry it out. Despite their varying emphases and approaches, both Redemption House and Recovery House use their religions to promote personal transformation as the antidote to addiction.

The main difference between the two programs' attempts at personal reclamation is the (presumed) source of the new start they offer their clients. Recovery House believes it is the inner resources of the self, awakened and "enabled" by the community and a Higher Power. Redemption House teaches that God, through the agency of the Holy Spirit, works in the hearts of the men to affect the changes. Both the brethren of Redemption House and the peers at Recovery House experience "truth" or "insight," respectively, about themselves, their pasts, and possible futures. The substance of the truth or insight, however, is decided not only by "inner lights" or "transmoral consciences," which are characteristic of mysticisms, but by the authoritative dogmas and directors of the programs.[18] Both programs attempt, rather, to build similar new moral consciences or consciousnesses in their residents, new logics of morality that are institutionally rather than individually determined. The same moral logics of abstinence and ascetic perfectionism, taught at both programs, also characterized the Revivalist and Temperance Movements and gave shape to the American religion of experience for the last two centuries. Harold Bloom and others have described how that religion has changed in significant ways in the direction of the post-modern American religion (see also Hunter 1983; Luckmann 1967). Ultimately, however, the Higher Power religion practiced by the men at Recovery House retains much of the same American Protestant moral logic that has dominated the American consciousness for two centuries. It is, in many ways, the same logic that is taught at Redemption House.

Max Weber (1969, 267ff, 323ff) drew a well-known distinction between mysticism and asceticism as religious forms, but he also distinguished between inner-worldly and otherworldly religious orientations.[19] Thoroughgoing mysticism entails an otherworldly orientation. It utilizes spiritual exercises of diverse kinds in the pursuit of union with the divine. Mysticism's distinctive goal is rejection of and escape from the world of daily responsibility and physical need, which are seen as material impediments to true spirituality. As Weber pointed out, this style or orientation is far more typical of Asian religions than so-called "Abrahamic" traditions of Judaism, Christianity, and Islam. With few exceptions, Western mystical groups and movements have used spiritual exercises and a spiritual union with the divine not as ends in themselves or as means of escape from material reality, but as sources of strength, support, and inspiration for the mundane struggles of everyday life. This surely is the case with the Higher Power spirituality at Recovery House. As Saul, once again, explains:

> I had a good talk with a young lady in my case load the other day. She's a level three. She's been here, oh God, 11 months, and she still has a tendency to be vicious when you touch a delicate nerve in her feelings. She becomes angry; she has a tendency toward attack. She was asking me how she could get better with that. I told her that had to come with becoming at peace with yourself, within. In order to do that, if you believe in a Higher Power, then you have to go to the spiritual aspect. You have to take your recovery to another level now [his voice softens here, implying intimacy, perhaps reverence]. You have to…ask God to give you the peace to help you deal with the things…that make you angry, that make you resistant to *better getting along with people*. You now have to go to God and ask him for inner peace. And once you begin to understand what inner peace is, acceptance of whatever the things are that make you angry; accepting them, working on consciously changing them, *then your viciousness and negative reactions to people will begin to change*. [Emphasis added.]

The self- (or mutual-) help spirituality characteristic of AA and Recovery House is not "escapist" (or world-rejecting) religion; neither is the religion of gnostic inclinations that both Ahlstrom and Bloom call the American Religion. This Emersonian religion of experience, as Ahlstrom (1975, II, 42) typifies it, is eminently practical. Certainly it shifts the balance of authority, the locus of the divine, in the direction of what might be called internal (spirit or contemplation) rather than external (tradition or institution), but it remains a religion *in service to the practical* side of life. American religion, including its twelve-step variety, remains inner-worldly oriented. The "spirituality" at Recovery House is not likely to devolve into the sort of "acosmic brotherhood" attempted by Dederich and the early Synanonites. It might, however, be argued that therapeutic communities do produce perfectionist-oriented "monks" who seek to escape the (seemingly) eternal cycle of relapse through perpetual attachment to the "sacred" community as paraprofessional counselors.[20] This, however, is not their manifest ideal, at least according to George De Leon, Director of the Center for Therapeutic Community Research.[21] Nevertheless, Higher Power spirituality at Recovery House operates precisely in the service of enabling people, like the woman Saul advises, to become better suited for selection within the circle of "purists," those deemed appropriately sober or recovered. Higher Power spirituality incorporates a quasi-mystical (but thoroughly contemporary) style of spiritualism in service to the *sectarian* therapeutic community. The explicit goal of the community is to return each man or woman to his or her appropriate role in the *everyday* worlds of work and family.

It is important to emphasize this latter point, that success *within* the sectarian community is not the ultimate end. The *independent* Emersonian individual remains an ideal in the therapeutic community. Its religion is individual or subjective, but it is supremely practical. The one caveat that is too often ignored by the Recovery House emphasis on *treatment* is that this independence is unworkable without *fellowship*. As Weber knew, the individual—especially the one who would be perfected in certain traits—must *depend* on the continued scrutiny of the sect (his circle or network) in order to maintain his character, his abstinent sobriety. I pursue this aspect in more detail in the following chapter on re-entry (see also my chapter on "reinforcement," Hood 2011a). For now it is important to see that the religion practiced at Recovery House, for all of its pretensions to being "not-religion," and its supposedly contrasting definition of the sacred, is a close, if not precise parallel with the religion of Redemption House, the avowedly faith-based treatment.

In both programs, withdrawal into personal religious contemplation or spiritual introspection (mysticism) serves the purpose of moral rearmament (to use the language of another Oxford Group descendent). The ultimate goal of this rehabilitation is absolute abstinence (a form of moral perfectionism) in a life of "Right living" (Recovery House) or "Christian living" (Redemption House) or, in Saul's variation on this theme, "good orderly direction." Each of these phrases refers to the same practical and ethical ideals embedded in American religion and bourgeois-industrial culture. The spirituality that has become part of the treatment process at Recovery House is also an American religion. By any sociological definition, it qualifies.[22] Higher Power spirituality has a clearly defined sense of the supernatural (if you want it), "your" Higher Power. It also features clearly defined distinctions between the sacred and the profane, especially its concepts of addiction versus abstinent sobriety, its communal hierarchy versus the anarchy of personal disorder, and its "Family" solidarity versus the addict's narcissism. Higher Power spirituality varies from the religion of Redemption House in some of its substance, but its "character" (or type) is categorically identical, especially with respect to the inner-worldly asceticism of its purpose and operation.

The Question of Tolerance

Skoll's Gramscian argument that therapeutic community hegemony is persuasively maintained by eliminating potentials for alternative identity formation (e.g., ethnic, racial, or gender referents) from the purview of residents in the therapeutic community domain would, on the face of it, not seem to apply to the element of religion. The Higher Power spirituality sanctioned at Recovery House purports to be an eminently tolerant approach to religion. According to its rhetoric, unlike whatever pretreatment religious sentiments or affiliations residents bring into treatment with them, the Recovery House orthodoxy allows for all forms of religious expression through the agency of Higher Power spirituality. In practice, this means that the clients can identify their Higher Power with whomever or whatever they wish. They can attach any name to it, God, Allah, Buddha, or no name other than "my Higher Power." Despite a democratic self-image, Higher Power spirituality nevertheless partakes of the very intolerance with which it attempts to tar other religions.[23] Presented as "anybody can believe whatever he or she wants," the religion of Higher Power turns out instead to have its own strict limits to ideological inclusiveness. Each resident can believe what he or she wants, but only if they keep it to themselves. That is, as long as it does not take a public, active, evangelical (i.e., proselytizing) form. If religion does not provide an alternative, non-treatment-based source for group identification and personal identity, then it is not inimical to the Higher Power spirituality of Recovery House. As long as a person's religion remains a religion *of* the self, and is kept *to* oneself, and does not become an(other) indoctrinating sectarian formation, it is permitted. Religion must fit the therapeutic community definition of the situation. If it does not, it will be unacceptable and not allowed publication of any sort.

As I have described, certain expressions of spirituality are acceptable to the "positive" orthodoxy at Recovery House, while other expressions of religion are not. This intolerance is clearly evidenced by the staff's continual suppression (nihilation) of alternative views: e.g., Juan's "put-down" when he publicly read the Bible, and the other spontaneous public client expressions that suggested an alternative religiosity (in Saul's group) or a desire to investigate one (Julio, discussed later in this chapter), which were also quickly dispatched. At the same time, however, every new resident is encouraged to claim her or his own version of God as Higher Power. Maria's simple exercise of going around the circle and asking everyone to name their Higher Power, for example, appears to signal a programmatic openness and tolerance for variety and individuality. She, certainly, sees it as a gentle introduction to the preferred spirituality of recovery. What can be coercive, repressive, or nihilating about that?

Despite the genuine intentions of Maria and the other counselors, I suggest that this practice accomplishes something more as well. While it manifestly appears to signal openness, Maria's seemingly innocuous exercise functions also (latently) as an initial ritual of engagement, an early exercise of *mutual witnessing* for new clients and a means of re-commitment for continuing or returning clients. As McGuire (1987, 71) writes:

> Mutual witnessing within existing [frameworks] appears to be especially effective in bringing about the recruit's conversion to a new meaning system.... Through these informal interactions, the recruit may gradually "try on" the interpretation suggested by members and apply their meaning system to [his] personal experiences.

In TC jargon, it is a form of "acting as if" (Perfas 2004).

Maria's exercise entices new residents to perform an overt, public act of identification with the therapeutic community's orthodoxy of Higher Power spirituality without full awareness of the consequences. The ritual of mutual witnessing does not constitute brainwashing, but it clearly parallels the indoctrination at Redemption House and other openly conversionist organizations. As McGuire's analysis shows, this tactic is favored by sectarian resocializing organizations that depend on ideological conformity as a means of social control over their members.[24] Mutual witnessing occurs regularly in so-called cults (e.g., The Unification Church), in the popular Catholic Charismatic Movement, and in more mainstream Pentecostal, fundamentalist, and evangelical churches. It is at the heart of the AA fellowship: "Hi, my name is Dan, and I'm an alcoholic..." Mutual witnessing is a potent commitment inducing technique common to numerous proselytizing movements and organizations: religious, political, and psychological (see Harrison 1974; Kanter 1972; Lofland 1977; McGuire 1992).

Also typical of other conversionary groups, Maria's ritual provides a point of contact between the individual resident's pretreatment religious sentiment and Recovery House orthodoxy. In the encapsulated setting, with Maria's gentle urging and the "correct" examples of a roomful of "supportive peers," the initiate palpably senses the presence of the "affective ties" that are the necessary prerequisite to more conscious and ideologically based acts of commitment. John Lofland (1977) referred to the "Moonies'" variant of this tactic as "love bombing." This ritual means of gently nudging novices unawares into a new cognitive universe, a new ideological domain, and onto the road of personal commitment is widely recognized in the conversion literature and continues to be widely practiced by various ideological movements (see Snow and Machelak 1984). Maria and her cohorts are almost certainly not aware of the theory of such inducement rituals, but they are certainly familiar with their effects in practice, and the counselors use these rituals regularly.

In this light, the vaunted tolerance of Higher Power spirituality, its "however you conceive of him (!)" quality, has to be seen—at Recovery House, at least—as an ideological smoke screen. The Higher Power allows for nominal variety, but demands or induces substantive orthodoxy (i.e., literally, conformity of belief). In fact, its ritual expressions of variety act as mechanisms for initiation to and maintenance of substantive conformity and submission to the "regime." Any resident may *name* her or his Higher Power whatever she or he likes at Recovery House, but they will have to keep its substance out of sight, only in his or her mind or heart! The *whatever you name it* religion must be internal, individual, immanent, ineffable, and substance-less. It may not entail doctrinal, ethical, political, or personal agendas or demands. It may not seek to convert other men to an externally located institutional center.[25] It may not confer elements of identity that conflict in any way with that proffered by the therapeutic community. "Religion must," as Saul put it, "be individual." It must not be collective, apart, that is, from the therapeutic community "Family" itself. The Higher Power, unlike the God of Moses at the burning bush, may not care much about its appellation, but it is nonetheless a jealous Higher Power, and in this sense looks very much like Yahweh, indeed—with no other gods before it.

Rationales for Orthodoxy

What I observed, then, is that the *in*tolerance of religious diversity practiced at Recovery House contradicts its own claims of tolerance for all religions. In analyzing the general religious discourse, as well as my interviews with staff members and residents, I uncovered at least three rationales or "accounts" for this contradiction between ideology and practice.[26] Two of these address ideological concerns; the third addresses more practical, organizational issues. All three rationales imply a continuing need for complete control of the therapeutic community environment by the treatment regime. All three further demonstrate how religion is used to promote treatment and organizational goals rather than the individual spiritual needs of the residents, except as those are conceived in terms of the organizational ideology.

The first and most common reason heard from staff members for suppressing certain expressions of religion among the residents is the fear of introducing heterogeneity and divisiveness into the (supposedly) ideologically homogeneous community, the therapeutic community Family. As Maria put it, open discussion of religion "leads to hurt feelings, arguments, dissension, and disunity." And Saul, who says, "yes, we believe that spirituality is incorporated in their recovery plan at any level; it can only help," also adds the condition that:

[a]s long as it doesn't *infringe on what we teach in recovery.*" [W]e don't want people to get lost in [religion]. Not that there's anything wrong with that. However, there

are certain things that recovering addicts need to do and that's catch the concept of [the] recovery process here.... So, we don't incorporate it [religion]..., but we don't have a problem with clients practicing, *within the limits here in the program*, their spiritual beliefs. [Emphasis added.]

Of course, "what we teach" is, among other things, Higher Power spirituality.

The second rationale for Recovery House orthodoxy is one that Saul and others claim repeatedly in many forums: interviews, groups, and chance conversations. The following is from an interview with Saul.

A lot of recovering addicts are afraid of God.... You know, a lot of our residents were brought up under the fire and brimstone theory of religion.... So they don't want to hear anything about God.

Thus, religion (defined in traditional, competitive sectarian terms) creates not only dissention within the ranks of the clientele, but it also has great potential for creating a wall between the treatment and the client, rendering the client resistant, the treatment ineffective, and the job of the staff more difficult. Both of these rationales are consistent with treatment rhetoric that the staff is protecting its clientele from the damaging effects of traditional religious ideas by maintaining a tolerant, nurturing environment safe from the ravages of the outside world; a haven where the "self-help process" can work itself out. It is the therapeutic community version of the well-known "it's for your own good" defense. After all, recovery must come before religion. Like any cloistered and intensely ideological organization, Recovery House must protect its ideological boundaries from enemies: internal and external. One way to facilitate moral encapsulation is to make it appear to be in the best interests of the cloistered. Thus, Higher Power spirituality, which provides for homogeneity of religious sentiment and allows the belligerently anti-religious as well as the complaisant their own space as well, fits neatly within the requirements of the therapeutic community now that the issue of religion can no longer be ignored altogether. These accounts thus support the active delegitimation of pretreatment religions that are common cultural baggage among the therapeutic community client population.

Julio, a Level III resident, first alerted me to the third rationale, a more instrumental accounting, for the suppression of alternative religious interests among Recovery House residents.

Any time I want to speak to anybody about religion, they don't want to talk about it. For example, when I wanted to go to church, I asked the counselors why they don't have these religious groups here. They didn't give me no answer.

Q: If you could change that and have outside groups come in for meetings, would it get a big response [from the residents]?

A: Definitely....

Q: Have you heard any other residents express this kind of desire?

A: Yes, a lot. But they just not bold enough to bring it up like I am. I don't care, if it's gonna help my recovery, you know, I will bring it up. And I would think that would help a lot in this program. I would add that into the struggle, that would help.

Q: Why do you think they don't?

A: Because it's *a clash of different religions*. They would have to structure [these meetings with outside groups], they would have to do a lot *more work* to get different religions involved in this.... so *many different religions* here that they have to change so many things, you know, the Muslims have to do this, the Catholics have to do this...have to go to different churches, so it's like [an] inconvenience. They say they have enough *paper work* to do. They afraid to try something new. But if that's gonna help us, that's their job. But when you go and tell them this thing, it's like you interfering, you adding more to their work.

Q: So you think inconvenience is the main reason they don't allow you to go to church or allow religious programs to come in?

A: Yeah. They should have them coming in *just like they have AA and NA*. That's important to our recovery here. They could have Bible study or class. I read the Bible, but what am I reading? I *need someone to explain* to me. I'm trying to get into spirituality, and I asked people and they say get a Bible and start with [the Gospel of St.] John. Okay, so I do that. Then what? If I don't know, then what do I do after that? So I just keep reading and reading, but is that what I have to do? I don't know. [All emphases added]

A few weeks later, during an interview with Saul, I confirmed Julio's story and his suspicions about staff reasoning.

Q: If an outside group, church or mosque, came to you and said, we'd like to come in and organize a prayer group or lead a bible study for those who are interested, how would the administration respond to that?

A: I don't know. I couldn't say. I could tell you that if we do it for one, then I believe we'd have to [do it] for everyone. We'd have to set up something for *every denomination*, and I think it would take away from the overall effect of what we try to do. We don't attack it [religion] head on here because we have people of *so many spiritual backgrounds* and religious backgrounds that we would have to bring in people who teach Buddhism, Islamic teachers. So we don't attack it [religion] primarily, because there are *too many beliefs and practices to serve.* [Emphasis added]

Here, Saul admits that in addition to the problems of client resistance and Family divisiveness, the staff sees a problem of systems maintenance, i.e., of simple bureaucratic efficiency, presented by the prospect of true religious pluralism at Recovery House.[27] Not only does the regime feel threatened, like any encapsulated, ideological organization, by the intrusion of alien meaning systems within its moral and geographical boundaries. It also senses danger in the potential challenge to the day-to-day efficiency of moving all of its residents through its treatment process. The more ideologically consistent that process can remain, the easier it is to approximate the stated goals. The fewer ideological focal points available to residents, the easier it is to keep them focused on the demands of the day. To introduce into the facility a series of externally centered, denominationally and doctrinally diverse sub-organizations that would process different sets of residents (i.e., attending to their spiritual needs), on different days and at different times, would add a serious degree of organizational complexity. This additional potential for inefficiency has to appear not only daunting but also unnecessary to any "right thinking" staff member at a correctional institution. It is much more appropriate, from a purely organizational standpoint, to process all of the residents through a single "spirituality" session. The Twelve-Step programs that are allowed into the facility on a regular basis provide that service with optimum ideological and bureaucratic efficiency. Despite his own strong personal commitment to the religious dimension of recovery, like all the staff, Saul recognizes the organizational as well as ideological threat of permitting residents to retain their traditional religious beliefs and practices (or perhaps entertain new ones) while encapsulated in the therapeutic community.[28]

All three rationales for the "apparent" contradiction between the ideology of religious tolerance based on the principle of a Higher Power spirituality and the practice of negation of independent or alternative religious expression at Recovery House have to do with social control. The explanations that seek to avoid client resistance and client divisiveness make the case for the necessity of client conformity and compliance over complete religious freedom of expression. Saul's diversity explanation is a paean to conformity for the sake of efficiency. Thus, the religious orthodoxy preached and practiced at Recovery House is ultimately not about openness and tolerance, democracy or individualism, but about conformity and compliance, or in the terms used by the practitioners themselves, "surrender" and "gratitude."[29] In yet another irony, Higher Power spirituality at Recovery House is a religion truly in the spirit that Marx would recognize, an *opiate* for the clientele. It allows men the illusion of choice and freedom in exchange for the reality of conformity, surrender, and submission to authority.[30]

An Apparent Exception to Orthodoxy: The Muslim Prayer Group

There is one apparent exception to Saul's rule of no outside religious groups within the therapeutic community. About twenty Muslim men meet daily for prayer at Recovery House. Their association is based solely on this ritual and does not include open proselytizing, nor does the group actively identify in public treatment settings as Muslims. They do not "hang together" and therefore are not segregated from "the Family" as a recognizable subgroup. They do not make an issue of doctrinal differences, neither does the program staff.

Allah is their Higher Power, both from the perspective of the program and from the perspective of the ritual group. This keeps them well within the working parameters of Higher Power doctrine as described by Saul, Maria, and others, despite their apparent deviation.

> Saul: [W]e have some people here who are Muslims that can identify with some Christian concepts and beliefs and vice versa. The beauty for them is that they are open to the religious and spiritual aspect and *enhancing* their recovery with spirituality.

Why is it that the practice of the Islamic ritual of prayer five times each day poses no threat to the homogeneity of Recovery House, while reading the Bible at Morning Focus does? One answer is that the Muslims do their thing in relative private, while Juan, the Bible-reader, did his in a public meeting of the Family with the clear (at least to Leroy and others) intention of differentiating himself vis-à-vis treatment and, perhaps, of recruiting others. The Muslims, unlike Juan, are not offering themselves as an alternative to or means of insulation from treatment, but as an adjunct, as Saul's comment suggests.

The ability to practice what to Saul is an alien, exotic religious rite and yet pose no threat of ideological heterogeneity to the presumed solidarity of the Recovery House community may also be accounted for by a distinction Herbert Danzger (1989) and others have identified between ritual-oriented and faith- or doctrine-oriented religions.[31] Louis Schneider (1970) used the term "orthopraxy" to refer to religions in which precise conformity in ritual behavior is required for the faithful rather than conformity in doctrine or theological interpretations (see Roberts 1995).[32] Religions such as, for example, Orthodox Judaism and Islam focus much more on concrete actions or ritual procedures and need not assign explicit doctrinal meaning to their ritual activities; it is enough that the scriptures (or other authorities) have prescribed the practice. Should an explicit meaning be required at some point, ritual-oriented groups have far greater flexibility to introduce rationales that are "new," that is, rationales that are not necessarily consistent with any precise historical orthodoxy.[33] Doctrine-oriented religions, on the contrary, tend to base their legitimacy on the claim to maintain such precision in creedal formulations over time. Ritual-oriented groups legitimate their correctness by claims to maintaining proper *performance* or orthopraxy. This focus on correct *observance* of ceremonies allows more creativity regarding specific ideological *explanation* or meaning of the performances.[34] The opposite seems true for the doctrinally oriented groups who pay less attention to precise performance, than to ideational content often disparaging the former. For example, there is a wide variety of forms for the Christian practice of "Communion" or "the Lord's Supper," which are accounted for by very few different creedal formulations.[35]

Like other groups that are ritual-oriented, the Muslim group at Recovery House seems not to be concerned with the specificity of belief. They can easily, that is, without much apparent cognitive dissonance, refer to Allah as Higher Power, as long as they can continue to perform their prayers as they deem appropriate. Their observance poses no apparent threat to the Protestant-based creedal patterns of AA-style Higher Power spirituality because it does not challenge the private, inner experience of religion or spirituality by, e.g., seeking to name or describe the character of the divinity. The Muslim ceremonies pose no threat despite the fact that they entail an active religious subgroup within the larger treatment community. Despite the regular observance of the Muslim ritual of daily prayers, the treatment-sanctioned spirituality of Higher Power maintains its religious hegemony within Recovery House.

Nevertheless, the Muslim group retains its *potential* for subversion of the treatment regime. The ability of groups of Muslims to challenge "authorities" has been evidenced in not a few "real" prisons and societies around the world (including the few months preceding the publication of this book!). However, this potential goes unrealized at Recovery House. The group continues to function as a prayer group and nothing more, presumably in tacit (or tactical?) agreement with the program administration to so limit its activity.

Conclusion

The Alcoholics Anonymous ideology of the Higher Power has "returned" to the therapeutic community after being repressed by Charles Dederich and the Eastern psychiatrists who adapted his method for treating drug addicts. The individual, inner, mystical form of religion such as that sanctioned at Recovery House has been identified by many sociologists, especially those with Durkheimian leanings like Thomas Luckmann and Robert Bellah, as appropriate to the modern world, imbued with strong notions of individualism. This form of religion recalls Durkheim's idea of the "cult of man," which he expected would be the modern form taken by religious evolution (Lukes 1973/1985). Bellah's "Sheilahism" or Luckmann's "invisible religion" are likewise considered the form of religion most appropriate to the modern rational sensibility (Bellah et al. 1985; Luckmann 1967). Although I was quite surprised to find any religion being "pushed" in a therapeutic community, it was not surprising to find that when it occurs it is a religion that has a strong affinity for the treatment *ideal* of a rational, *self-directed* individual whose guidance systems are all internal. This, of course, is a system of thought most congenial to those "scientific" professionals who formulate and/or rationalize (systematize and standardize) the ideology that is promoted in the therapeutic community. It is a form of religion that, within proper bounds, does not threaten the Enlightenment orientation of the therapeutic community's philosophical ideals of reason, science, and inner-direction.

It is likewise not surprising, at least in retrospect, to find that the introduction of religion raises such an interest among the residents. Many, if not most, of the men come from backgrounds that are anything but Enlightenment-oriented.

The backgrounds of the residents more often include exposure to traditional sectarian and/or ecstatic religions; in many cases these are deeply embedded in their family histories. Whether a particular man practiced or disparaged them, traditional forms of Christianity and, in some cases, Islam were part of the taken-for-granted reality of most of the men interviewed at Recovery House. In virtually all cases these religions included some form of concrete, external authority (e.g., priest, scripture, minister, tradition) that was considered necessary to religious life and practice above or, at least, in addition to inner experience. However, this aspect of religious experience, one that is most appropriate to the sensibilities of the general population of its clientele, is actively discouraged by the therapeutic community. These religions are perceived as antithetical to its purpose and ideal. Recovery House has no interest in producing people who are religious in any traditional sense or in facilitating that process by any outside organization. Indeed, the Recovery House regime, much like that at Redemption House, represses any religion but its own.

The manifest reason for this repression—the rationale—is that traditional religions create controversy due to the reality of religious pluralism and the "fact" that junkies off the street do not want God pushed down their throats.[36] But also, in Skoll's framework, these "former" religious traditions represent potential sources of alternative social identities and world views that could disrupt the treatment. They may create multiple antithetical identities and thereby threaten the ideal of the homogeneous and harmonious community that is considered the core of the therapeutic process. That is, outside religions could offer alternative interpretations of the addict experience, particularly redemptive interpretations that see the addict's experience as "part of God's plan" rather than merely "poor decision making," "dope fiend" behavior, or "diseased thinking." Residents could "learn" that they have value to others (including "the Other") and are not alone in the world condemned to make their own way because of their past errors, character flaws, or disease.

Conventional forms of religion, like that promoted at Redemption House, would also make rational planning based on scientific (medical and/or behaviorist) rationales more difficult to impose on the clientele. Because modern, empirical science is the worldview within which therapeutic community treatment is legitimated, historical religions could present potential alternative realities and rationales for both "abuse" and treatment, rationales that must be kept at bay. The AA notions of Higher Power and spirituality, as opposed to specific, historically identified "Gods" and "religion," accomplishes this ideological task and, as such, effectively "cools out" any potential religiously oriented opposition or alternative. Higher Power spirituality, as adapted from AA, thus offers a functional form of religious social control within the therapeutic community. It has become another technique or procedure in the arsenal of the treatment staff for inducing commitment to the true higher power at the therapeutic community, i.e., the institution, which is represented ideologically as "the treatment" or "recovery process" and rhetorically as "the community." The Higher Power of Higher Power spirituality is not the highest power at Recovery House. Recovery House, itself (i.e., "the treatment"), is the *highest* power of all.

* * *

Treatment at Recovery House actively encourages a recognizable religious outlook and discourages most others. It disguises its approach as all-inclusive, but in fact Higher Power religion is exclusive, especially in relation to the historical "theisms" (e.g., Christianity, Judaism, or Islam) that clients typically bring with them from their lives prior to treatment. This exclusionism is evident in the reactions of the Recovery House staff to attempts at public consideration of other religious dogma. Does this mean that the therapeutic community is a religious program, too? There can be little question that it qualifies as a "functional equivalent" of religion (McGuire 1992). Kurtz's analysis of AA with its Higher Power spirituality, and Pagel's explication of gnostic religion also clearly apply to the Recovery House version of spirituality. What the implications of this "religiosity" are for policy and understanding "addictions," I leave for later consideration. One thing seems clear: the therapeutic community's self-image is illusory at best. It "hobnobs" with medical and scientific treatments for "real" diseases, and fancies itself a secular and rationalist, objective and non-ideological form of "treatment." The therapeutic community is, rather, simply another in a long line of American agencies for the resocialization and social control of people who have been labeled deviant. It "pushes" a particular moral logic, one that is socially and historically bound to specific classes and cultures and not objective in any sense of the word, certainly not in the sense of "value-free."

The ease with which Recovery House has made the transition from the therapeutic community movement's early opposition to the spirituality of Alcoholics Anonymous to its current acceptance and promulgation of the same Higher Power religiosity may be an indication of this movement's affinity with (and historical roots in) other classic American movements for moral reform, including those that were explicitly religious such as Revivalism and Temperance. The numerous similarities the therapeutic community form of treatment bears to that of the discipleship training at Redemption House only strengthen this suspicion. The use of a religious orthodoxy as a means of social and ideological control described in this chapter is yet another indication of the overall similarity between the two supposedly distinct programs for the treatment of addictions.

Notes

1. For total institution, see Goffman, *Asylums*, 1961.
2. See http://www.daytop.org/history.html (5/18/11) regarding the role of Father William B. O'Brien in the development of Daytop Village. In this regard, Daytop

was something of an exception, but regardless of the religious motivations of some of its founders, the psychiatric viewpoint ruled the treatment process.

3. The founding psychiatrists typically depended on "experiential input" from Synanon alumni and refugees, many of whom had been leaders under Dederich, but who had become disillusioned with the direction in which he took his organization. Also, some of these psychiatrists were not entirely devoid of charisma. Judith Densen-Gerber (1973) is perhaps the best example.

4. Deitch, for example, holds a Ph.D. in clinical psychology and the title of Clinical Professor of Psychiatry at the University of California, San Diego and has had faculty appointments in Psychiatry at the University of California, San Francisco, the University of Chicago, and Temple University.

5. At this early stage, virtually all heroin addicts were men. Therefore, virtually all therapeutic community clients were men as well.

6. The chemical leg of this double threat to independence was, of course, soon compromised when the prospect of psychotropic drugs as medication appeared, and with it the promise of quick cures and quicker fortunes. Some chemical crutches are okay, as long as they have the correct legal definition. Some modern therapeutic communities have dropped their strict "drug free" treatment regimen to include "dual diagnosed, MICA patients" who use antidepressants and other prescribed mood "adjustment" medications as part of their addiction treatment.

7. As far as I have been able to discover, this change has not been documented elsewhere.

8. See Frankel (1989) for a somewhat different view of therapeutic community as non-coercive.

9. Goffman (1961, 12) refers to a "'presenting culture' (to modify a psychiatric phrase) derived from a 'home world'—a way of life and a round of activities taken for granted until the point of admission to the institution."

10. The orientation level is the primary site of the attack on the client's ideas about himself and his drug use; it is a period of identity de-formation. At this early point in treatment (the first four to six weeks), the client just in off the street is bombarded with critiques of his "junkie mentality," the essence of which in recovery ideology is manipulation, dishonesty, and "jive." In turn, the resident learns that he must be "open and honest," confront his manipulations of self and others, and replace such attitudes with attitudes of e.g., "surrender and gratitude," if he is to "make it in recovery."

11. The "Big Book," the bible of AA was often invoked, but was never in evidence on the treatment floor. Interestingly, in my interviews with residents, the Bible and/or the Quran were mentioned numerous times. One client happened to have his Bible at his interview. It was a Recovery Bible, structured and with commentary for recovering addicts. It has an AA orientation. The Big Book was never mentioned, although almost everyone used the terminology of Higher Power spirituality interchangeably with that of God or Allah, when referring to a deity.

12. Clients at the orientation level are expected to do little work, simply get their bearings by learning the rules, regulations, and philosophy of the house. Level I clients (six weeks to three months in treatment) are still getting oriented, but have work details and other assignments (e.g., remedial education classes). Similar orientation groups, with various names, are held daily, Monday through Friday, at nine, eleven, and one o'clock in the Recovery House "living room" (a spacious, former auditorium also used for meetings of the entire 100-person population). Other residents temporarily with no outside assignment are also expected to attend regardless of their treatment status. Attendance is taken at each meeting; lower level clients

(O-I) are expected to attend twelve sessions per week, upper level clients (II–III), six. (See Hood 2011a, chap. 2 for more detail.)

13. Obtaining a degree is increasingly necessary if people like Leroy are to maintain their careers in the treatment industry, let alone gain advancement in a time of both rapid professionalization and cutbacks. During the four months I spent at Recovery House, the program length was cut from 12–18 to 6–12 months by government oversight and funding agencies. Several employees were laid off, including the criminal justice system liaison (who coordinated client's court dates and parole hearings) and several paraprofessional counselors.

14. These terms are virtually interchangeable. Rhetorically, they include the staff, but the always evident hierarchical system of privileges allows staff to avoid this early morning cheerleading session when not immediately involved with its supervision. It is my unsystematic observation that the term Family is preferred when the collective role of support or "care of souls" is at issue, and the term Community is more commonly used when its role of moral arbiter or corrections officer is called for.

15. This is typical of the stereotypes circulated via therapeutic community rhetoric. In the course of my research, several participants told me they had active religious lives during the times they were active as drug users. Also, in my role as volunteer at a local needle exchange, I have known several active users who are devoutly religious. Contrary to treatment rhetoric, there is no necessary contradiction or conflict between religion and drug use.

16. In this case, it happens to be the lingo of paraprofessional staff. I discuss the religious language of residents in a later section. No one at Recovery House uses the language of twelve steps per se. However, residents and staff alike regularly refer to various individual steps or related AA concepts, e.g., "one day at a time," "each one teach one." Higher Power spirituality also specifically rejects many aspects of American popular religion. I consider the issue of religion *versus* spirituality later in this chapter.

17. Bloom finds the inner, spiritual quest a congenial religious style. He writes (p. 36): "Like poetry, religion is a culmination of the *growing inner self,...* religion is the poetry, not the opiate, of the masses, the inner structures of the imagination prevail in religion as in poetry." Bellah, the sociologist and communitarian, on the other hand, finds this trend, at best, detrimental to our democratic republic.

18. On inner light and transmoral conscience, see Nelson (1981, 49–53) and Tillich (1948).

19. Weber (1969, 325) writes:

> Active asceticism operates within the world... [it] seeks to tame what is creatural and wicked through work in a worldly 'vocation' (inner-worldly asceticism). Such asceticism contrasts radically with mysticism, if the latter draws the full conclusion of fleeing from the world (contemplative flight from the world)."

The importance of "vocational" discipline as preparation for post-treatment life at both Recovery House and Redemption House, its religious counterpart, evidences their mutual commitment to the inner-worldly asceticism that remains one of the foundations of modern American culture and character, despite inroads by opposing forces of consumerism and other "escapist" moral logics. On consumerism, see Barber (2007) and Reinarman (1994).

20. See Chapter 2; also Manning (1989).

21. Personal communication in various forms and formats over the years, including the seminar he co-taught with Charles Winick on therapeutic communities. This

seminar was jointly sponsored by the City University of New York (CUNY) Graduate School and the Center for Therapeutic Community Research in the late 1990s–early 2000s.

22. McGuire (1992, 10ff) writes:

> It is useful to approach sociological definitions as strategies rather than as "truth.... Two major strategies...are **substantive** and **functional** definitions. Substantive definitions try to establish what religion *is*; functional definitions describe what religion *does*...[T]he critical feature of [the substantive definition] is that beliefs, patterns of action, and values, refer to "superhuman beings," [or] similar concepts, including..."transcendent reality."...A functional definition...emphasizes...what religion does for the individual and social group...The most important element is the provision of meaning...[others include,] the attempt to interpret the unknown and control the uncontrollable...the effort to deal with the ultimate problems of human experience. One distinction used in many functional definitions is...the **sacred**. Whereas the natural/supernatural distinction of...substantive definitions refers to the intrinsic quality of the *object* of worship, the sacred/profane distinction refers to the *attitude* of worshippers. The realm of the sacred refers to that which a group of believers sets apart as holy and protects from the "profane" by special rites and rules. Functional definitions...are usually much broader [than substantive ones]...Functional definitions often include as "religion" phenomena such as nationalism, Maoism, Marxism, psychologism, spiritualism, and even atheism.... From a functionalist standpoint, a good case could be made for considering psychotherapeutic groups as essentially religious.

Wuthnow et al. (1984, 81) write regarding Mary Douglas's thought: "For modern society...the very things we consider the most real—hence scientific [truth]—are, in fact the most religious."

23. This intolerance, appears to be intrinsic to all virtuoso religions, or other sectarian, ideological movement organizations. On virtuoso religions, see Weber (1964, 162ff). Also see Hood (2011a, chap. 5).

24. Recovery House displays many characteristics of a sect. As McGuire (1987, 33–34) writes:

> Sectarianism is an orientation by which a group tries to maintain its distinctive world view by...[among other things] distancing [members] from...real or perceived opposition...limiting outside influences...and restricting members social contacts.

In Hood (2011a), I have referred to this practice as "discourse deprivation" and described its use at both Recovery House and Redemption House.

25. External with respect to Recovery House, that is.

26. On accounts, see Scott and Lyman (1968). Scott and Lyman refer specifically to "deviant" behavior. However, Saul et al. are accounting for behavior that might otherwise be deemed in violation of their stated norms of tolerance, if not accounted for by the "higher" motives of recovery. Scott and Lyman expand on Sykes and Matza's (1957) "techniques of neutralization," which include the explicit example of "appeal to higher authority" as a means of "neutralizing" internalized controls (norms) in specific instances, while not denying the general principle involved. Here, Saul is "neutralizing" the principle of tolerance. In general tolerance is good. In treatment, in certain instances at least, it has to take a back seat.

27. Both Saul and Julio echo Goffman (1961, 46f): "In total institutions...the various rationales for mortifying the self [which would include the denial of religious liberty

afforded "civilians"] are very often merely rationalizations, generated by efforts to manage the daily activity of a large number of persons in restricted space with a small expenditure of resources."

28. It is also curious that this third account, while expressing sympathy toward the religious diversity of American culture, also poses it as an interest that is inherently inferior to that of maintaining the dominant behaviorist world view. Democracy (or pluralism) is good, but the disease of drug addiction is so devastating that its treatment via the regnant ideology of abstinence takes precedence over any other, lesser consideration. The parallel here between "treatment" or "recovery" and "national security" as a claim that is deemed self-evidently superior to all others seems, well, self-evident.

29. These terms, among others, are constantly used to describe appropriate attitudes that clients should cultivate. I attended orientation sessions that focused on one or the other of these concepts exclusively for entire ninety-minute sessions. One such group on gratitude utilized a variant on Maria's method of going around the circle. After a brief homily on gratitude, the paraprofessional leading the session strolled around the circle and every few minutes would suddenly thrust his finger in the face of an unsuspecting participant and ask, "What is gratitude?" Each selected client was expected to "testify" what gratitude meant to him or her. Generally this involved a supporting anecdote about a treatment-related experience, for example, "I'm grateful for my counselor, or my peers, because…"

30. However, this conformity may be only public and collective. Frankel (1989) argues that this requirement may not be a complete straitjacket. Higher Power spirituality does permit variant expressions *in private*. However, if identities are dependent upon continuous—or at least regular—social maintenance, as Peter Berger and others (1966, 1981) argue, then different religious expressions in private and public would seem a formula for identity confusion rather than the stability the therapeutic community claims to be promoting. On another level, the passivity that Skoll (1992) identifies in the therapeutic community and that Kaminer (1992) identifies in the general recovery movement may be the most likely outcome of this situation. In my research, interviews with residents, held behind closed doors and with the solemn promise of anonymity, elicited somewhat varied accounts of religious sentiment, including both passive disinterest and active pursuit of religious interests.

31. Danzger (1989, 4) writes: "Christian rebirth requires belief primarily and ritual acts only secondarily. Judaism in contrast emphasizes acts, the performance of *mitzvot* (commandments)."

32. Roberts (1995, 93) reports that Schneider is "actually citing…observations by…Gustave von Grunebaum," the classic historian of Islam, as well as other observers.

33. Used here in its literal sense of correct opinion or idea.

34. Danzger (1989, 130) explains that the aim among "returnees" to Orthodox Judaism

> is not to learn *about* the rituals but to learn to *perform* the rituals…. the person first performs the action and only afterward speculates on its inner meaning…[which] allows…a range of explanations, as the act, not the explanation, is primary. [Emphasis added.]

35. Christian denominations differ as to time (weekly, monthly, quarterly, yearly) and place (altar, sanctuary, home) of performance, appropriate elements of performance (wine vs. grape juice, bread or wafer only vs. both elements), officiates (male only

vs. both genders, clergy vs. laity), and more. Creedal formulations are limited, in practical terms, to transubstantiation (Roman Catholic), consubstantiation (traditional Lutheran), and "purely symbolic" views (Baptist and other sectarian traditions).

36. This idea is traceable to the earliest thoughts of Bill W. in his quest for an organization that could ensure his sobriety (Kurtz 1991).

4

Reentering the World:
Beyond Recovery and Redemption

Of the seventeen guys we got here right now,
maybe two of them will be walkin' with the Lord a
year from now. That's because most of these guys
don't have a church. Got to have a church. [A]nd
they don't do they devotionals. Th[at's] what they
supposed to do. They need that authority in them
to tell them when to get up and where to go. That's
one thing [I've learned] by working in a Christian
program. You can always stay ahead. Hearing the
Word every day...I need that. A lotta times I sit by
the door while Harry is teaching [his daily Chris-
tian Life class] so I can get some word that helps
me through the day.
　　　　—Ervin, Redemption House Intake Director

I always tried to base my recovery at work [on] be-
ing a hard worker and having two or three friends
at work in recovery who I can talk with about any-
thing. And then, of course, my spouse. This is my
circle of recovery. Other friends that I have, [they]
have to go to [AA or NA] meetings every day. But
the people that work in the [treatment] field....
They're talking about the things [at work] they're
gonna talk about at the [outside] meetings.
　　　　—Louie, Recovery House Counselor

Three chapters in the previous volume based on the same ethnographic
project described and analyzed the major transformational process at the core of
treatment and training at Recovery House and Redemption House, respectively
(see Hood 2011a). This chapter looks at the reentry process at both houses and
the problems encountered by residents as they attempt the transition back to
the "real" world after treatment and training. The final step in the treatment and
training process focuses on the resident's preparation for the transition to the

outside world. From the perspectives of both programs, the key to successful continuation of abstinence from drugs and other "life-controlling" behaviors is essentially the same: find or create a social network or structure that shares and supports the moral logics and meaning systems advocated by the programs, Christian living (at Redemption House) or Right living (at Recovery House). In its course, this chapter also discusses issues of staffing at both programs and concludes with a detailed account of one graduate's attempt to get beyond both treatment and recovery—to "normality."

Plausibility Structures

At Redemption House, Harry, the director, says repeatedly to residents that joining a local church and making oneself "accountable" to its leadership and congregation is essential for success after leaving the training program. For Recovery House, as the staff counselor Maria and others preach persistently, success means either maintaining regular contact with a support group of fellow recovering addicts constructed while in the reentry phase of treatment, or regular attendance at and participation in an organized support group such as Narcotics Anonymous (NA) or Alcoholics Anonymous (AA).

The instructions residents receive from both programs regarding individual practices are similar as well. At Recovery House they teach the techniques ("tools" is the term they use) deemed necessary to avoid relapse. These include continued contact with one's support group, but also they involve practices and outlooks that prevent not only relapse, but are claimed to minimize temptation and resist "cravings" for forbidden activities. These include obvious methods such as avoiding places where one used or "copped" drugs prior to treatment, contacting a friend from the support network when experiencing urges, cravings, or fantasies about drug use or other tabooed behavior, and continuous use of "consequential thinking" (see Hood 2011a, chap 4). The prescriptions are more or less the same at Redemption House: do not frequent former drug-using places or associates; make new friends who are believers at a local church; maintain a personal devotional life (regular personal prayer and Bible reading), join and attend services regularly at a local evangelical congregation.

What is central to the entire plan for post-treatment or post-training success is establishing effective "plausibility structures, that is, the specific social base and social processes required for...the maintenance of [one's] subjective reality" (Berger and Luckmann 1966, 154). Wuthnow et al. (1984, 52) view this concept as "a rough parallel [to] the symbolic interactionist term, reference group." They continue:

Though the concept can and does refer to macro-societal phenomena.... It is principally through *interaction* with significant others that reality is maintained as *subjectively* plausible. The vehicle of reality maintenance is...*conversation*.... [C]onversation with others...mediates the reality of the symbolic universe. When this...is interrupted...as in the case where a plurality of definitions are in…competition…the reality ceases to impose itself as self-evident truth. [Emphasis added.]

Graduates must establish or find social and cultural networks and patterns that will effectively support their new beliefs about self, world, drug use, and abstinence adopted in the process of treatment or training. Both programs trumpet this principle loudly and often to potential graduates. It is old hat to the evangelical establishment at Redemption House, much newer to the therapeutic establishment at Recovery House. A basic shortcoming of therapeutic community (TC) thought has been a psychologistic tendency to believe that socialization can be entirely successful. TC personnel seem tempted to assume that each individual can so thoroughly internalize the new recovery identity that she or he needs no permanent community to sustain the new self in sobriety. They seem to crave the notion that internal social controls can, for all practical purposes, replace external controls entirely.[1]

The faith communities, being tied to an older tradition, and perhaps not quite so theory-driven, seem more aware that new converts are vulnerable to even the most cursory challenges in the outside world. Therapeutic communities, on the other hand, may tend to believe their Emersonian and (William) Jamesian assumptions too much. They have too much faith in the notions of socialization built on individualistic and essentialist notions of identity and personality. Interactionist and constructionist, i.e., sociological, notions of socialization are rarely so sanguine. The better models always leave room for the necessity of ongoing processes and structures of reality maintenance, especially at the level of everyday association and conversation as well as in overt systems of social control (Berger and Luckmann 1966). Over the last decade and a half, however, the TC movement has apparently conceded that graduates need continuing treatment-like structure and association to assist their continuing sobriety after they leave the program. In light of this, it should come as little surprise that many if not most of the graduates who remain true to the ethic of right living are those who become staff members in a TC or similar treatment program.[2] There is little, if any, hard evidence to substantiate this, because no one has bothered to do the necessary research. Anecdotal evidence, however, points clearly in this direction (Manning 1989; Skoll 1992).[3]

It is this point of comparison that may go furthest toward establishing that what treatment and training are, at their cores, is a conversion, a transformation of belief, of outlook, a change of world view and view of self (identity). The initial belief that is central, as described in the previous volume (Hood 2011a), is the belief that one is a sinner and/or addict, i.e., someone in need of correction or rehabilitation. But further, remaining residents of both houses come to believe that abstinence is the sole solution to this particular problem and that adherence to program-generated principles of Right living or Christian living are required to maintain abstinence or are, perhaps, synonymous with sobriety. That is to say, treatment—like training—involves the establishment and maintenance of a faith in the essentialist notions of addiction and recovery on a theoretical par with evangelical notions of sin and redemption. Although, in sociological terms, both "addiction" and "recovery" as well as "sinfulness" and "saintliness" are best understood as socially and historically contextualized patterns of association, both programs tend to reify these experiences as static "qualities" or "traits" of individuals. These beliefs and the changes in belief affected in the confines of the programs are established and maintained in the context of a group of "like-minded" people (community or congregation; treatment or training) who share these same beliefs. The same sense of plausibility or taken-for-grantedness experienced there is not readily available in the face of a generally indifferent and occasionally hostile outside world.

One of the clues about this is that whenever Redemption House or Recovery House presents their programs to the public or to funding groups, the testimony of "success stories" is a primary source of evidence for their effectiveness.[4] At any such meeting featuring the therapeutic community modality, the witnesses are likely to be graduate staff personnel, like Louie at Recovery House and Martin at Redemption House. As Louie reports:

> I used to go on speaking engagements with Daytop. And you met all these teachers and professors and medical doctors who were trying to convince other people that treatment works. So I [was a case where it] worked. Here I was: a living example. They made you feel like a king on most of these interviews.

Redemption House presents a slight variation on this process. Each year they sponsor a Gospel Music concert to raise funds, spread the word, and celebrate their successes. The year of this research, it was held at Symphony Space, an auditorium on Manhattan's Upper West Side. During the concert intermission, several program graduates came on stage to testify about their experience at Redemption House and success on the outside. A number of the men who testified at this concert were *not* staff members there or at any other discipleship training program. They were civilians! However, virtually all of them held service positions in evangelical Christian organizations, often in programs directed at drug users or groups considered particularly vulnerable to drug abuse.

Each man that testified introduced himself to the capacity audience in much the same fashion, following a typified, almost ritual, pattern. James, the first to offer his testimony, established the pattern:

> Hello, I'm James _____, I graduated from Redemption House twelve years ago. There, God delivered me from fifteen years of drug addiction [applause, whistles, cheers]. Today I'm married, I have two children, I'm a supervisor at the Department of Sanitation, a member of [unintelligible] Gospel Church in [an upstate NY] County. I'm involved with jail ministry and children's ministry [as a volunteer].

Evangelical ritual patterns do not eschew spontaneity, but channel it, as a later testimony evidences. The third graduate of the night introduced himself with a bit of humor to relieve his obvious stage fright, but otherwise followed the common script:

Good evening ladies and gentlemen, I'm Nervous. [Audience laughter.] I am a senior accounts representative for an inter-school youth program called Project Express. I'm also an associate pastor of Calvary Baptist Church. I'm in charge of Christian education. [Applause.] At Redemption House, God delivered me from drugs. I just wanna thank Him for that.

Paul, a more recent graduate, followed "Nervous":

I graduated from Redemption House last March. Jesus Christ delivered me from a life of alcoholism and depression. And I'm glad to be working at Samaritan Center, which is a ministry of Redemption House for men with full-blown AIDS.

Then there was Vinnie:

My name is Vinnie [from the audience: "Hey Vinnie,"] the Lord delivered me from an eighteen year habit. Today I'm the Director of Outreach at Church of the Savior. We implement a Christ-centered support group for [people with] life control problems [i.e., "addictions"]. I also teach at Redemption House and I'm two semesters away from obtaining my BA in Human Services. [Applause.]

From the perspective of the discipleship program, these men *are* staffers. Each is intimately involved in a Christian service organization—as staff member or volunteer—that is actively and philosophically part of the evangelical subculture. They remain enmeshed in the culture and institutions (the plausibility structures) of evangelical Christianity, which is the training culture of Redemption House.[5]

Interestingly, this is one important way that Redemption House differs from Recovery House. It may be easier for the discipleship training program to send its graduates directly into an organizational setting that conceptually, if not structurally, replicates Redemption House. The evangelical community, as a whole, maintains the same world view and ethical outlook that pervades Redemption House. No comparable and identifiable institutional segment of the American populace professes or practices the therapeutic community ethic and outlook to the same degree. AA and NA programs are comparable organizations, but they consist only of former and current drug users. Evangelical churches include former and current "sinners," but most of them have not engaged in illicit drug use. It would seem, given the sociological notion of the means of success, that Redemption House could expect greater accomplishments from its graduates than Recovery House, since the requisite plausibility structures (evangelical congregations) are more readily available for its graduates. As I discuss in

Chapter 5, however, success rates appear to be more or less the same for both groups—rather dismal when read without treatment industry spectacles. The problem that graduates of both programs face equally is that the plausibility structures that are most readily available to them after treatment and training are their former drug-using cultures and socioeconomic milieus (read: poverty and discrimination).

The Reentry Process at Recovery House

At Recovery House, reentry, the last phase of the tri-partite longitudinal structure of the therapeutic community, by and large continues the same rituals of treatment, especially group therapy.[6] The major difference from earlier phases is that the reentry candidate is separated from the general program population and eventually finds his or her own living arrangement outside of the treatment facility. Louie described the reentry phase. As always, he combined his own experiences in treatment, a decade earlier, with the process of Recovery House, where he was employed at the start of our conversations.[7]

The reentry portion of the program at Recovery House involves a radical decrease in program demands and requirements on the part of the resident. Those that remain are merely variations on the rituals that have become second nature to the residents over the previous twelve to eighteen months. At Recovery House, for the first month of reentry the resident remains in the regular population, but attends special reentry groups whenever the rest of the House is in group meetings. The only exception to this rule is caseload groups, which, as described in the previous volume (Hood 2011a), are the only groups that maintain any continuity of membership and leadership over the course of a resident's treatment. Residents advanced to the reentry phase continue to attend the all-important caseload group until they are transferred to the separate reentry facility in the second month. Louie explains:

> When you get to [reentry], everything is gonna be on you, y'know. It becomes a constant focus for maybe two months. All of the groups you're in, this becomes the focus of everything. So all the peer groups you're in are: "What the fuck you gonna do when you're out there asshole, you can't do that shit out there." The only groups at this level where you mix with other lower levels is in your caseload, otherwise it's all people ready for reentry. Whenever they are doin' groups, you are in the reentry group. This is during reentry at the main facility. You have about a month of reentry there, and then when you get a job, you move to the separate facility.
>
> In [the reentry facility] it's more like a boarding house. I mean, there's things you have to go to, like a house meeting [each night], but there's no Morning Focus, except Saturday. You have to sign in and sign out of the facility. There's a curfew; but compared to the other facility, its nothing. But it's really like society, in a sense. [You] got your own place; [therapy] group, like once a week, but if you have a valid reason, you can miss. Have to make one outside NA or AA meeting a week. All the counselors who work there have been in recovery a very long time, they're very rational people. Y'know, it's not about getting you in trouble [like the earlier

levels]. Once in a blue moon you get a new jack asshole [counselor] who treats you like you're in the other place, but you don't respond to that stuff.

The process of treatment continues to be group work, practicing being (i.e., acting-as-if) an ex-addict, developing the new identity—or, at this phase, polishing and presenting it to the peers and staff for evaluation, reinforcement, and on occasion, correction and adjustment (see Hood 2011a, chap. 5 on reinforcement). The next major step, while still in reentry, is "move out." The resident in reentry remains in treatment, but begins living outside, in society as Louie puts it, while still attending Recovery House groups, AA meetings, following prescribed treatment criteria, and meeting with a counselor and/or therapist.

Then you present [apply] to move out. It took me six months. Some have stayed in as long as two years, but that's a special case, medical problems or whatever. Most people are out by twelve to fourteen months.[8] You have to move out with a roommate from treatment unless you're married or have a really good job or whatever. You have to fulfill certain criteria: have to have a budget, money saved, bank account and so forth.

I moved out with a staff member who lived in Jersey City. Still had NA, AA meetings once a week, had to bring a slip [i.e., proof of attendance]. [Louie repeats this in a sing-song style with flattened affect to indicate the matter of fact character of these requirements; no big deal.] I had to report back once a month for "live-out" groups for another six months. These groups are a lot like the caseload groups from treatment. You go once a month, you know most of these people, so you don't mind goin'.

It's really fun at this stage, like being a senior in high school, near graduation. We often go out after [group], together, to Manhattan, whatever. The theme in group is usually "how you doin' out there?" Generally you have somebody doin' bad, someone doin' well, some in between. Some may even mess up and get high. But they don't necessarily have to start over again. Usually they can't graduate, but they don't go all the way back to [a lower level] because they come to group and confess, say I fucked up, whatever.

Caseload therapy continues to be the model ritual process for this level of treatment as well as earlier phases, and obviously preferred by Louie. However, encounter is also utilized—as a part of this same process, when deemed necessary—again, just as in earlier levels. Louie's description of the process is instructive.

Q: What happens if I'm in move out and I come into the group and say I fucked up?

L: Well there's a lotta different degrees of fuckin' up, y'know. In a typical treatment program, "messing up" is like snortin' some dope or takin' a drink or smokin' some weed. But "*Fuckin' up*" [with strong emphasis], that's like shootin' dope [injecting heroin] or smokin' crack and you're in real trouble. 'Cause most of the time you're gonna do it again where you developed some sorta habit or routine about it. So there's some concern about that, 'cause you went all the way to shootin' dope. 'Cause usually your most typical addict's gonna come in and say he drank or smoked pot or sniffed some coke or whatever. Very rarely would someone come in and say, "I shot dope," and expect to leave the group and come back the next meeting.

Q: What's the reaction to messing up?

L: It turns into an *encounter group*. Y'know. "You fucking asshole, why did you get high, what did you do, tell us what happened."

Louie continues this role play, but shifts his part, taking the "defendant's" position:

> [So he says something like] "Since I been out it's been lonely, I don't have a girlfriend, so I went out one night and had a drink and said fuck it and I started gettin' high." That's usually the routine. Then we give them our concern, which is usually a haircut, like: "You shouldn'ta done that, you shoulda called me, [you] fuckin' know better. You better hope they don't throw you outta here or rotate you back to [level I]," or whatever. [Again, in sing-song, indicating the predictability of the ritual process of encounter.]
>
> After that, you have to meet with staff and you're on a urine list. You have to give urine every time you come in, [you] might have to report in during the week, or they call you up and say come in and give urine, y'know, try and bust you. But usually when somebody messes up and comes in, we try to help 'em. And generally when they come in and admit it, they don't mess up any more. Usually, the worst thing that happens is they can't graduate with the group and have to wait 'til the next one.

Reentry at Teen Challenge

The shape of the Teen Challenge program, where all Redemption House residents spent the final months of their training during my period of research, is organized differently than is Recovery House reentry.[9] The goal is the same, however, as is the principle behind it. Jake, who was introduced in my discussion of work discipline (Hood 2011a, chap. 2), described for me his experience of reentry preparation at the Mid-America Teen Challenge Training Center in Missouri.[10]

The Teen Challenge emphasis on job training continues after graduation, especially for those men who do not plan to enter "full-time Christian service." For many of these men, Teen Challenge arranges apprenticeships or mentorships in the geographical areas to which they return after graduation. Ideally, this means each man is assigned to the care of an alumnus who learned the same job skill in training and can either offer the new graduate a job or assist him in finding one.[11] This relationship is supposed to assist the new graduate spiritually as well, to find a "home church," and provide a readily available and experienced evangelical Christian former addict who can act as spiritual counselor during the critical early weeks and months after graduation, when relapse is most likely. This arrangement is supposed to help protect the new graduate from the temptations of the world. It tries to provide a ready-made plausibility structure. As Jake put it:

> With Satan as lord of this world...the world is a garbage pit, because he's running things. [There's] greed, pornography, drugs, abortion, adultery...

However, these "babes in Christ" are sometimes led astray in spite of the arrangements that are supposed to assist them in their quest for the straight and narrow. Jorge was a Teen Challenge graduate who relapsed and was mandated to Recovery House (where I met him) in lieu of prison time. Teen Challenge had assigned him a mentor who gave him a job in his construction business and introduced him to his home church. Unfortunately, while working there, Jorge met other laborers who regularly had a few beers after work and often smoked marijuana on breaks. Jorge eventually began joining them, and several months later began using heroin again. Treatment spokespersons and other drug warriors might be inclined to attribute Jorge's relapse to his casual use of these "gateway" drugs.[12] However, he had another explanation. As he accounts for his relapse, Jorge mixes the idiom of the two different programs in a way that suggests the very parallels described here between the relapse prevention techniques they each prescribe.

> I *stopped praising* the Lord *and witnessing* for him, that's why I fell. I *stopped using the tools*. I took my eyes from my goals and just kept working overtime. I *stopped going to church*. [Emphasis added.]

As in the therapeutic community movement, many of the men who make it to graduation at Teen Challenge are encouraged to become staff members or, what amounts to the same thing for the evangelical subculture, enter some form of "full-time Christian Service" or "ministry." Most of the counseling staff members at Redemption House are Teen Challenge graduates.[13] Manning (1989) suggests that a reasonable way to understand the therapeutic community treatment programs is as a recruiting program for the abstinence-oriented treatment movement in the United States and other temperance cultures (Levine 1992). Recovery House fits very well a resource mobilization analysis of varied commitments among movement memberships. Much the same can be said of the discipleship training programs in the evangelical and Pentecostal movements. They are in many ways just what their name implies, trainings. Despite the assistance provided to others like Jorge, the reentry process at Teen Challenge Centers emphasizes this ideal of training for "full-time Christian service," which may mean a staff position at a Teen Challenge facility.

One day, while I was assisting Jake in the Redemption House kitchen by preparing an industrial-sized green salad (for twenty-five men) to accompany his even larger (and very tasty) cauldron of spaghetti, he described his reentry training.

> As it got close to time to leave Teen Challenge, they began to ask what I was gonna do. [Q: Who?] The guys in charge of the Thirty Day House in Cape Girardeau, [MO], where they teach [new] graduates to do all sorts of ministries: nursing home, street witnessing, food pantry. The big [ministry] is the Super Saturday. They get 200 kids from the neighborhoods, drive buses all around Cape Girardeau, pick 'em up and bring 'em to the church. For the older kids they had preaching services. But for the

five to eleven year-olds they have games and puppet shows and all that. The big part is the puppet shows, all with a Gospel theme.

The guy running the house said I should come to the Thirty Day House. I said, "No, I don't own anything, don't even have a decent pair of shoes. I need to go out, get me a job, 'cause I want a nice little job, nice little family, nice little house, go to a nice little church." Y'know, live real? 'Cause I was tired of the city. I liked living on the farm, and that's what I wanted, be out in nature to commune with God. That's what I wanted, to live on a farm.

When I told Tito this, he said, "Jake, your problem is you don't trust God to take care of your needs." Right then I determined, okay, I'm gonna go to the Thirty Day House. If God has a need there for me, He'll show me. So I took over Tito's spot, 'cause he was leaving. So I became the Puppet Master.

I fell in love with it, the puppets, the kids. I used to do five puppet shows a week along with the food pantry, children's church on Sunday, and all that. But my big thrill was Saturday. Super Saturdays! I loved doing the puppets, because I got to be myself and be the comedian I never was. I did Dan Blather with the world news tonight and Spiritual Man. I did all the voice characterizations.

[Then, all of a sudden] I'm junior staff. The third month there they put me in charge, and I'm running Super Saturday, and in charge of the new staff of new graduates.

After another month at Thirty Day House, Jake was told he would have to leave because they could not have men on staff who were HIV positive. He was informed that a position was available at Redemption House in the Bronx as manager of their AIDS hostel. After considering it for a time ("much prayer and fasting"), he decided to take it, because he was convinced it was God's will, what God wanted him to do, despite his own desire ("craving"?) to live on a farm rather than go to another city.

Jake was the ideal Teen Challenge graduate. He was committed to the movement and willing to do whatever its leadership decided was best for him. When asked what advice he had for men leaving Redemption House for the Farm, he said:

I'd tell 'em something Tito tried to tell me a long time ago. Ninety-nine percent of problems are we don't trust God. [I'd tell 'em] Trust God, do what you're told. Just shut up and do it.

This unquestioning commitment was, arguably, the reason that Jake was fed back into the system that created him. Despite his stigmatizing condition, he was to do his part to produce the next generation of committed, "ex-addict, ex-juvenile delinquents" as disciples of evangelicalism. In Jake's case that meant a Goffmanesque take on the mission:

do whatever has to be done to help run Redemption House, [which] is like a boot camp or field hospital. You take 'em in off the street and clean 'em up…clean off the rough edges, teach them respect…and send 'em on to the Farm.

Both Redemption House and Teen Challenge personnel are quite clear about the fact that the central role of each graduate is to attract more recruits to the evangelical movement. This is the role of all evangelical Christians, "to be soul-winners." Graduates of these discipleship programs are drawn to (placed in) familiar circumstances to do their recruitment. Like, they believe, attracts like. Or, no one can understand an addict like a redeemed addict! Or, in Jake's case, no one can help someone who is HIV positive or suffering from AIDS better than someone with the same condition who has found Christ. As described in the preceding volume (Hood 2011a, chap. 5), both programs share this basic myth about the nature of work with people who have certain deficiencies (addiction, AIDS, sin), especially those that bear heavy stigma, either from the perspective of the general populace (addiction, AIDS) or from a particular subpopulation like evangelicals (sin). This notion goes back at least to the beginnings of the Temperance movement and its temporal, and in many ways, ideological and structural parallel, the Revivalist movement: recovered drunks seeking drunks; redeemed sinners seeking sinners (Kurtz 1991; McLoughlin 1959). This notion itself was redeemed by Bill Wilson, the founder of twelve-step practice.

Ervin was another staff member at Redemption House who got there because of his T-cell count. Ervin does not have Jake's natural loquacity or ease with people, his evident charisma. Nevertheless, as part of its reentry program, Teen Challenge at Rehersburg (PA) prepared Ervin for a full-time service position in its ranks. However, things did not work out exactly as planned. As Ervin tells it:

> My ministry was the Walkathon. I loved the Walkathon. I loved witnessing to the peoples. You know, you meet a lotta peoples, tell them about Teen Challenge. And you get a chance to witness to them, tell them what the Lord is doing in your life, and that feels good. A lotta ladies want the information so they can get they sons in it.

After his ministry training, Ervin graduated and sought an internship like Jake, but in an entirely different field. However, what got him from Pennsylvania to Redemption House was quite the same process. It seems that Teen Challenge, unlike Harry Evans' program in the Bronx, prefers to isolate their HIV cases from the rest of their population. Ervin continues:

> Then, after I graduated, I put in [an application] for internship, to work there as a custodian. They accepted [me]. Then I got sick: PCP pneumonia, stomach virus, I had ulcers. I had a lotta different things wrong with me. I had this black spot on my chest. I said, "Oh…, I was depr…, I was really upset. [This memory is obviously troubling for Ervin, and he has difficulty getting his thoughts together and his words out.] It was because I had did everything right and I thought the Lord had healed me.[14] He didn't. I spent two weeks in the hospital, [then] went to renew my internship and they said no.[15] They said they thought it would be best if I went to another center to work with guys that have the virus.

Q: Did you think they were trying to get rid of you because you had the virus?

A: Exactly. I was mad. I really was mad at them until I spoke with Sonny. He's the director of the HIV groups and AIDS section at the Farm. He informed me about a program for men with the AIDS virus at Redemption House in New York. He said you could work there and at their induction center. They would like to have you. So I prayed about it and prayed about it, and came here to work. But I was still angry with Teen Challenge. I was angry a long time.

Christian Living Right After Graduation

Although he was supremely disappointed because he was denied the second internship and effectively banished from the Farm, Ervin seemed, to me at least, settled at Redemption House. He seemed convinced that working there was his salvation. His account of his post-training position as a staff member at Redemption House displayed his sense of the principle means of relapse-avoidance and successful abstention from drugs and other sinful activities.

I had decided [while in training] that I was gonna be a staff [member] at the Farm. I was gonna live in one'a those nice trailer houses they give staff to live in. They get a car. Teen Challenge really fix you up nice, if you a staff [member] up there. When they sent me here, I didn't wanna be here.[16] Then Sonny asked me, "Who you doin' this for? They need you more where you at than they do at the Farm." And we prayed about it and prayed about it. I did a report about it and sent it to Sonny. After I was here for a while, I began to see how I was being used by the Lord here. I began to see how this was the best place for me, 'spite of what I felt. Now, I wouldn't wanna be no place else.

Ervin's experience at Redemption House has reinforced for him several pertinent notions about the means of living a Christian life after training is complete. In particular, he is beginning to see the practical effectiveness of maintaining the necessary plausibility structures.

I'm Intake Director. When guys leave here with a bad attitude, it hurts me. I have three guys on the waiting list now that been here before, completed the whole program and left instead of going to the Farm. That's a major mistake. Harry said he's been doin' this 25 years, and in that time only two guys completed just this stage and is still walking with the Lord. That's because they had a home church backing them up. Most of these guys [residents] don't have a church.[17]
    That's one thing [I've learned] about working in a Christian program. You can always stay ahead of the other guy [who doesn't work in one].[18] Hearing the Word every day, staying in contact with my director and pastor (Harry is my pastor), I need that. A lotta times I sit by the door while Harry is teaching [his daily Christian Life class] so I can get some word that helps me through the day. I look up to Harry as a role model. His walk with the Lord keeps me going. All the roles he has to play—he's not just Director, he's teacher, he's doctor, he's plumber, electrician, everything. And everything he's doin', he's doin' it with a Christ-like attitude. That's hard to do. If I was working outside, it would be hard for me. I would probably be cleaning boilers, like I did before, where I worked with 20 guys and only one used to read his Bible.

The rest, from 7:30 to 4:30, all them guys used to do was drink and clean, and get smutty [talk dirty] and clean [boilers], drink and raise bills at the liquor store. I think it would be hard for me.

Ervin also has developed his own relapse prevention mechanism. He protects himself, first of all by recognizing the main source of inducement to sin, then by taking an inventive, yet age-old, precaution to avoid seduction. His prevention program is one part magic and two parts solid social psychology.

What I do, what keeps me going when I go out, I take a Bible with me. I don't know, maybe it's superstitious, but I will not do nothing, drink or do anything [sinful], as long as I got a Bible in my pocket or somewhere on me. On holidays, if I go to visit my family, the urge always comes, because they swear, they smoke, they do they thing. If I go to my mother's, I take one of the students with me. Not the staff, but the students. The staff, you can con them easy, but the students, that's different. I'm setting an example. I can't be messing up. And that way, I'm *protecting myself* from temptation.

Ervin is, of course, using a mutual witnessing technique here, in which he reinforces his own faith by being a role model for a less advanced trainee (Hood 2011a; McGuire 1987/1992).

Living Right After Recovery House: the Circle of Recovery

The (unknowingly) shared doctrine that successful avoidance of relapse following treatment and training requires the maintenance of a support network (plausibility structures) was something I discussed at length with Louie, the counselor from Recovery House who was my most intimate contact in the world of drug treatment.[19] Much of what he had to say seems to apply equally to both types of programs, which should not be surprising given the fact that they have so much else in common.

Ervin has described what it takes for him to maintain his "walk with the Lord." The counterpart at Recovery House is "stayin' clean," or, as Louie put it (paraphrasing DeLeon's "right living"), "living responsibly." Much of the reentry group discussions at Recovery House are about "how're you gonna do out there." As we have seen, Recovery House offers a set of relapse prevention tools that is by now more or less standard throughout the treatment industry. These tools are concepts and practical advice "to be internalized." These "tools" were developed by research largely independent of the therapeutic community movement.[20] The tools include such basic advice as, e.g., avoid the "people, places and things" that were associated with past drug use or criminal activity and associate only with "people, places and things" that are associated with conventional activities and legal pursuits.[21] Another "tool" that is closely associated with "people, places and things" is the notion of a network of people in recovery that can support each other through regular social contact and, especially, in times of crisis, when temptation to relapse is the greatest—or so it is universally claimed throughout the dominant treatment discourse. Louie had an interesting perspective on this particular tool, considered central to relapse prevention.

During his reentry, Louie had a good position in the placement department of a Manhattan center for the physically disabled. He had completed a three-month internship there late in his main treatment phase and was offered a regular position as job coach.[22] His success on the job led to the opportunity to advance to the "live out" stage of the reentry process and he moved into a small apartment in Jersey City with a staff counselor. Louie did well in live-out, and graduated. Some eighteen months after graduation, Louie was offered a job as counselor at Recovery House. Louie stayed there for almost three years, which included part of my research period. Then, when Tommie French, his mentor from Phoenix House became Director of Programs at another large TC complex on Long Island, he hired Louie as an Assistant Director in charge of the adolescent program. At this point, Louie was chief operating officer of a community of one hundred teenagers diagnosed as problem drug users, many because of their contact with the juvenile justice system. He was not yet thirty years of age.

Like Ervin, Louie offered an account of what keeps him straight and living responsibly. His account provides both empirical support and a new phrase for this particular version of plausibility structures—both their necessity and their grounding in conversation.

> I always tried to base my recovery at work on being a hard worker and having friends at work, [who are also] in recovery, who I can talk with about anything. After I graduated, I mainly socialized with six or seven people from Recovery House; and I was in touch with Tommie [as well]. Basically, you find two or three people at work who you can talk to about anything. This was my *circle of recovery*. [Emphasis added.]

> Ç: Where does the phrase "circle of recovery" come from?

> A: I heard it in treatment somewhere. To me it means having a *routine* of how to stay straight. Which means for me, goin' to work, goin' out, uh, there was always somethin' you had to do, a routine. Work every day, kept appointments, went out with friends, socialized, had fun, movies, had excitement in my life. The last thing is being honest, y'know, talking, which is something that has kept me straight. Just talking. As a matter of fact, a month ago, it happened to me. I was working in my garage and a big white thing fell on the floor and it looked like crack and I thought about crack for fifteen minutes. So I went and called someone. [I told him] "I got this urge," and you just express the real truth.

Like Ervin, Louie believes that his position as a full-time staff member at a TC is crucial to his recovery. He sees friends outside the movement as being at a distinct disadvantage.

And at work, when I run a group, I have a *dual purpose* in being there. Not only am I doin' a job, but I'm also *doin' somethin' for me*. That's one of the reasons I stay in the business. When I left the business I had a harder time. If I wasn't in the business, I could see myself goin' to meetings, or having to be involved with a support group, and goin' to a therapist. I don't doubt that at all. [Emphasis added.]

But other friends that I have, go to meetings every day. Some of them don't work in the field, and I can understand that. But the people that work in the field, I don't understand why they have to go to meetings every day? They're in recovery [at work] talking about the things they're gonna talk about at the [outside] meetings. One guy I know is in four different kinds of recovery [groups]. When we do get together, we have dinner, whatever. We talk about old times in treatment, assholes who did whatever, how we got over, laughing and so forth. A lot of these people are not staff, so I become like their pseudo-counselor. They call me up with questions.

From Recovery to Normalcy

Louie has experienced a number of years of sobriety and has developed a further perspective on recovery, one that I did not hear discussed in any treatment facility. Neither did I find it in any professional treatment industry assessment. Louie is attempting, cautiously and with sensitivity, to transcend the recovery paradigm that he sees as responsible for his success in sobriety and that he now experiences as an increasingly unnecessary burden. It has become another stigma that carries over from "addiction" to recovery and infects, or perhaps, "disorders" his quest for identity in the outside world. After several years of married life and recent fatherhood, Louie is ready to shed the label of "recovered addict" and live, as he puts it, "like a normal person."

When I get home at five o'clock, I want recovery to, like, shut off in a sense, and [I want to] be a *normal* person. Some people have problems with that, but not the "old school" people. They understand that rationale. Even after [my earlier treatment at] Daytop, I tried to look at it [addiction and treatment] as an *episode*. It's ended now and I want to move on now to be with people that are…uh…[he's searching for the right term] *normal*. [Emphasis added.]

Something that still aggravates me is feeling like you're not like everyone else. Y'know? Like you have this thing, this dragon inside that really makes you feel different. But now when you're trying to join the human race, you wanna be just like everyone else.

As we talked more about this, it began to become clear how this "craving" for normalcy evolved. As Louie's life took on more and more of the accouterments of a conventional rather than a contraventional life style, as he gained more and more of a personal "stake" in conventionality, he began to feel differently about his life, himself, and his past unconventionality—both as "addict" and as "recovered addict." The responsibilities of this new role in life, e.g., of fatherhood, became not requirements to be complied with, but purposes that shaped his consciousness of who he was and what his life was about. The more conventionally he lived, the more others—especially non-treatment others—

acknowledged him as normal, and the more he came to see himself as normal. And, as the meaning of his present life was being reconstructed, his past had to change as well, at least certain aspects of it.

But as I got married and did a lotta things I [had] always wanted to do, y'know, I started seein' myself differently.[23] Hey, y'know, I started seein' myself as *normal*. This [i.e., addiction-recovery] was an *episode* in my life. I was a fuck up. I made mistakes; I did these things wrong. I just messed my own life up. Now I can make it better. Now, since my baby's born, a lotta my old tendencies, like not wanting to get up in the morning [i.e., being "negative about initiating a day" (see Hood 2011a, chap. 2)] and all'a these things that contribute to being an addict, have changed in a lotta ways. I have a different goal. I don't just worry about me and my wife, I worry about this baby. I have to do this for the baby, have to be responsible, go to work. [Emphasis added.]

    Like all the episodes we've gone through since the baby was born. Like the baby getting sick, y'know, when he was first born? He had an infection. We thought something was wrong with his kidneys. All'a these crises, they were real-life crises; I had no time to think about being a fuck up. I had to think about being responsible and goin' through this pain, seeing the baby with a friggin' IV. Or the baby's nose is stuffed up: does it have anything to do with SIDS? All'a this craziness you go through as a parent. It gives me a whole new incentive that makes it better, because it makes it [i.e., life] more realistic. I'm not doin' this 'cause I'm an ex-addict and I'm in recovery and have to do these things; I'm doin' 'em 'cause that's the way life is.

As Louie discoursed on this issue, he began to recognize the contradiction between his spontaneous comments and recovery rhetoric. At first he backed off, taking refuge in traditional recovery nostrums. But the more he talked, the more his ambivalence resolved itself into what he began with: "I don't wanna be an ex-addict, I wanna be just like everyone else. And, I think I can." He even began to build a rationale in support of his normalcy: everybody's screwed up in some way or another; us addicts are no different. Here, he *normalizes* his past.

Q: You keep coming back to one theme, seeing your drug use in the past as an episode, as not an essential part of your personality or your identity.

A: Yeah.

Q: My understanding of therapeutic community treatment is that they drill into you that you're a drug addict. Once an addict, always an addict. What I'm hearing in the last 20 minutes or so is that your recovery is in some ways dependent upon your ability to put that in your past, to have it be an episode that's over. I think the way you expressed it is quite eloquent. So, in a sense, your continued success in recovery is part and parcel of your ability to say: "I'm not an addict, I'm a normal person." If that is right, isn't there a contradiction there?

A: The contradiction is because some of us don't wanna feel that way about our life. We don't wanna feel that we're ex-*addicts*. We don't wanna be labeled in any way.

Y'know? Yeah, there's a part of me that rejects that this thing has to be a life-long shadow over my life. I think I reject the theory "once an addict always an addict" for the fact that somebody's gonna get high again. Because I don't believe people have to get high again. I don't believe I had to relapse again to learn. It's just something that happened. I also look at my environment and see no other alternative than to do the things I did. I believe there's a genetic disposition, but [it's] also my environment. What if my parents didn't get separated and my older brother didn't die and my neighborhood wasn't rampant with drugs, y'know? What would I have done?

There is a point before you go into treatment where you feel totally abnormal. Y'know? You're a fuck up, unique and all'a this stuff. But then you go into treatment and identify with all'a these other people and most of the time the identification [i.e., rationale] is, "Hey we all made mistakes, now we're gonna put our lives back together." That's always the premise I stuck with. Y'know, these things happened to me and I'm just like anybody else with a disability or disadvantage or [who] made mistakes. And that's what continues to make me feel normal today. Yeah, there's TCs for people who do drugs, but there's also self-help groups for people who eat too much, y'know? And you start identifying with [i.e., believing in] the fact that everybody has, ummm, some inadequacy or something they're screwed up about.

As Louie and I continued our discussion, the main source of this desire to reconstruct his identity from "ex-addict" to "normal person" came to light.

Q: Can you locate a time in your life when you became aware of this: that you didn't want to see yourself as an addict? That this was an episode you could leave behind?

A: When I met my wife and began to meet her family and all that stuff. For obvious reasons, in the beginning, of course, you don't want anyone to know, except your partner. But even after that y'know, you're just beginning to know, y'know, your brother-in-law, and you find out his views on somebody who has AIDS or who was a junkie or whatever. So you think, jeez, do I want him to know? So you start trying to disengage with the reality that you're an addict. Doesn't mean you give up the principles of not being an addict [maintaining sobriety]. But, I know a lotta people, a good forty of us in recovery who have this attitude—some in recovery a lot longer than me, who live normal lives.

Louie does not use treatment terminology to describe his wife's place in his current circle of recovery. However, his description of their relationship and her role in his continuing success confirms a point that has been raised about treatment of addictions by William L. White (1998, 333).

The delivery of effective services to addicts begins with the transcendence of contempt.... What recovered people brought to this field was, first and foremost, a capacity for moral equality.... But, *contrary to treatment industry mythology*, this is not a quality limited to people with a history of addiction. [Emphasis added.]

White notes that non-addicts as well as ex-addicts have accomplished much in the field of addiction services. To describe what they all seem to have had in common, he cites Ernest Kurtz (1991).

They…all…experienced tragedy in their own lives. They all had *kenosis*; they had been emptied out; they had hit bottom…whatever vocabulary you want. They had stared into the abyss…. Each had encountered and survived tragedy.[24] [Emphasis in original.]

Louie's account of his relationship with his wife can be seen as a case study in what White refers to as the "kinship of common suffering."

Q: Was it a conscious decision to look for a partner who was not from a TC background?

A: Not really. What was conscious was that I wanted someone that was gonna understand me. Y'know't I mean? 'Cause I tell all'a [my dates] after the first night what the deal is, 'cause I want them to know, and then either not call me or whatever. My wife happened to call me seven times after [our first date] for three to four hour conversations about my life. I found [in her] someone that I can tell anything to. Y'know, like, she don't ever throw it out [at me], like, "Why [are you upset], because you feel like smoking pot?" [Said in mock anger]. Y'know, and this kinda crap? It's more of an adult, mature, two-in-the-morning talk after sex kinda thing that becomes, y'know, your counseling, your guidance. Your partner should be your best friend.
    The greatest thing about my relationship with my wife is…Other women, from recovery, were very protective of the fact that I was in recovery. Some would question me constantly. Or, God forbid, you are watching a movie like *Good Fellas*. I have to fast forward the part where he has these golf balls of cocaine. I can't watch that, because I start getting this internal physiological reaction to it. I start getting nervous and sweaty and urgent. That's a change I go through, but I wanta be able to say to my wife, "Oh my God, does that drive me crazy." Y'know? And I've had relations with women [from treatment] who I couldn't even tell I felt like smoking a joint. I couldn't say I seen someone who "kicked up the shit" and I felt like doin' it.[25] They would suspect me constantly. For me, as an ex-addict, I don't want to go there [i.e., have that sort of relationship].
    I had girl friends who were, like, prim and proper, and probably still had virginity. Y'know? But what they didn't have was a reality. Yeah, they understood my reality, but they were always wantin' to make sure that I was "okay" [feigns a weak, patronizing "feminine" tone] and it wasn't a two way street.
    When I met my wife, she was a person that had a lotta trauma in her life. And, see, that is something I did look for. My wife had more trauma than I did without drugs. She lost her first husband to brain cancer only two years after they were married…. [It involved] a year and a half of suffering on his part and mental anguish on hers. Then she lost her brother two years ago and her father died three days after I met her. Just major losses and problems growin up, y'know? [This] gave us a bond. We struggled through something; we made it. Y'know, its more of a mutual relationship.

What seems most refreshing about Louie's comments is the lack of program rhetoric. More than any other person interviewed for this project, Louie had constructed for himself a reasonable structure of plausibility that enabled him to navigate both the world of the TC, where he earned his living, and the world outside, where he did his living. He accomplished this by using elements of both worlds that he found helpful in his quest for sobriety, after periods of searching and discarding or relinquishing other elements that did not work so well. Louie comes as close as any graduate from any program that I have spoken with to being the independent, inner-directed, "Emersonian" individual envisioned by treatment ideology.[26] However, he has done it by maintaining close associations with the community that nurtured (controlled) him and by structuring his (independent) associations with the wider world outside the TC in a way that supports his ongoing belief in (modified) abstinence, which he also defines with a bit of independence. Louie claimed to be entirely drug-free when it came to illegal substances, but would take a drink now and then in appropriate social settings.

Beyond Recovery: Discussion

Louie, at least, has been able to carve out an identity for himself that is increasingly similar to "normal" people. He justifies this in part by use of the disease model of addiction and the fact that other disabled persons claim similar degrees of unavoidable debility in pursuit of normalcy (e.g., overeaters, smokers, anorexics, neurotics). This is perhaps a clue to what the treatment and training programs actually offer their graduates.

Using the literature of "natural recovery," Currie (1993, 239) suggests that what is crucial to recovery is that addicts "resolve to develop an entirely new identity…and must translate that resolve into permanent changes in their lives." As Biernacki (1990, 117) claims, they must "become ordinary." And as Ray (1962, 132f) has shown, they must be able to be seen and accepted *by others* as "normal" rather than as ex-addicts, if they are to have a good chance of success. As Louie put it, "at some point recovery [has] to, like, shut off in a sense, and [I have to] be a *normal* person." According to the natural recovery paradigm, successful recovery requires significant "stakes" in conventional life (see also Waldorf 1983; Waldorf and Biernacki 1981; Waldorf et al. 1991). Louie seems not only to be finding these stakes, but—to twist the metaphor a bit—sinking them into solid social ground, as perhaps the testifiers at the Redemption House fund-raiser were also doing.

What the programs of treatment and training seem to provide their residents is not so much the programmed or paradigmatic identity (recovered or redeemed addict), especially in Louie's case, but the experience of the possibility of *any* new identity other than that of "loser-user." After all, from the perspective of most members of conventional society, the identity of "ex-addict" is not much farther along the road than addict. "Ex-addict" is barely enough of an identity to build a conventional life upon if one remains within the confines of the redemption or recovery subculture by becoming a treatment or train-ing staff member.[27] To establish a foothold in conventional life—in another line of work outside the encapsulated culture—seems quite difficult. Perhaps this explains why Louie's ex-addict friends outside of the treatment industry make such a fetish of recovery group meetings (as many as four a day!). But, just maybe, what the lucky ones learn in treatment and training is that personal transformations of identity are possible—with the right resources, e.g., Louie's wife, treatment skills, and industry connections, i.e., plausibility structures.

Once outside the treatment context, graduates may be able to shed the "heroic ex-addict" self, which rarely flies outside this subculture, and blend back into the conventional world on the basis of other available or creatable self-defining elements. Perhaps what the most fortunate, like Louie, can learn in the treatment process is to transcend its reifications, to step outside the confines of socially prescribed identities and piece together a new cognitive world that is more meaningful than that of either addict or ex-addict. As Peter Berger (1963) suggests in his now-classic book, *Invitation to Sociology*, once one has experienced one radical change in consciousness (a conversion or alternation of identity) others are not quite so shattering. Some people even develop a skill for it. The common experience of "serial conversions" to various religious groups provides some weight to this suggestion. The phenomenon of confidence men and women provides another. The therapeutic community does not provide a real stake, material or ideal, in conventional society, because it is transitory; residents cannot move in for life unless they can qualify as staff members. It may, however, allow some few perceptive and resourced residents to discover the necessary skills of self-creation or self-transformation that will enable them to negotiate the necessary re-adaptation to normalcy—or perpetual chameleon-ism—once on the outside. And even Louie has yet to get entirely outside.

Also, it is important to remember that treatment (or training) holds no true monopoly on former drug users changing their lives. As the natural recovery literature aptly demonstrates, many people free themselves without resort to formal treatment programs. They, like Louie, free themselves not so much from chemical enslavement, as—to use a Bergerian image—from the prison of reified social identities (Berger 1963). This view, of course, runs counter, once again, to the disease or disorder notion that addicts are somehow constitutionally different and must retain the "recovered-addict" mentality if they are to survive, a notion that is increasingly prominent in the daily discourse of Recovery House. With such a complex path to follow, is it any wonder that Louie is one of the very few who make it "all the way home?"

Notes

1.   See Erich Goode (1996) for a similar critique of the Chicago School sociologists as middle-class ideologues.
2.   The therapeutic community movement still resists (read: denies) the correlative notion that their horrendous relapse rate is a result of returning their converts to the general population via graduation where these new converts lose their plausibility structure, i.e., the believing community. Personal communication with executives

at the Center for Therapeutic Community Research. See also, Hoffman (1987); Johnson (1976); White (1998).

3. The treatment industry will not do the research, presumably, because they can only lose. The drug research industry ignores the issue, presumably, because there is nothing to gain. If they were to prove that only—or mostly—staffers succeed, treatments would come under heavier criticism than they currently garner and research groups would likely lose research sites. Also, this would be an expensive and time-consuming job. Locating the staffer-successes is easy. Locating those who have "melted" into the general population and may not want their previous identities known would be much more difficult.

4. The therapeutic community movement also presents voluminous statistics, often published in scientific journals, purportedly demonstrating the effectiveness of its method. However, these are based largely on the very same success stories that are presented at public forums that often feature graduate staff personnel.

5. Even if all of these tales are not strictly truthful, the fact that these men find it necessary to report their association with such organizations is significant. It further demonstrates their recognition of the necessity of continuing support from evangelical plausibility structures that is central to the rhetoric of Redemption House and the wider evangelical community.

6. See Frankel (1985, especially chap. 7), for discussion of the relation of this structure to general theories of socialization and learning.

7. The data for this aspect of treatment and training is based largely on retrospective reports of staff members, most of whom had completed their programs within one to five years prior to these interviews. This was necessary because of the resistance of the Reentry Director at Recovery House. She successfully avoided allowing me access to her program. It was necessary at Redemption House, because it did not have a reentry program at the time of my research, but sent its residents to Teen Challenge for reentry. I was able to spend only one week at the Teen Challenge facility, much of which was spent re-interviewing transfers from Redemption House and observing the training program there.

8. Louie is referring here to his own treatment sojourn that ended well before my research began. By then, the treatment time at Recovery House had been trimmed to twelve months, overall. That is comparable to the Teen Challenge program. Reentry at Recovery House was geared to a three-month move out, with a maximum of six months.

9. Redemption House no longer transfers men to Teen Challenge, but has expanded its program to include the entire twelve-month stay. The last three months residents spend primarily in apprenticeship or other work training or educational programs that Harry arranges or approves. They continue to attend church in the evenings and/or chapel in the mornings, depending on their work schedules. They are encouraged to participate in as many prayer meetings as possible. They are also held to strict curfews, and weekend passes are required. However, these restrictions are much less stringent compared with the residents in earlier phases and curfews are individually modified to fit work and other scheduling necessities. In these structural respects, Redemption House has come to resemble Recovery House more than it did during my research.

10. I spent several hours with Jake, often in the kitchen preparing meals, discussing the training programs at Redemption House and Teen Challenge—always with the tape recorder on. He was the most cooperative informant among the Redemption House staff who were Teen Challenge graduates. Jake loved to talk and he loved company while he worked in the kitchen. He often repeated the same story more

than once, which was fortunate, because it allowed me to evaluate the consistency among the versions that appeared at different interview sessions. Suffice it to say that I have very little reason to doubt Jake's veracity. I cannot evaluate his stories against actual events, but each of his versions varied little from its counterpart in essential content, even though Jake was a vivid storyteller. There is another reason to trust Jake's veracity and accuracy. He was HIV positive and just beginning to show signs of active disease. He saw these interviews as an opportunity to get his testimony "on the record" before he died. He wanted his experience to benefit others after he was gone.

11. In certain cases, a man returns to a local church that includes members of his family in its congregation. In others, where there is no church background, and no "ideal" apprentice connection, some form of mentorship is arranged with a local pastor or alumnus. By all appearances, this program operates in principle similar to the AA big brother or mentor program.

12. The classic *post hoc ergo propter hoc* error of the "gateway" argument has been more than adequately disputed by research (see, e.g., Zimmer and Morgan 1997, 33ff). What is more likely is that Jorge believed the rhetoric typical of virtually all treatment programs in the United States, that one drink or one use of any psychoactive substance re-triggers the "disease" (or character disorder, or [dormant] sinful nature) and the user is virtually helpless to stop his total relapse. Thus, the rhetoric often becomes a self-fulfilling prophecy, a conventionally supported (and convenient?) rationale for returning to a life focused on the misuse of an intoxicant. In other words, TC rhetoric set him up to give in to the enticements of the drug culture, which is what he encountered forty hours a week, while church consisted of barely two or three. Jorge, certainly, did not attribute his relapse to the slippery slope.

13. Harry, the Director, and Martin, the House Manager, were the two main exceptions to this generalization at Redemption House. At other, less independent, Teen Challenge induction centers many of the directors, and virtually all staff, are graduates of the system. At Redemption House, Ervin and Jake as well as Teddy (the one man who declined to be interviewed) were Teen Challenge graduates.

14. Ervin tested positive for HIV while in a Teen Challenge induction center in Philadelphia. He had been symptom-free throughout his time at the Farm. This is a typical pattern for the disease—a reality he was apparently not prepared for during his training.

15. To become a regular staff member at Teen Challenge at this time, two six-month internships were required.

16. Recovery House provides room and board and a modest salary for its staff members. There is no car for personal use and no private trailer to live in.

17. Here is yet another confirmation of the basic similarity between the populations of the two Houses. Redemption House does not attract men primarily from evangelical backgrounds or men who are actively religious. This is evidence counter to earlier claims by Langrod et al. (1972); Muffler et al. (1997).

18. Ervin implies no competitiveness here. Rather, he simply means it is easier to remain committed and faithful in this environment than it is outside Redemption House, in "the world," where the "other guy" has to struggle with constant temptation and competing universes of meaning. Unfortunately, Ervin is unfamiliar with Durkheim's notion of the universality and relativity of social deviance. During my research, Ervin was punished for a minor infraction of the rules in place for Redemption House staff. He was suspended briefly, without pay.

19. As mentioned elsewhere, we had six separate taped interviews of two or more

hours each, plus numerous informal conversations about these issues over a period of two years. During that time, I was privileged to develop with Louie the kind of relationship that is most appropriate to the method of participating observation traditionally practiced by anthropologists. Before my research began, Louie was a student in two sociology classes of mine at a local college. All but one of our taped interviews took place following the completion of those classes. By the end of my research, Louie and I were engaged in the kind of dialogue that allowed us both to press issues and challenge responses in ways that are often not possible in less textured relationships or more incidental interviews.

I do not mean to dismiss the significance of other interviews used in this treatise. There is substantial evidence that I gained a reasonable degree of confidence from many, though not all, residents represented in these pages. I believe that their responses to my nosy intrusions into a difficult period of their lives were, for the most part, as genuine and reliable as any comparable research process, whether done with men in drug treatment, in full clerical vestments, or three-piece business suits. Nevertheless, Louie provided me with the lengthiest and most nuanced look at the practice of drug treatment in a therapeutic community. Without his assistance, this project would have been much more difficult and much "thinner" (in the Geertzian sense) than it is. I am deeply grateful for his selfless and self-sharing contributions. (See Geertz 1973; Hood 2011a, chap. 1 re "thick description.")

20. See Marlatt et al. (1985).
21. The jargonistic tendency of drug treatment discourse has abbreviated this advice to the phrase enclosed in quotation marks. It is commonly repeated as an *explanation* for one's drug use or other behavior considered unsavory, as well as a *tactic* for future sobriety. It is so well integrated into the vocabulary of motives (Mills 1940) at Recovery House that it was confusing, at first, to hear the same response given for why one used drugs in the past and how one would avoid this problem in the future. The meaning, as with so much else, is contextual not literal (Geertz 1973; Hood 2011a, chap. 1). This advice, not surprisingly, is consistent with the tenets of "social control theory," developed by Travis Hirschi (1969). See also Goode (1996).
22. Louie was selected for this position because of his earlier experience working with a mentally retarded population in a facility in Texas. This was between the time he finished his initial period in treatment at Daytop Village and his subsequent relapse, which resulted in his more recent treatment experience at Phoenix House, which he describes here, in part.
23. Whether he actually always wanted these things or not is an open question. However, the actual truth is irrelevant. Louie and all of us build the meanings of our lives out of what readings are currently plausible to us and our audiences and interlocutors, our reference group(s). For a similar re-reading of past desires at Redemption House, see my description of Keith in the chapter on "Ritual, Miracle, and Myth" (Hood 2011a).
24. I have serious doubts about the "hitting bottom" notion, especially as necessity for recovery (see Fingarette 1998a/b). But Kurtz (1991) likely has a point about the source of empathy. While personal suffering may be a necessary ingredient in empathy, I doubt that it is sufficient by itself, however.
25. "Kicking up the shit" means stirring up urges to use drugs.
26. Several of the long-term graduates of Redemption House that I spoke with at the concert impressed me as similarly independent men grounded in strong support networks. However, that impression is based on much thinner evidence than my hours of conversation with Louie.

27. This may be less so for Redemption House residents than for those at Recovery House. The evangelical subculture does offer a relatively conventional (perhaps hyper-conventional) potentially supportive community on the outside for graduates of discipleship programs. Each grad must, nevertheless, make his or her own way into a particular local incarnation of evangelicalism. No mean task, that. There is, however, no comparable "mainstream" community for TC grads. They must remain in the treatment context as staff (or return as client again?) or find a way to re-create themselves yet again in terms that some conventionally oriented social community will find acceptable.

5

Success and Failure at Redemption and Recovery

For traditional TCs, national surveys indicate that 30 percent of clients achieve maximally favorable outcomes (no crime, no illicit drug use, and pro-social behavior). Success rates among graduates exceed 75 percent after treatment.
—George DeLeon, Director,
Center for Therapeutic Community Research[1]

Conventional outcome statistics tend to be circular and self-confirming; they tell us, in effect, that the programs are likely to be successful for those who are most likely to succeed.
—Elliott Currie[2]

If the argument advanced in the two volumes (Hood 2011a, 2011b) has merit, if, indeed, both secular and religious programs operate by the same social media on the same population of drug users, it would be reasonable to expect that rates of "conversion" (or successful treatment and training) would be more or less the same for recovery as for redemption. I *believe* that this is the case. However, there is no easy means of empirical comparison on this issue. In fact, I would argue that there is ultimately no way—with existing data—to establish positively (i.e., positivistically) what the facts are on this issue. Nevertheless, in this chapter, I attempt to make a case for my "conclusion" based on the ethnographic results as presented and this ethnographer's assessment of the numbers the treatment researchers have been able to assemble.[3]

The Numbers: Recovery House

In one important way, Redemption House and Recovery House held quite similar attitudes regarding the question of program successes and failures. Representatives from both programs suggested that each individual's redemption or recovery is what is important, not the aggregate numbers. This, of course, is a classic true believer's hedge. However, closer examination revealed radically different assessments of success rates at both programs. Harry Evans, as Ervin described in a previous chapter, claims something akin to a 10 percent success rate. That is, based on his twenty-five years of experience as Director of Redemption House, Harry Evans has learned to expect no more than two men from any given group (average $n = 20$) to be "walking with the Lord" a year following graduation. Recovery House demonstrated a different response. There, very few staff members wanted to talk about success rates, on or off the record. Residents were often unaware of such things, except in the contradictory programmatic terms that "splittees" were doomed, even though most graduates had been second or third timers in treatment. On the other hand, some administrators would talk about aggregate rates of "success" in terms of reduced drug use and criminality after treatment, but no one would make any claims about abstinence rates of graduates, the stated goal of therapeutic community treatment. Most administrators referred me to the statistics department at the Manhattan office.

According to the official numbers graciously supplied by the "Computer Specialist" at the Recovery House Foundation central office in Manhattan, the rates of *graduation* from this therapeutic community compare well with "official" research assessments. Recovery House, like all therapeutic communities, graduates residents with the hope that they will maintain absolute perfection in abstinence, without relapse. When being candid, most staffers will admit that most graduates can be expected to relapse. However, this admission is not part of their official self-presentation, nor is it something they emphasize during treatment. That is, Recovery House intends to produce totally recovered addicts; it does not take credit for relapses. Relapse, like addiction, is always seen as the user's fault or failing, not the treatment's.[4]

In this light, it is interesting to look at the Recovery House numbers. These numbers cover admissions and discharges for the six-month period prior to my participant observation at Recovery House. These numbers cover all four segments of the main facility of which Recovery House is part, each of which accounts for approximately 25 percent of the total population (Table 1).

This is not a precise statistical evaluation of the program. For example, the two total lines (admitted and terminated) do not match because they do not account for arrivals prior to this six-month period who were terminated during the period. However, if we can assume that this is a relatively normal six-month period, it does give a rough measure of what happens to the residents of Recovery House. During a period when 347 people were admitted, 46 moved out as part of the approved reentry "move out" phase of treatment discussed by Louie in a previous chapter. That is, fewer than *15 percent* of the number *admitted* during the six-month period were processed out in keeping with program protocol. Or, to look at these raw numbers another way, just over *15 percent* of the people who left for any reason, left for program-sanctioned reasons. In other words,

Table 1. Six Month Admissions and Discharges at Recovery House

	Male	Female	Total
Total Admitted	208	139	347
Left w/o consent	137 (68%)	97 (76%)	234 (71%)
Admin discharge	27	5	32
Medical discharge	10	6	16
Graduated	27 (13%)	19 (15%)	46 (14%)
Total Terminated	201 (137+27+10+27)	127 (97+5+19)	328 (234+32+16+46)

by these measures, the "success" (i.e., program completion) rate of Recovery House for that six-month period hovers around *15 percent*.

How does this compare with other evaluations? George DeLeon (1984), the foremost "inhouse" researcher and defender of the therapeutic community modality, writes that in seven therapeutic communities studied, "12-month retention rates ranged from 9% to 15%." In a subsequent evaluation of drug treatment by the U.S. Office of Technology Assessment (1990), therapeutic community retention rates are also found to be quite limited: the first thirty days in treatment, drop out rates are 35–50 percent; after three months up to 70 percent of clients have left against staff advice.[5] As the DeLeon study noted, the percentage of clients that complete the program is 10–15, which corresponds well with my ad hoc numbers. In fact, by DeLeon's measure, Recovery House was on the high end of the scale during the period covered by the numbers cited above. In sum, I think DeLeon captures the picture quite well when he states that in therapeutic communities, as in "all drug treatment modalities...attrition is the rule."[6]

The treatment chronicler, William White (1998, 248) also comments on therapeutic community success rates. First on his list of "Criticisms of the Therapeutic Communities," is that

> the oft-quoted statement that 90% of those who graduate from TCs remain drug-free belies the fact that only a very small percentage of those admitted graduate...partly because as many as half [of TC clients] leave against staff advice within the first year [of treatment].

Moreover, many graduates become staff members of a therapeutic community or other treatment program after graduation, which is tantamount to not leaving treatment at all.

The Numbers: National Treatment Evaluations

The further question, of course, is how many of these "move outs" remain abstinent for any length of time. It is this sort of question that the independent evaluation studies appear to address.

The national and regional treatment research bureaucracies trumpet the message that "treatment works."[7] First of all, the standards of these large surveys are not the completion of a program, but "success" or "failure" to maintain treatment goals *after leaving* treatment. Treatment goals, of course, can be variously defined. For these "independent" studies the goals are usually defined as abstinence from (at least illegal) drug use, from criminal activity, and from unemployment. (Some more recent evaluations have included general health variables and interpersonal skills.) However, they are not looking for "perfection" (i.e., absolute abstinence), but e.g., *reduced* frequency of use," "*reduced* amounts of drug use," "*fewer* arrests," "*increased* days of employment."[8] By these aggregate standards, drug treatment programs appear to reduce drug use (though not necessarily create abstinence), reduce criminal activity, and (slightly) increase employment rates among the treated population.[9]

In its March 1998 "Report to Congressional Requesters," The Government Accounting Office noted four major independent evaluations of drug treatments over the past three decades (USGAO 1998, 21). These are: DATOS, the Drug Abuse Treatment Outcome Study, sponsored by the National Institute on Drug Abuse [NIDA] (1991–93); NTIES, the National Treatment Improvement Evaluation Study, sponsored by the Substance Abuse and Mental Health Services Administration [SAMHSA] (1993–95); DARP, the Drug Abuse Reporting Program, sponsored by the National Institutes of Mental Health [NIMH] (1969–73); and TOPS, the Treatment Outcome Prospective Study, sponsored by NIDA (1979–81). According to the GAO report, "much of what is known about typical drug abuse treatment outcomes comes from these studies."

The numbers that have been produced by these studies might lead anyone to conclude that treatment is effective.[10] A few examples should suffice to indicate the general conclusions: "DATOS, the study most recently completed, found that the percentage of individuals reporting weekly or more frequent drug use...declined following treatment." For cocaine users in long-term residential treatment—the majority of men interviewed for this study—use dropped from 66.4 percent in the year prior to treatment to 22.1 percent during the year following treatment. But there is more. "Previous studies found similar reductions...the TOPS study found that... 40 to 50 percent of regular heroin and cocaine users who spent at least three months in treatment (of any kind) reported *near abstinence* during the year after treatment [emphasis added]." Additionally, "DARP found that...61 percent [of clients] *in* therapeutic communities...reported abstinence from daily opiate use [emphasis added]." And that is not all. "NTIES found that 50 percent of clients in treatment reported using crack cocaine five or more times during the year prior to entering treatment, while 25 percent reported such use during the year following treatment." These are indeed impressive numbers. However, it must be recalled that they are based, for the most part, only on those clients who remain in treatment at least three months. This is one of the major criticisms leveled at evaluation research by Elliot Currie (1993, 222): it seriously inflates its numbers. For example, Currie, one of the few researchers to seriously evaluate the evaluators, writes that the TOPS numbers are based only on "those who remain in treatment three months or more." The study does not take into account the "55 percent of therapeutic community clients [or] the 64 percent of outpatient drug-free program clients [who] discontinue treatment...in the first three months," according to the same GAO report (1998, 25). This caveat should be added to the several pages the GAO report spends justifying the practice of basing "hard" statistical numbers on "soft" self-report studies. When these two criticisms are added together, they seem to raise serious questions about the effectiveness of the effectiveness studies of drug treatment. As I have suggested regarding my own informants' self-reports, when properly evaluated, they can be useful as data. However, they cannot be taken simply at face value. This is especially true with "true believers" who are likely to report the proper orthodox line whether it is strictly true or not in their own case.

Currie has other complaints about these evaluations. Not only do they inflate their numbers, but they also "stack the deck" in favor of the "treatment works" position. By comparing the first-year post-treatment with the year immediately prior to treatment, researchers compare what is often the very "best" with the very "worst" periods of a drug-using career, rather than comparing life after treatment with the user's "typical pattern before treatment." As many of the men I interviewed suggested—in agreement with a large body of street ethnography on drug use—users often manage their habits for extended periods of time with minimal "dysfunction." Miguel's (Recovery House) heroin habit is one example and Stanley's (Redemption House) comparatively controlled crack use is another (see Chapter 1). Many users consider treatment only when things get beyond their control—things like Miguel's failing a urine test and facing several more years in prison, or Stanley's suicidal depression over lost love, or Andrew's ultimate sense of self-degradation when his mother locked him out after yet another crack binge. Most users come to treatment as a last resort, when all other social resources are depleted. Therefore, to compare their lives at such nadirs with the immediate post-treatment period, when the newly converted sense of self is strong, hope is at its peak, and a new social network (the treatment community) is still in place (at least mentally), is tantamount to biasing the research in the direction of the "treatment works" hypothesis. It evaluates the best of treatment outcomes in the light of the worst of the user's career. Currie (1993, 222) cites a different approach that compares crime rates of treated users *two years* after treatment with their *average* crime rates from the onset of their drug use to their treatment entry. The results showed that their rates of criminal activity were actually 28 percent *higher* post-treatment! Perhaps, like prisons, therapeutic communities also can be schools for crime.

Currie's final criticism is that treatment evaluations completely ignore the majority of users and abstaining or moderating former users who have never had to resort to treatment. I have discussed this issue at length elsewhere, so I will not belabor the point again here (Hood 2011a, chap. 6). Suffice it to say, however, that to the degree that treatment researchers ignore the common process of "natural recovery" from all so-called addictions, they further bias their results. This error seems especially marked in evaluations supported by government and mainstream foundation monies. Treatment research focuses entirely on formal, fee for service, and publicly funded programs like therapeutic communities, where they have captive populations. This "sample selection" process alone gives aid and comfort to the taken-for-granted notion that all illicit drug users become abusers and need treatment, a form of treatment whose effectiveness they also continue to inflate at public expense. This research is thus too often the worst sort of institutional self-congratulatory effort rather than the critical, discriminating, and incisive work it could be and ought to be (see also Reuter and Pollock 2006; Robinson and Scherlen 2007).

But, let us suspend disbelief for a while, just for the sake of "evaluation." If we look at the TOPS or DATOS numbers in light of the retention and completion numbers, what do we find? All the studies reported by the GAO show 40–60 percent decline in drug use after treatment. There is no way of knowing, however, from the published results, if this means all graduates use only half the drugs they used prior to treatment or if it means one half of the graduates are totally abstinent while the other half are not, or some other real-world variation on these aggregate, abstract numbers. But, if we assume the best-case scenario outcome for the abstinence paradigm and apply the 60 percent decline to the 10–15 percent completion rate, we get a rate of 0.09 (0.6 x 0.15), or approximately 7–10 percent of all graduates of drug treatment programs are abstinent during the year following treatment. More recently, Reuter and Pollack (2006, 343) reflect the real-world variation on these numbers: "most clients *will* continue their drug use at some level after treatment [and] even five years later most respondents report some *recent* use of at least one targeted substance." [Emphasis added.]

If my earlier suspicion, unsubstantiated by nothing other than anecdote (even worse than "soft numbers"), that many therapeutic community graduates end up as drug treatment staff, how many of the 9 percent I just created do they account for? Also, as the GAO study reports, and most researchers acknowledge, follow-ups are very difficult to complete. Since this is the case, how many of the follow-ups that were completed (for any of the major evaluations) are drug treatment staff personnel? Is it possible that the positive numbers that are created are a result not only of all the machinations that Elliot Currie has uncovered, but also a result of the fact that a "significant" percentage of the "year after treatment" respondents are staff members of therapeutic community organizations and, thus by definition, committed members of the movement, i.e., converts (Manning 1989)? This would be an interesting survey research question for some budding social scientist or graduate student.

The Numbers: Redemption House

Despite the questions surrounding all these statistics, one set of numbers seems to be reasonably accurate: the completion rates determined by DeLeon and others, including my own "straw" survey above. Although they do not tell us whether the graduates remain abstinent, they can supply a rough means of comparison regarding rates of relative retention of residents between the two types of programs highlighted here. While Redemption House does not keep statistics of its residents, graduates, and dropouts, it does keep somewhat haphazard records of admissions and terminations in a large ledger book kept at the front desk, which I was allowed to peruse at will. I was able to accumulate composite numbers for the period that covered my active research efforts at Redemption House plus five months. In this nine-month period, sixty-nine men were "inducted" into the discipleship program, seventeen transferred to the Teen Challenge Farm for continued training after approximately three months in the Bronx. Although these numbers cover a period of nine months, they have to be considered as three-month retention rates, because transfers to the Teen Challenge "finishing" facility occur between three and four months at Redemption House. That is, all dropouts in this nine-month period occurred prior to the three-month length of the Bronx discipleship program. This means that the three-month retention rate at Redemption House for that nine-month period is 24 percent, which corresponds fairly well with the 30 percent three-month retention rate DeLeon found for therapeutic communities (see OTA 1990).

I was also able to learn the fates of the men who recorded interviews with me and who transferred to the Farm (Teen Challenge) during my active research at Redemption House (five of the men were interviewed at both programs). Of these seven transfers, four (57 percent) completed the program at Rehrersberg, PA. Of those four, at least two (50 percent) joined the staff of a Teen Challenge program after graduation. Of the four graduates of the discipleship training program (Redemption House and Teen Challenge combined), one (25 percent) is currently "drug-free" and "walking with the Lord," the other three "slipped back" at one point or another. One of these is currently in a drug program in another state following a "two year relapse into crack use."[11]

These data do not easily compare with those from Recovery House because of the different ways in which they were recorded and collected and the different structure of the program. However, for the sake of my straw poll, I will attempt to extrapolate from the Redemption House total numbers that can be compared across programs. I do not intend these calculations to be definitive, nor do I contend the outcomes are necessarily very accurate. They are simply what I have to work with, and I intend them only to be suggestive of what seems, from my observation, to be the case at the discipleship program. To get a completion rate figure to compare with that of the Recovery House totals, I will do two extrapolations from the Redemption House numbers cited above. First, I reduce the total inductions (sixty-nine) and transfers (seventeen) by one-third so they correspond to six months rather than nine months.[12] Thus, inductions equal forty-six, and transfers equal eleven. Next, I assume that the ratio of three-month completions (transfers) to program (or twelve-month) completions is relatively constant at 50 percent (four of eight that transferred during my research). This means that completions for the extrapolated six-month period are six (5.5). If six men out of the initial forty-six complete the full discipleship program, the extrapolated completion rate is 13 percent. This corresponds very well to the 15 percent tabulated in the straw poll of Recovery House, which reproduces the rate considered to be accurate by more extensive statistical studies (DeLeon 1989). This also corresponds with my equally "unpositivistic" and impressionistic sense of the situation at the two rehabilitation programs, namely that they are doing the same things at more-or-less the same rates, if not with the same absolute numbers.

The Numbers: Teen Challenge

Despite the serious questions about "independent" treatment evaluation research, it might be interesting to compare what studies are available on "religious therapeutic communities," (White 1998) with those summarized above on secular treatments. Although the Redemption House staff seems unconcerned with statistically derived rates of success, Teen Challenge (its "parent" organization at the time of my research) is not averse to this sort of endeavor, but is not included in the large-sample studies done by government agencies that traditionally include secular therapeutic communities. Such inclusion would be quite interesting and might be more bureaucratically justifiable when/if the faith-based initiative provides similar monies to Teen Challenge as other government programs do to therapeutic communities!

There are four studies available that attempt to establish a sense of the completion rates at Teen Challenge.[13] The first was a follow-up study on an early (1968) Teen Challenge graduating class seven years later (Hess 1993). Another was completed in September 1994; a third in 1999; the most recent in 2007. The principle investigator for the first study was Catherine B. Hess, MD, a widely respected medical researcher and treatment physician since the early days of the "war on drugs." Dr. Hess' study was funded for one year by NIDA and for an additional year by Teen Challenge. The main interest of the study was to evaluate Teen Challenge claims of 70 percent cure rate. The survey was able to do that, as was the 1994 poll by Roger Thompson, EdD at the University of Tennessee at Chattanooga. The Thompson study was also funded by Teen Challenge.[14] However, in both cases, response rates, while considered acceptable by general survey standards (Thompson cites Babbie 1992), were in the 50 percent range for graduates, which is likely to indicate that the survey's results are inflated by at least 50 percent.[15] The Hess study indicated a self-reported success rate with regard to opiate abstention of 71 percent (114 out of 161). However, a fact sheet generated by the Teen Challenge website indicates 67 percent of graduates were drug-free according to the urinalysis test administered at the time.[16]

The Hess study can be compared with both the straw poll of Redemption House and with the larger evaluation studies of secular drug treatments. As indicated above, most of the independent evaluations claim a ballpark figure of 50 percent use reduction for people following secular treatments, in some cases only three months of treatment. Teen Challenge, based on the Hess study, can claim at least a 67 percent success rate for its graduates. Hess also adds that 54 percent of three-month drop-outs report being opiate-free after seven years, although not for the entire intervening period. These numbers clearly rival those of the secular programs. Dr. Hess claims to have experienced a "conversion" herself as a result of this study, from a "severe and doubting critic" to a new belief that "Teen Challenge…basically a spiritual center…[is] a unique and successful rehabilitation center" (Manuel 1993, 130). To the degree that this means it is just as successful as a science-based therapeutic community, the results of this study would not contradict her conclusion.

It is perhaps more interesting, however, to look at the numbers Dr. Hess produced regarding the question of program completion. Although this was not a question she was particularly interested in, her data allow a relatively clear picture of this issue for the population she counted. The Brooklyn induction center she focused on started with a population of 335 inductees for the class of 1968. One hundred and thirty-three of these transferred to the Farm after three months. This calculates as a 40 percent retention rate at three months, a little higher than DeLeon's count at therapeutic communities and mine for both Redemption and Recovery Houses. Unfortunately, things get a little muddy after these men get to the Farm. Here, Hess includes thirty-one transfers from other locations, from populations of unknown size. This skews the final results in ways that cannot be determined. But this is probably no worse than the extrapolations above, merely a more obvious source of error.

Despite the difficulties with her numbers, Dr. Hess concludes with a graduating class of 67 (47 percent of total transfers) out of 144 for 1968. Assuming that the rate is more or less the same for the 133 men who came from Brooklyn as it is for all 144, the number of graduates in that cohort would be 61. Forty-seven percent as a graduation rate for three-month transfers corresponds well with the same category at Redemption House (four of eight). Moreover, the *overall* completion rate for the Brooklyn cohort at Teen Challenge (using the correction factor) calculates as 18 percent (61 of 335). This, too, compares well with the completion rates at Recovery House (15 percent) and that extrapolated for Redemption House (13 percent), not to mention DeLeon's extensively researched evaluation for therapeutic communities in general (10–15 percent). Thus we have a four-way comparison of overall completion rates (Table 2). As with all other categories of comparison considered throughout this work, the rates at which residents complete the treatment and training processes are virtually identical.

Professor Thompson's study consists of a sample of fifty men who were chosen to receive his questionnaire. These names were selected at random from 213 names of men who completed 3–4 months of training at the Chattanooga induction center (comparable to Redemption House) covering the thirteen-year period (1979–91). Of the fifty questionnaires sent out, Thompson reports a 50 percent response rate. Of those twenty-five respondents, 96 percent (twenty-four) attended a Teen Challenge center, and 79 percent (nineteen) of those graduated. This implies that some 80 percent of transfers to the Farm completed the entire (twelve months) program. This is quite different from my straw poll number of 50 percent. Thompson supplies no other indication of completion rates in his survey. (He is primarily interested in the success rates of men who pass through the three-month Chattanooga facility, unlike Hess' focus on the larger program.) If, however, we assume that his twenty-five-man response rate includes the vast majority of his fifty-man random sample of three-month finishers *who also finished the entire training*, that rate would lower the actual completion rate considerably, perhaps to the neighborhood of 50 percent—similar to all previous findings by DeLeon and myself for this category.

This, of course, is the most outrageous of my assumptions and flies in the face of statistical theories of probability upon which Thompson rests his conclusions. There is, nevertheless, good reason to believe (see note 15) that most respondents to questionnaires like Professor Thompson's are, in fact, program "successes." This is likely the case because successful program graduates have the (personal, psychological) incentive to engage in activities that lend them a positive sense of self, like completing survey forms. More importantly, this is likely so because those former trainees who have slipped back into a self-destructive pattern of behavior associated with use of illegal drugs are less likely

Table 2. Four-Way Comparison of Completion Rates

Program	Pct.	Details
Teen Challenge (Hess)	18%	47% of 3-month transfers
Redemption House	13%	50% of 3-month transfers
Recovery House	15%	In-house statistics
TC (DeLeon study)	15%	Seven TCs

to be personally motivated to respond. Perhaps more important, relapsers or backsliders are also less likely than their successful counterparts to be locatable, because of the relatively unstable residential patterns of people with drug-use problems, criminal involvement, or unemployment. While large population surveys that investigate matters of taste (like preferences in automobiles or perfumes) and imply no stigma are likely to adhere to mathematical models of probability, surveys that test stigmatized behavior like illicit drug use are less likely to do so. Therefore, Thompson's study, although highly touted at the time by Teen Challenge, is both highly suspect and not very useful here.

The third study is the 1999 doctoral dissertation of Aaron Bickenese, "The Teen Challenge Drug Treatment Program in Comparative Perspective," completed for Northwestern University. A summary of his findings can be seen on the Teen Challenge website (http://www.teenchallenge.org) where his results are reported in the most favorable light. This study compares outcomes of graduates of the three Teen Challenge full treatment sites (in MO, CA, and PA) with clients of several unidentified "secular treatment interventions" (STI) and Alcoholics Anonymous programs based on telephone interviews. Both comparative types are short-term out-patient programs rather than in-patient programs like Teen Challenge and therapeutic communities. The summary on the Teen Challenge website (not written by Bickenese) includes the report of the "phenomenal success [of] Bickenese's research [that] found 86% of those Teen Challenge graduates interviewed for this study were abstaining from drugs."[17]

Bickenese himself is much less sanguine about the validity of the numbers his study produced. As reported by Wineburg (2007, 38), Bickenese writes that his findings are "of limited external validity due to low response rates in both...dataset[s]." Those response rates were less than 40 percent (59 responses) from Teen Challenge graduates and only 30 percent from the comparison groups. Bickenese continues: "we can compare the two datasets with one another reliably enough, but much caution is in order before extending these results to compare with other studies." In other words, as Wineburg (38) writes, "much more work must be completed to determine if Teen Challenge is more effective than its government-funded counterpart."

The fourth study (Gerrard et al. 2007) was also found on the Teen Challenge website. It was produced by Wilder Research, a firm with a Saint Paul, MN address and a summary of this study can be found on its website http://www. wilder.org/research.0.html. It is a straight forward follow-up survey of graduates from 2001 through 2005 with the medium not indicated, probably telephone. They report a 55 percent response rate with 73 percent of those 174 respondents reporting no current use of psychoactive substances (nicotine and caffeine not included). The highest rate for response (68 percent) came from 2005 graduates. The next highest rate was 33 percent from 2004. The lowest rates were 22 percent from both the class of 2001 and 2002. This seems *prime facie* evidence for my claim that successes respond more often than non-successes and therefore skew numbers produced in this fashion. Neither Bickenese nor Gerrard et al. deal with the issue of graduation rates. Teen Challenge, not unlike the secular programs, is able to bend what research is available to its own public relations purposes. However, that research does not supply any truly reliable accounting of its successes and failures as drug treatment or training programs.

Despite my "unscientific" skepticism of all these studies, it may be instructive to compare them with the evaluation studies sponsored by the government. Thompson, for example, reports that

> 75% of those who graduated from Teen Challenge 1-15 years ago are abstaining from any use of illegal drugs. Of the 25% that are currently using drugs, none reported heavy use (at least once a day). Of the active users, one-third use 1-2 times a week and two-thirds use drugs occasionally, at least once a month.

The Hess study resulted in comparable numbers: 71 percent of 1968 graduates reported being drug-free one year after training (67 percent passed the urinalysis test). Bickenese claims 86 percent of graduates are cured (my word) and Gerrard et al. put that number at 73 percent for adult graduates. All of these numbers are comparable to—or even better than—the claims of the alphabet studies (DA-TOS, TOPS, etc.) of secular programs. It seems, if we take these results at face value, that treatment and training both work with amazing degrees of success. Certainly, both regimes claim successes at something like equivalent levels, and have produced numbers from both programmatic and independent researchers to support those claims. Yet, completion rates are woefully low, even as represented by program-inspired research when compared to program entries (ca. 10 percent). Moreover, critiques like those of Elliot Currie are applicable to the research on both programs. His analysis brings the whole process of treatment and training, as well as treatment and training research, into serious question. This is yet another way in which the two types of programs are one.

A Revivalist Comparison

As with all issues considered at length throughout this and the previous book (Hood 2011a) (e.g., demographics, conversion, ritual process), the outcome rate parallels are yet one more demonstration that the transformational programs of Recovery House and other therapeutic communities are but secular incarnations of religious programs for individual betterment via cultural technologies of the self/soul developed in earlier centuries under the aegis of explicit religious perspectives. In this light it is interesting to see the success claims and realities of evangelical religious revival movements over the last two hundred years.

Extended American (and British) revivalist campaigns have typically claimed thousands of converts only to have the results revealed by independent or skeptical reviewers as considerably fewer. William McLoughlin (1959, 204f), an historian of revivalism, cites contemporary critical evaluations of the "inflated claims" of nineteenth century evangelists like C. G. Finney and D. L. Moody. These popular revivalist preachers typically claimed to have converted *masses* of "anxious inquirers" during various regional, month-long revival crusades during America's Second Great Awakening. (By the way, Finney sought to convert his masses to what he called "right living," which included abstinence from alcohol as well as other activities that would be termed addictive today, card-playing, i.e., gambling, as well as all forms of sexual activity outside traditional marriage. He also condemned dancing, attending the theater, and divorce.)

Among McLoughlin's assessments of the Revivalists' claims to convert large numbers of the unrighteous masses are the following:

(1) 400 anxious inquirers [were] found to be mostly Christian men [already]…many [were] helpers in the [revival] work…*not a score* of anxious [unconverted seekers] among them.
(2) The blessing [of conversion] has fallen chiefly on those who may be called the church-going portion of the community…little effect has been produced on the [unrighteous] masses…the masses have not been reached and there is no perceptible change in their moral condition. [Emphasis added.]

More recently, the Billy Graham crusades have incorporated the same sort of strict attention to numbers while "fudging" the meaning of the constructed categories in much the same way seen in the alphabet treatment studies. One of his crusades, for example, reported 8,161 "decisions for Christ." A follow-up investigation cited by McLoughlin learned that 75 percent of these "decisions" were taken by people who were already regular churchgoers. More than 500 of these were children, another 654 "decisions" were made at a "dedication service" for church workers. McLoughlin (1959, 516f) reports that "the net result…appears to have been 102 new members and 339 new attenders out of 8161 decisions" (5.4 percent). Nevertheless, Graham continued to refer to *each* of the 8,161, "as persons who 'gave their lives to Christ,'" as if, McLoughlin adds, "they were all a statistical and qualitative gain for Christianity."

This tactic seems quite similar to the reporting strategy of treatment researchers and advocates who report that "treatment works," implying that abstinence is accomplished when, in reality, something quite different is happening. Their numbers and claims are presented "as if" all successes were "statistical and *qualitative* gains" for abstinence-based treatments (i.e., cures). Actually, these are at best only statistical variances within an aggregate population toward fewer instances of deviancy among a generally marginalized population. Like the revivalists' converts, the numbers generated by the alphabet treatment studies are not really an accurate test of what treatments are or do—and they certainly are no test of the exaggerated claims made by therapeutic communities, religious or secular.

Treatment and training undoubtedly have an influence on the behavior of the men and women who pass through them, perhaps the largest influence on any subsequent cessation or diminution of use. But the mere passage of time also has a well-established effect, as indicated previously. This effect is known in various literatures as "maturing out," "ageing out," or "burning out" (see Waldorf et al. 1991; Winick 1962). Therefore, to claim that "treatment works" seems as much an obfuscation as the claims of Graham, Moody, and Finney regarding their successes at inducing religious conversions. One might be tempted to suggest that the claim "treatment works" has a similar empirical validity to that of the slogan "Jesus saves."

In addition to this ideological smoke screen regarding real successes, treatment researchers do not ask what effects treatment has on those who stay only a short time. In his TC ethnography, Skoll (1989) suggested, that the treatment ideology of abstinence may well influence dropouts ("splittees") in the direction of more "committed" use. Their "consequential thinking" (see Hood 2011a) may be: "If it's a disease, and I can't cope with treatment, why bother trying to adjust my risky using patterns. Perhaps I should let them intensify."[18]

In this context, it is also interesting to look at the research on conversions to modern religious groups and movements that emphasize missionary work or proselytizing. Whether one speaks of relatively mainstream groups like the Mormons or more harshly stigmatized organizations like the Unification Church (the Moonies), Heaven's Gate, or Hare Krishna, research demonstrates that even the most successful conversion rates are typically below 10 percent of contacts and these, like at the treatment programs, occur among encapsulated captive audiences—at ashrams or orientation camps (see Rambo 1993, 87f). What this suggests is that this form of changing people's "images of self and world" as a means of changing their behavior—or as the TC behaviorists would have it: of changing their behavior in order to change their outlooks—simply is not very successful in the long run. Rambo (1993, 87–88) reports:

> Even the relatively successful Latter-Day Saints report only one in one thousand contacts eventually becomes a Mormon...seeking proselytes is extremely difficult.

This is especially true when, like the Mormons, your audience is not encapsulated, but continues to live amongst the unbelieving world. This is precisely why intensive treatments like the therapeutic communities and Teen Challenges require in-patient formats.

Interesting also is the fact that this research corresponds well with the "clinical" assessment of Harry Evans, the Director of Redemption House, and that of my own experience with reference to the men interviewed who completed the discipleship program.[19] Something on the order of 10 percent of those originally admitted to the program seems to be the average successful completion rate whether of recovery or redemption. And, even if the five-year post-treatment and training rate of successful abstinence among TC *graduates* is 90 percent (which seems highly unlikely), that means the overall success of abstinence treatments is no better than 10 percent *of initial program admissions*. Moreover, program entries are far fewer than all who are presumed to need treatment or training. This does not seem to support the claim that "treatment works," unless, again, that phrase can be understood as the practical equivalent of the slogan "Jesus Saves." In this regard, Michael Tonry (1990, 2) writes:

> The major [treatment] modalities "work," if by that word one means not that instant miracle cures are possible but that sustained treatment efforts over time, generally after a series of relapses in drug use, criminality, or both, can...help people reclaim their lives.

What this all means is that treatment success rates are not likely to improve, just as Billy Graham's (real) numbers were no better—and no worse—than those of Charles Finney or Dwight Moody a century before him. The same is true for discipleship training at Redemption House: it works for those it works for (Currie 1993, 223). And "addicts with more severe problems or fewer resources simply fall out of the picture altogether."

Louie, Saul, and Maria at Recovery House and Jake, Ervin, and Martin at Redemption House are testimony to the real successes that do occur in treatment and training—as Tonry suggests, usually after several tries over years, if not decades of cyclical relapse. But, did they occur because of the treatment and/or training they received? Or, as Martin claims in his case (see Hood 2011a, chap. 3), did they occur in spite of treatment and/or training? None of the hard work to demonstrate one or the other of these possible answers has been done. Perhaps it is not possible, at least not in the positivist terms that would be acceptable to those who control the treatment research industry and usually monopolize the ears of the media. One of the consequences that I hope will come from this study—the whole study—is at least a conversation about what treatment actually does, what actually happens in the process of treatment and training, and whether this actually creates change or is just a way to pass time while the natural recovering process of maturity occurs (Winick 1962). This is one of the main reasons I have attempted in the ten substantive chapters of this two-volume study to present a "thick description" of the very processes (with the rhetoric left out) that claim to transform troubled users into abstinent non-users. Here is what happens day-in, day-out in treatment and training. Does it add up to "treatment works," or does it make more sense as "it works for those it works for" and does not for those it does not?

My somewhat playful attempt in this chapter to compare success rates and statistical studies was also motivated by an attempt to contextualize such "scientific" rationales for the continuing mythology of abstinence and its attendant methodology of zero tolerance. My methodology was, as throughout, to compare, to compare the scientifically legitimated research with the similar but more transparent research hired by Teen Challenge in order to demonstrate their deep affinities. If I have succeeded in catching the attention of the treatment industry and the treatment research establishment, then I have succeeded, perhaps because my stake in the process of assisting distressed drug users has been greater than my stake in the conventional approach to "subjecting" them to treatment or to research.

Notes

1. DeLeon (1988, 75).
2. Currie (1993, 223).
3. The available outcome studies for secular treatments, including the therapeutic communities are numerous, as will be seen. Those for religious programs are far less so. I have been able to find a few outcome studies for what William White (1998) refers to as "religious therapeutic communities." All were done on Teen Challenge populations.

   I take this issue of successes on, in part, because it is of great concern to the therapeutic community movement, the entire treatment industry, and its professional researchers. This issue is, perhaps, the only one this tradition of research is really interested in. Research into "treatment process," such as this study, has been severely neglected (DeLeon 1990a; Wuthnow 2007). I suspect this is so because it is not really of interest except as it explains how to increase the success rate. I expect my study will not interest this tradition much.

   One of the more obvious indicators of this interest occurred when I ran into a Vice President of the Recovery House Foundation shortly after completing my research. At the outset of this project, he questioned me extensively about my "hypotheses," recommended several books and articles, and offered me advice about research, which was his background, although he was not an ethnographer. When we met by chance at a seminar a few years later, I reintroduced myself. After a minute he recalled my work and asked, "Well, what did you find out? Is the religious program as successful as the TC?" When I then reminded him that mine was not an outcome study, he lost interest and quickly excused himself from the conversation.
4. This is a classic case of "blaming the victim." See Ryan (1976).
5. Congress of the United States, Office of Technology Assessment, *The Effectiveness of Drug Abuse Treatment: Implications for Controlling AIDS/HIV Infection* (Washington, DC, 1990), 83. (Cited hereafter as OTA.) It is interesting to note that the OTA attributes these numbers to "a compilation of studies," but cites only DeLeon (1989), an article which is essentially a repetition and update of his 1984 study based on seven other program-related studies. See also Currie (1993).
6. DeLeon's major triumph within the treatment research community and the treatment industry was his demonstration, in this article, "that the TC had a therapeutic effect that increased with the amount of time spent in treatment and that the dose-related positive effects...accrued even to those who failed to complete treatment" (White 1998, 248). The minimum "dose" is about four to six months, which compares well with my analysis of cognitive affiliation in the previous volume, Hood (2011a).
7. Alan Leshner (1999), the Director of NIDA, writes, "there is already abundant scientific data showing that drug treatments are...effective." See similar arguments in Leshner (1997) and OASAS (1999). The latter reports an OASAS review that "shows treatment works."

8. These "treatment goals" are taken from a sample table of "types of outcome measures to assess effectiveness of drug treatment," in "Drug Abuse: Research Shows Treatment is Effective, but Benefits May Be Overstated," the GAO Report to Congress (HEHS-98-72), March 1998, 16; emphasis added. (Hereafter cited as USGAO 1998.)

9. These results have never been evaluated in light of true control groups. The reasons vary from the difficulty of creating such groups—or locating "natural controls"—to the claim that it would be unethical to deny treatment to someone who wanted it in order to create a control group of "treatment ready" individuals, a common practice in clinical studies of medical and pharmacological therapies. (Personal communication with George DeLeon. See also, Anglin and Hser (1998).)

10. The caveat noted in the title of this report, "Drug Abuse: Research Shows Treatment is Effective, but Benefits May Be Overstated" refers primarily to methodological questions regarding self-report studies. Its general conclusion is that caution should be used since users tend to under-report drug use at certain stages of the treatment process, although not at all stages. The following statistical statements are from pages 22 and 23 of the GAO report.

11. This "anecdotal" information was supplied by Martin Davis, the Redemption House Manager, based on his personal knowledge of the men. When I asked him if they had records of the progress of the men I interviewed at the Farm and after, he said, "Give me a name and I can probably tell you his progress." He supplied significant details on the fate of each man. Martin also pointed out that this five-year success (my word, not his) total of one man, was precisely what was predicted when I was in the course of interviewing and participating at the Bronx facility. It is interesting to note further that the single success is from a family that attended a Pentecostal church regularly throughout much of his childhood, and both of his parents are committed members of this movement. Furthermore, his sister graduated from a discipleship program for drug users as well. This man is one of two Farm transfers in my sample with a strong religious background.

12. This is reasonable, since all numbers are really three-month numbers due to the length of the program at Redemption House.

13. I discovered a third, older, evaluation, but too late to include in this analysis. See Calof (1967).

14. Professor Thompson (1994, 4) provides all assurances that his study was carried out independent of any contact with the funding agency.

15. Consider that those contacted are likely to be the ones who have not changed address often in the intervening years between program completion and survey, while those not contacted may have several changes. The latter corresponds with heavy drug use more than does the former. This suggests that most non-respondents were also non-successes, while most successes would be respondents, or at least most respondents would be successes. Dr. Hess' study tends to bear this out. She was able to contact 97 percent of graduates, but only 33 percent of three-month dropouts. These surveys, like those of the secular programs are, thus, biased in favor of successes.

16. This is somewhat confusing. The report of the Hess study included in Manuel (1993, 150) states that the second year was "to validate the facts [by urinalysis] given in the questionnaire [but] this phase was not carried out."

17. This twelve-page summary, entitled, "Teen Challenge's Proven Answer to the Drug Problem: A Review of a Study by Dr. Aaron Bickenese" is attributed to "Andrew Kenney a professor at Vanguard University," who was "commissioned" to write

it by Teen Challenge (http://www.teenchallenge.org). The Vanguard website (http://www.vanguard.edu) describes itself as a "comprehensive university of liberal arts and professional studies [with a] Pentecostal/charismatic Christian community..." Professor Kenney is not listed among its faculty. A Linkedin site lists an Andrew Kenney as Online Marketing Director and Campus Pastor at Teen Challenge International and Webmaster and Adjunct Professor at Vanguard University.

18. See Fingarette (1998) for a similar argument about AA and its "little white lie" (viz., "one drink equals one drunk").

19. Recall that Harry's comment was two out of every class, at best. My experience was only one remaining after four years from the class I observed.

6

Conclusion to Redemption and Recovery

After almost one thousand pages of manuscript, it seems we have arrived at the point of conclusion to this study of Redemption and Recovery. Actually, I wrote a partial conclusion at the end of the previous book (by now you know the reference). That conclusion focused in part on possible alternatives to the types of programs that Redemption House and Recovery House represent. What is left to do? Well, certainly, I can summarize what I have done in the five chapters in this book and how that fits into the larger argument of the entire corpus…or two corpi. In the Introduction to this volume, I said I would give the layout of the entire ten chapters of the manuscript as originally submitted—and accepted—for publication. That is not difficult. The original table of contents looked like this:

Introduction: Redemption and Recovery as Addiction Treatment
Chapter 1: Two Houses: People, Places, and Programs
Chapter 2: A *Prima Facie* Case: Parallels in Redemption and Recovery
Chapter 3: Resident Demographics: The Men of Redemption and Recovery
Chapter 4: Resident Accounts: Rationales for Treatment and Training
Chapter 5: Redemption House: The Social Construction of a Calling
Chapter 6: Recovery House: The Social Construction of Pathology
Chapter 7: Religion at Recovery House: Orthodoxy and Nihilation
Chapter 8: Reinforcement: Ritual, Miracle, and Myth in Addiction Treatment
Chapter 9: The Reentry Process: Beyond Recovery and Redemption
Chapter 10: Conclusion: Success and Failure in Redemption and Recovery

Chapter 1 of the first book ("People, Places, and Programs") described the two central programs and the different treatment modalities and cultures they represent as well as my methods of data collection and analysis. Chapter 2 of the first book made a "Prime Facie Case" for the broad and deep similarities between Redemption and Recovery in terms of organizational structure; treatment and training processes; the modes of discourse; resident populations and staffing sources; and central assumptions about "addiction" and "treatment." Next in the original scheme came the first chapter of the present volume, "Resident Demographics," which was followed by the "Resident Accounts" Chapter 2 in this book. Then came the two central process chapters, first one on Redemption House and then one on Recovery House. They are now Chapters 3 and 4 in the first book. Next came the chapter on "Religion in

Recovery House" that is Chapter 3 here and describes the return and use of Higher Power spirituality in the TC movement. This was followed by the chapter on myth and miracle, that compared the means of reinforcing or solidifying the faith of clientele at both Houses, Chapter 5 in book one. The last two chapters in the original manuscript were the reentry and success chapters, respectively. The success chapter also included an extension as the conclusion to the whole project. The latter was revised and expanded as a result of the two-book approach to publication.

There were compromises and sacrifices that had to be made when the decision to break the whole into two parts was conceived. Perhaps the biggest was whether to include the Accounts chapter or the Reinforcement chapter in the first volume since both are direct adjuncts to the central descriptions and analysis of the conversion processes. I finally decided to include the Reinforcement chapter in the first book because of its important focus on the mutual witnessing processes in both houses, a central element in the transformations that occur among the residents. However, I consider the story of "Resident Accounts" as equally important, because it is where I introduce the idea of reconstruction of biography that is also a crucial process. This process is also laid out in detail in the two following (in the original scheme) social construction chapters, one on each house. The justification for my use of this particular source of data, however, is explicitly spelled out in the "Accounts" chapter and less fully developed in the social construction chapters. So, I trust that any reader who is truly interested in working through the entire argument—not an insignificant task given its length—can now sort through some of the ellipses and perhaps cryptic internal references to get to the heart of the matter. I apologize for this complexity, but am only partly responsible for it. Publishing necessities dictated these choices; I made them as best I could.

Given these matters of layout, let me turn to content for a bit. The initial chapter in this book, on contextualized demographics, has attempted to demonstrate in detail just who are the residents, the clientele who avail themselves of these two programs. This entailed an extensive biography of two men, one from each program, whose backgrounds as marginal men caught between the worlds of convention and contravention (conformity and deviance, at least from the perspective of the former world's view) demonstrated the social conditions typical of drug users who end up in treatment or training. This tactic also, I hope, demonstrated that the typical addiction mythology of uncontrollable collapse into an inevitable downward spiral of personal degradation and desperation due to some "inner impulse" (demon or disorder) provides little help when attempting to understand most problems of drug misuse.

Other "minor" characters from both houses were included in Chapter 1 to demonstrate that no single schema of explanation—not even mine—can account for all those who experience problems with drug use. There is no single explanation for what we call drug addiction, and there is no single social or psychological profile that fits all or even most addicts. It did seem true, however, among the men (and women) I witnessed at both houses that social marginalizations of various sorts and combinations (poverty, underemployment, minority status) do much to describe the people most likely to wind up in one of our modern day "inebriate asylums."

What this evidence suggested to me, although I was not unfamiliar with this notion previously, was that what misusers need more than religion or science is genuine opportunities to create decent lives for themselves, lives that might include religion and/or science in many of the possible manifestations of each. First they need the opportunity to remain healthy while they continue to try to maintain or cope with their habits or demons; they need things like sterile syringes and unadulterated medications, preferably available in legally or legally tolerated form and format. The provision of other more conventional services like various psychotherapies as well as alternative therapies (e.g., acupuncture or Reiki) and referrals to abstinence or maintenance treatments on a purely voluntary basis would also seem appropriate.

This prescription describes many current harm reduction agencies in cities like New York, Philadelphia, LA, Seattle, and Chicago and others. In the long run, however, what my informants seem to require most are the requisite skills and opportunities to create (in some cases re-create) a reasonably satisfying life. Many of them, like Stanley and Andrew, already have at least some of the skills. What they need is not to have to face unreasonable impediments to the opportunity to use them. They may also need some personal therapy to help adjust to occasions when they are impeded, as do we all. What they do not need is to be told they must abstain from all psychoactive substances (except caffeine and, perhaps, nicotine). They do not, I suggest, need to become someone else (converted or transformed) to cope with their drug problems any more than the rest of us need those processes to cope with whatever demons or disorders occasionally—or regularly—disrupt our lives. My depiction of Miquel in this chapter was intended to indicate that the major impediment to a normal life for him and his family was not so much his drug use as the legal prohibitions against what one needs to maintain a safe and healthy use of opiates, which are not in themselves necessarily physically detrimental in any serious way as long as they are used with knowledge and care, which Miguel seemed to display. The major dangers to drug users today are the punitive prohibitionist laws and the treatment industry's perpetual and perpetuated mythologies and ritual prescriptions, not the substances they consume (assuming they were available in safe, regulated dosage and purity, as are alcohol, nicotine, and caffeine).

The second chapter here, on residents and their rationales or the accounts they offer for being in the confines of a drug treatment program or discipleship training program, demonstrates perhaps the clearest similarities between the two programs and their clienteles. The various literatures cited in this chapter that analyze conversionary groups agreed that "sad tales" of converts regarding relative deprivations and/or depravities prior to entering the new group were typical if not universal. Redemption House and Recovery House were no exception to this rule. What was equally noticeable after spending some time in both locations was the high degree of similarity between the tales told at each house. The majority of these resident accounts were easily categorized into four groups: fear of AIDS; fear of death; female troubles; and self-degradation. I heard virtually the same tales at both houses, only the personal details varied from individual to individual; the themes of the drug-use dangers remained constant. What this demonstrated to me was not only intense similarities between the two groups of residents which I then cast as a single population in their pretreatment incarnations. But also, based on the Millsian notion of "vocabularies of motive," I proposed that these tales were also significantly shaped by the presence of the tellers in the very programs of redemption and recovery. Drawing on several other studies in the Millsian and NRM traditions, I proposed that the similarity of tales not only indicates the affinity of the residents but also the close similarities of the paradigms preached at both programs regarding the typified experiences of drug users based on the same mythology of the downward spiral of addiction.

Again, the "data" are best explained by the fact that Redemption House and Recovery House draw on the same marginal, drug-using populations for their clientele AND then insist the clients adapt their own biographies to the same underlying paradigm(s) of the addiction myth. I also found that the same was true, even more so, regarding the rationales the men shared across programs to explain the success of some of their number and the failure of most in their quest of redemption or recovery. In both houses the men blamed themselves, the victims of addiction, for failing to escape their demons or disease. Only those who truly want to be saved or cured will be, they all claimed. This clearly mirrors the programs' own ideologies that successful transitions to discipleship or recovery are the true effect of the treatment community or the discipleship training (or the Lord), while any failures are due to the resident's own denial of need or resistance to transformation. Addiction treatment in America is in the business of blaming the victim (Ryan 1976) and, as such, does little more than systematize the negative "junkie" stereotype that has plagued the American collective consciousness for at least a century (Acker 2005).

In Chapter 3, I explored the use of Higher Power spirituality (HPS) at Recovery House. This system of belief was created by Bill W. for his Alcoholics Anonymous (AA) cronies, but dismissed by Charles Dederich who founded the original therapeutic community, Synanon, as he picked and chose among AA ideas and practices. Higher Power spirituality has returned to TC practice and now infests its entire process. TC ideologues, like those at AA, claim that faith in a Higher Power is not religion, but something different and non-threatening to drug-using clients. I demonstrated that there is no necessary antipathy between religion and drug users, some of whom like to quote scripture and admonish others in biblical language until the TC taboo on outside religious systems steps in and quashes overt religious language. I also described how mistaken HPS is in its claim to be not a religion, since it is merely a recent American incarnation of a venerable religious tradition, mysticism, that can be traced to ancient origins. The use of this religion is also very practical from the perspective of the Recovery House regime. Insisting that clients use the language and concepts of HPS rather than those of any other historical religion, especially those typical of resident pasts (Catholicism or "fire and brimstone" forms of Protestantism), facilitates conformity, which in turn promotes the smooth processing of the relatively large number (one hundred) of residents during the course of the day. Conformity in the exclusive discourse of HPS rather than, say Christianity, Islam, or Judaism, precludes the formation of alternative bases for identity among residents, identities that may be at odds with the ideologies of addiction and treatment, identities that might challenge the orthodoxy and orthopraxy of the TC. The Higher Power is quite functional in "cooling out" any potential for internal conflict between religious views and or identifications that would impede recovery as well as daily scheduling. Use of HPS exclusive of any other religious system is functional for Recovery House process in many of the same ways exclusive use of evangelical Christianity is functional in maintaining orthodoxy and orthopraxy at Redemption House. Yet again, similarities of operation outweigh, or at least offset, differences of discourse and rhetoric in similar ways at both the religious and secular programs.

The main theme of the reentry chapter (Chapter 5, here) is the similarity in the programmatic attempts of both Houses to prepare their clients for ideological survival in the outside world. The focus of these attempts is primarily ideological, solidifying residents' beliefs in abstinence teachings and preachings. However, both also attempt minimally to create other protective plausibility structures, both cognitive and social, to assist the graduates to stay on the straight and narrow (no pun intended). These consist largely of information about local churches (Redemption House) and local AA or NA "rooms" (Recovery House) where clients can receive regular doses of evangelical or recovery orthodoxy and have the opportunity to continue the processes of mutual witnessing to reinforce their new paradigm of self and confidence in their respective program. These material and spiritual structures of plausibility supposedly maintain new graduates in sobriety via abstinence perfection.

The graduates from each house, however, share a similar problem. The major responsibility for maintaining the structures of plausibility is their own. They are no longer encapsulated in the physical confines or the social discourse of the treatment or training program. They are not required to go to morning meeting or chapel. They cannot easily follow the rest of the residents to prayer meeting or group meeting—there are none where they reside as post graduates. The pressure of constant peer surveillance no longer exists, and they must muster their own motivation for church or AA meeting sometimes in the face of, "Come on, man; let's get high." Treatment and training reliance on internal controls for the post-grad situation is much higher than on external controls which is just the reverse of the encapsulated pre-graduate situation. The outcome is predictable. Most graduates revert to drug use. They "re-pick up again," in the common phrase of Recovery House, or the Devil gets a hold of them, and they fall again, à la Stanley from Redemption House in Chapter 1.

Do people survive and maintain sobriety? Indeed they do. Louie and Saul (Recovery House), Ervin and Jake (Redemption House) are testimony to that, as I have shown. The vast majority of successes, however, are "retreads," men and women who have passed through programs of treatment and training more than once. Many of them have been through several different kinds of programs several times. Several of my informants in this study had been through both treatment and training; men interviewed at each program had been in treatment or training previously with men I interviewed at the other program. Treatment (and training) professionals, the experts, admit it often takes more than one time to "get it." It is quite possible, however, that the issue is not getting "it"—or being ready to get it (DeLeon and Jainchill 1986)—but the passage of time, maturity, or simply ageing (Waldorf et al. 1991; Winick 1962). Which answer you choose depends largely on what you believe about the nature of addiction.

Can more scientific research on treatment solve this riddle for us? Yes, say the positivists, like the treatment survey folks who operate and fund the alphabet studies discussed in Chapter 5. The TC experts, like DeLeon, agree. They are typically psychologists or social workers, usually methodological individualists (a form of positivism) who believe that addiction is an individual "disorder" or disease that results from some inner, individual pathology. Other "experts" like myself, who take a more sociological or anthropological view, are much less sure. First, we do not believe that addiction is an inner or pathological condition, at least not in the vast majority of cases. (In fact, I believe that most of the men I met in treatment or training were not addicted in any pathological or physiological sense. But that's another issue.) The behaviors that get labeled addiction and the people who get labeled addicts often have more to do with the "labelers" than the "labeled." Many people engage in "bad," "risky," or "antisocial" behavior, including serious drug use. Only a few end up in treatment programs (or prisons). They are typically the ones with the least in the way of economic, social, or familial resources. They are poor, alone, unskilled, and, disproportionately, ethnic minorities. Remember Stanley, AJ, Andrew, and Louie? It is these social conditions that drive whatever "abusive" cycle they experience, as I demonstrated in Chapter 1 in this book.[1] If this view has any validity, building up the inner resources of AJ or Louie through treatment or training will do little to impact the real sources of their problems. It can help, but when they graduate…if they graduate from one of these programs, they will, in most cases, have to return to the same economic, social, and familial conditions they inhabited prior to entering their program. As a result, for most of them, reentry equals relapse. Will more treatment or "refined" treatment help? Perhaps. But, then, so may the passage of time, assuming they survive, as many do. If surviving is the issue, harm reduction services (including decriminalization) make infinitely more sense than treatment or training.

Can more research help? I think not, at least not the positivist kind that gets all the public monies for drug research and washes it down the drain counting (self-reporting) heads (again, no pun intended). That is why I (and others) have tried something else. Ethnographies that get at the histories and stories and experiences and thought processes of users in and out of treatment—via thick description—may furnish the kind of data that will demonstrate the point I have been making. But, positivists have a methodological bias against seeing things from the "subject's" viewpoint, because that, they say, prejudices the outcome of research. Only trained positivists can attain a "scientific" viewpoint—and that's gospel (pun intended) in "scientific" research circles. It is interesting, however, that most of their data are based on self-reports of users and former users, while researchers avoid getting too close to the sources. There may be prejudice anyway you look at it—reality, that is. And, ethnography on a grander scale would be expensive.

My brief methodological rant brings me to summarize Chapter 5, where I—the ethnographer—use my anthroposociological nose to analyze the research that goes on around treatment and training issues. This research typically involves questions about success and failure rates and little else. "Scientific" treatment research very rarely includes questions about process, or how treatment or training is actually carried out. In Chapter 5, I looked at the success rates of the very programs where I did my participating and observing and interviewing and informal conversating. Since my data were not gathered with any pretense of scientific precision, my conclusions are, indeed, tenuous. Nevertheless, given that caveat, I blundered on in much the same way conclusions are arrived at in positivist research reports. I interpreted the numbers that were available to me. What did I find? Lo and behold, Redemption House and Recovery House graduated virtually the same percentage of their clientele—about 10 percent each.

Then I looked at the official treatment industry survey numbers, the alphabet studies (NTIES, DATOS, etc.). They do not evaluate graduation rates, but rates of graduates' (and former residents') self-reported declines in drug use, crime, unemployment, and sometimes increases in health status.

As a general rule, most of these surveys found around 50 percent or more subjects benefitted from their treatment. Fifty percent decline in drug use; 50 percent decline in criminal activity; less than 50 percent decline in unemployment. As a result many treatment and treatment research advocates and organizations declare that "treatment works." However, these studies are not without their critics. Some criminologists, like Currie (1993), point out that the graduates that are surveyed for most of these studies represent only 10 percent of the people who have been in treatment. Thus these *numbers* have little if any more substance, positivistically, than my own.

I also looked at a number of evaluations done at Teen Challenge, the premier faith-based drug treatment program, according to George Bush's office of faith-based initiatives. There has been one government-sponsored outcome study of Teen Challenge (Hess, 1993) and four or five additional studies sponsored by the program itself. The results of these studies vary somewhat depending on whose version you read. Versions found on the program's website, written by Teen Challenge employees, tend to be far more sanguine about the successes discovered than do the original authors or other critical evaluators (Wineburg 2007). In general, the studies find large amounts of success, again around 50 percent, sometimes more, among the self-reporting Teen Challenge alumni. Of course, these studies are suspect on obvious grounds. But it is also possible to question the widely accepted research assumptions (dogma) about the random nature of research survey responses. Finding graduates of a drug treatment or training program like Teen Challenge is not the same as doing so for, say, users of a certain gasoline or shopping mall. Respondents to drug treatment surveys are far more likely to be "successes" than "failures" for at least two reasons. First, people successfully reintegrated into the mainstream after drug treatment will be far easier to locate than relapsers, many of whom may be unhoused or insecurely housed and therefore difficult to locate. Second, "successes" are more likely to respond once found by surveyors, because they get to tell a success story. Doing the survey helps reinforce the very beliefs they brought back from training and on which they depend for continued success. Again, these are highly questionable numbers for many reasons, including Currie's point about much higher rates of drop out than graduation.

Finally in Chapter 5, I looked briefly at research on success rates in more traditional religious conversion campaigns, for example, nineteenth and twentieth century evangelical revivalist campaigns (Charles Finney and Billy Graham, for example) and some of the New Religious Movements (like the "Moonies") as well as the intensive proselytizing Mormons. Although numbers again are highly questionable as to precision, social science research demonstrates that even the most successful conversionist groups accomplish success rates of no more than 10 percent. Most programmatic attempts at proselytizing fall well below this rate. This is true even when prospective converts are approached under the most opportune circumstances, for example, when they are separated from alternative life influences (family or job) and encapsulated in organizational enclosures for "orientation weekends" or other "educational" sessions. Despite this evidence, conversionist organizations like the Billy Graham Crusade continue to *claim* thousands of converts to their cause. This "conversion disorder" seems typical of all such organizations, including Redemption House and Teen Challenge. The number 10 percent seems fairly common despite more sanguine (delusional?) claims to the contrary. The only "official" I met during my research whose claims did not overreach the evidence was the Director of Redemption House, Harry Evans. Harry actually claimed from the outset of this research that his program of discipleship training was successful in about 10 percent of cases. As reported by his deputy, Martin Davis, "We only expect one or two men out of each class (20-25) to be walking with the Lord a year after graduating." Although numbers and success rates were of minor concern to me in this research, at the end of it all, this appears to be the best assessment of that issue—and that makes Harry and Martin exceptions to the rule of "conversionist disorder." (Diogenes would be pleased.) It also reinforces my contention that the "treatment works" claim of the addiction treatment crowd is tantamount to the discipleship trainers' claim that "Jesus saves," at least as it has to do with scientifically measurable successes.

If my analysis has any merit, is there any place for programs like those at the center of this study? Although my analysis has been pretty rough on them at times as systems of manipulation and "voluntary coercion," they are essentially—or at last legally—voluntary organizations.[2] In this respect, they are just like the other religious organizations I suggest they emulate. They are as legitimate as the "mosque at ground zero" (which is neither mosque nor at ground zero), which is causing so much uproar as I write these last lines. Both Synanon and Teen Challenge arose in the same era of moral panic over heroin use and "addiction" via the vision of a motivated individual who thought he had a/the solution when no other existed. The history of the United States, indeed the world, is littered with similar charismatic collectives created to solve the problems—or perceived problems—of evil, danger, or social threat. As with both Dederich and Wilkerson, most people involved in the movement organizations that have resulted from their efforts and charisma are well-meaning; many are true believers. And their organizations have resulted in redeemed and/or recovered lives for some people. However, despite all these beliefs, therapeutic communities and Teen Challenges are little more than churches (or exceedingly church-like organizations) that work for those they work for and don't work for those they don't.

Billy Sunday, the famous ball player-turned sawdust revival preacher, believed that alcohol prohibition would end all the crime and other social problems that America was heir to in the early twentieth century. He was wrong. In fact, it made things worse! The Teen Challenges and therapeutic communities of today are little more than training grounds for personal prohibition (abstinence practice). They are as mistaken as Rev. Sunday. Part of the reason for that is that our real—or at least more serious—drug problem is not addiction but our prohibitionist impulse to mistreat addicts and other users.

First we panic at any report of (apparent) new drugs or new drug users. Then we try to protect ourselves by banning the "new" substance and/or intensively stigmatizing "new" users. Think here of the 1980s panic over "crack babies"—perhaps well-intended initially, but ultimately a complete fraud. That largely baseless scare sent many women to jail and deprived them of their children and vice versa for no legitimate reason (Reinarman and Levine 1997). Drug treatments are not alternatives to this impulse, but institutionalizations of it. Where current "macro" drug policies try to interdict drugs or indict users or dealers, "micro" policies (i.e., treatment and training) try to instill prohibition (abstinence) at the personal level. While it does not try to accomplish social control of unpopular behavior or unpopular persons by external coercion, treatment preaches internal coercion that co-opts the subject to participate in his or her own "self" control. If someone desires this with full knowledge of its process and effects, that is freedom of choice. However, when the full knowledge of the processes and effects are deliberately hidden—for the "patient's" own good or from institutional self-delusion, that is less than freedom and akin to fraud or manipulation. Earlier, I suggested regarding drug treatments that we should let a hundred schools of thought contend. However, those thoughts should not be hidden in medical rhetoric when what they really supply is something more akin to religious practice or, at best, social placebos. In today's world, medicine is the much stronger cultural authority, with much greater coercive power than religion. Borrowing medical or other scientific rhetoric and discourse does not make the therapeutic community's tactics and techniques any more objectively curative than were those very same tactics and techniques—or their close cousins—when they were used 150 years ago by the Washingtonian Houses or inebriate asylums or, indeed, by Recovery House or Alcoholics Anonymous today.

Both micro and macro approaches to drug problems in this country are misguided by the twin ideologies of abstinence and zero tolerance. There are reasonable alternatives to both that have demonstrated their effectiveness in places like Amsterdam and Vancouver as well as New York City and San Francisco, Chicago and Detroit. They will reduce the micro problems of drug addiction and abuse as well as the macro problems of crime and violence associated with drug distribution. If/when we adopt harm reduction approaches to our drug problems, therapeutic communities and Teen Challenge (probably more so the former) will wither away like the jack-leg preacher of prohibition and the jake-leg victims of unregulated alcohol during the 1920s. Perhaps the 2020s will see some of this prophecy fulfilled. But I do not plan to hold my breath in the meantime.

Notes

1. I use "drive" here in the same sense that Inciardi (1986) did when he wrote that "heroin use drives crime."
2. The recent increased acceptance of "drug courts" as alternatives to incarceration for "addicts" (i.e., drug users) accused of criminal behavior may radically decrease the number of people in treatment who are there voluntarily. See Nolan (2001/2002) and Whiteacre (2008).

Bibliography

Acker, Caroline Jean. *Creating the American Junkie: Addiction Research in the Classic Era of Narcotic Control*. Baltimore, MD: The Johns Hopkins University Press, 2005.

Addictions Newsletter 8, no: 1 (Fall 1998): [entire issue].

Agar, Michael. *Ripping and Running: A Formal Ethnography of Urban Heroin Addicts*. New York: Seminar Press, 1973.

Ahlstrom, Sydney E. *A Religious History of the American People*. Garden City, NY: Doubleday, 1975.

Alexander, Jeffrey C., and Steven Seidman, eds. *Culture and Society: Contemporary Debates*. Cambridge: Cambridge University Press, 1990.

Ammerman, Nancy. *Bible Believers: Fundamentalists in the Modern World*. New Brunswick, NJ: Rutgers University Press, 1987.

_____. *Southern Baptists Observed*. Knoxville, TN: University of Tennessee Press, 1993.

Anglin, M. Douglas, and Yih-Ing Hser. "Treatment of Drug Abuse." In *Drugs and Crime*, edited by Michael Tonry and James Q. Wilson. Chicago: The University of Chicago Press, 1990.

Antze, P. "The Role of Ideologies in Peer Psychotherapy Groups." In edited by Mary Douglas, 1979.

Asch, Solomon E. "Effects of Group Pressure on the Modification and Distortion of Judgments." In *Readings in Social Psychology*, edited by Eleanor E. Macoby, Theodore M. Newcomb, and Eugene L. Hartely. New York: Hope, Rinehart and Winston, 1958.

Babbie, Earl. *The Practice of Social Research*. 6th ed. Belmont, CA: Wadsworth Publishing Company, 1992.

Bainbridge, William Sims. *The Sociology of Religious Movements*. New York: Routledge, 1997.

Bainton, Roland. "The Left Wing of the Reformation." *The Journal of Religion* XXI (1941): 127ff.

Bakalar, James, and Lester Grinspoon. *Drug Control in a Free Society*. New York: Cambridge University Press, 1984.

Bankston, William B., et al. "Toward a General Model of the Process of Radical Conversion: An Interactionist Perspective on the Transformation of Self-Identity." *Qualitative Sociology* 4 (1981): 279–96.

Barber, Benjamin. *Consumed: How Markets Corrupt Children, Infantilize Adults, and Swallow Citizens Whole.* New York: Norton, 2007.

Barker, Eileen. *The Making of a Moonie: Choice or Brainwashing.* New York: Basil Blackwell, 1984.

Barron, James. "N.Y. Court Let's Inmate Refuse Alcohol Program." *New York Times,* June 12, 1996, http://www.nytimes.com

Baumohl, Jim. "On asylums, homes, and moral treatment: the case of the San Francisco Home for the Care of the Inebriate, 1859–1870." *Contemporary Drug Problems* 13, no. 3 (1987): 395–445.

Baumohl, Jim, and Robin Room. "Inebriety, Doctors, and the State: Alcoholism Treatment Institutions before 1940." In *Recent Developments in Alcoholism,* Vol. 5, edited by Marc Galanter. New York: Plenum Press, 1988.

Becker, Howard S. "Notes on the Notion of Commitment." *American Journal of Sociology* 66, no. 1 (1960): 32–40.

———, ed. *The Other Side: Perspectives on Deviance.* New York: Free Press, 1964.

——— *Outsiders: Studies in the Sociology of Deviance.* New York: Macmillan, 1963.

Bellah, Robert N., Richard Madsen, William M. Sullivan, Ann Swidler, and Steven M. Tipton. *Habits of the Heart: Individualism and Commitment in American Life.* Berkeley: University of California Press, 1985.

Berger, Peter L. *Invitation to Sociology.* Garden City, NY: Anchor Books, 1963.

——— *The Sacred Canopy.* Garden City, NY: Doubleday, 1967.

Berger, Peter L., and Hansfried Kellner. *Sociology Reinterpreted: An Essay on Method and Vocation.* Garden City, NY: Anchor Books, 1981.

Berger, Peter L., and Thomas Luckmann. *The Social Construction of Reality.* Garden City, NY: Anchor Books, 1966.

Berger, Stephen D. "The Sects and the Breakthrough to the Modern World: On the Centrality of the Sects in Weber's Protestant Ethic." *Sociological Quarterly* 12 (Autumn 1971): 486–89.

Bettelheim, Bruno. "Individual and Mass Behavior in Extreme Situations." *Journal of Abnormal Psychology* 38 (October 1943): 424.

Bicknese, Aaron. "The Teen Challenge Drug Treatment Program in Comparative Perspective." Ph.D. Dissertation, Northwestern University, 1999.

Biernacki, Patrick. "Recovery from Opiate Addiction without Treatment: A Summary." In *The Collection and Interpretation of Data from Hidden Populations,* edited by Lambert. Rockville, MD: NIDA, 1990.

——— *Pathways from Heroin Addiction: Recovery without Treatment.* Philadelphia, PA: Temple University Press, 1986.

Biernacki, P., and Dan Waldorf. "Snowball Sampling: Problems and Techniques of Chain Referral Sampling." *Sociological Methods and Research* 10 (1981): 141–61.

Bloom, Harold. *The American Religion: The Emergence of the Post-Christian Nation.* New York: Simon and Schuster, 1992.

Blumer, Herbert. "Society as Social Interaction." In Rose, 1961.

Bourgois, Phillipe. *In Search of Respect: Selling Crack in El Barrio.* Cambridge: Cambridge University Press, 1996.

Brecher, Edward M., and the Editors of Consumer Reports. *Licit and Illicit Drugs: The Consumers Union Report on Narcotics, Stimulants, Depressants, Inhalants, Hallucinogens, and Marijuana - including Caffeine, Nicotine, and Alcohol.* Boston, MA: Little, Brown and Company, 1972.

Brill, Leon. *The De-Addiction Process.* Springfield, IL: Charles C. Thomas, 1972.

Bromely, David G., and Anson D. Shupe. *The Moonies in America.* Beverly Hills, CA: Sage, 1979.

Brown, B., ed. "Aftercare." Special issue of *International Journal of the Addictions* 25, no. 9A+10A (1991): [entire issue].

Caplovitz, D. and F. Sherrow. *The Religious Dropouts: Apostasy among College Graduates.* Beverly Hills, CA: Sage Publications, 1977.

Carroll, Jerome F. X. "The Evolving American Therapeutic Community." *Alcoholism Treatment Quarterly* 9, no. 3/4 (1992): 175–81.

Casriel, Daniel. *So Fair a House: The Story of Synanon.* Englewood Cliffs, NJ: Prentice Hall, 1963.

Castel, Robert. "Moral Treatment: Mental Therapy and Social Order in the 19th Century." In *Social Control and the State: Historical and Comparative Essays,* edited by Cohen and Scull. New York: St. Martin's Press, 1983.

Cerulo, Karen A. "Identity Construction: New Issues, New Directions." *Annual Review of Sociology* 23 (1997): 385–409.

Cohen, Patricia. "Experts are Reassessing a Tumultuous Decade." *The New York Times,* June 13, 1998, B7:2.

Cohen, Peter. "The Drug Prohibition Church and the Adventure of Reformation." *International Journal of Drug Policy* 14, no. 2 (2003): 213–15.

_____. "Is the Addiction Doctor the Voodoo Priest of Western Medicine?" *Addiction Research* 8, no. 6 (2001): 598.

Coleman, James William. *The Criminal Elite: Understanding White-Collar Crime.* New York: St. Martin's Press, 1998.

The Compact Edition of the Oxford English Dictionary, vol. 1. Oxford: Oxford University Press, 1971.

Conrad, Peter, and Jos. W. Schneider. *Deviance and Medicalization: From Badness to Sickness.* Columbus, OH: Merrill, 1985.

Cooley, Charles Horton. *Human Nature and the Social Order.* New York: Scribners, 1902.

Coser, Louis A. *Masters of Sociological Thought: Ideas in Historical and Social Context*. 2nd ed. Long Grove, IL: Waveland Press, 2003.

Courtwright, David T., Herman Joseph, and Don De Jarlais. *Addicts Who Survived*. Knoxville, TN: University of Tennessee Press, 1989.

Currie, Elliot. *Reckoning: Drugs, the Cities, and the American Future*. New York: Hill and Wang, 1993.

Cushman, Philip. *Constructing the Self, Constructing America*. Reading, MA: Addison-Wesley, 1995.

Cuzzort, George. *Using Social Thought: The Nuclear Issue and Other Concerns*. Palo Alto, CA: Mayfield, 1989.

Danzger, M. Herbert. "Signposts along the Road Home: An Analysis of the Rhetoric of Return to Judaism." Presented at the annual meeting of the Israel Sociological Society, Tel Aviv, Israel, 1976.

_____. "Recruitment to Orthodox Judaism: Jerusalem and New York Compared." Presented at the annual meeting of the Association for the Sociology of Religion, New York, 1986.

_____. *Returning to Tradition*. New Haven, CT: Yale University Press, 1989a.

_____. "Motivation, Rhetoric, and Ritual in Religious Conversion and Return." Unpublished manuscript, 1989b.

Darnton, Robert. *The Great Cat Massacre: and Other Episodes in French Cultural History*. New York: Basic Books, 1984.

Davies, John Booth. *The Myth of Addiction*. Amsterdam: Harwood Academic Publishers, 1997.

Davis, Nanette J. *Sociological Construction of Deviance*. Dubuque, IA: William C. Brown, 1980.

Davis, Natalie Zeamon. *Society and Culture in Early Modern France*. Palo Alto, CA: Stanford University Press, 1975.

Deitch, David and J. Zweben. "Synanon: A Pioneering Response to Drug Abuse Treatment and a Signal for Caution." In Lowinson and Ruiz (eds.), 1981.

DeLeon, G. "Aftercare in therapeutic communities." *International Journal of Addictions* 25, no. 9A and 10A (1991a): 1229–41.

_____. *Elements of the Therapeutic Community* (videotape). New York: Outreach Project, 1990a.

_____. "Program-Based Evaluation Research in Therapeutic Communities." In Frank Tims and J. P. Ludford (eds.), 1984.

_____. "Retention in Drug Free Therapeutic Communities." In *Improving Drug Abuse Treatment*. Rockville, MD: NIDA Research Monograph 106, 1991b.

_____. "The Therapeutic Community and Behavioral Science." In *Learning Factors in Substance Abuse*, edited by B. A. Ray. Rockville, MD: NIDA Research Monograph, 88, 1988.

_____. "The Therapeutic Community and Behavioral Science." *International Journal of the Addictions* 25, no. 12A (1990–91): 1537–57.

_____. "Therapeutic Community Research: Overview and Implications." In DeLeon and Ziegenfuss (eds.), 1981.

_____. *The Therapeutic Community: Theory, Model, and Method.* New York City: Springer Publishing Company, 2000.

_____. "The Therapeutic Community: Toward a General Theory and Model." In Frank M. Tims, George DeLeon, and Nancy Jainchill (eds.), 1994.

_____. "Treatment Strategies." In *Handbook on Drug Controls*, edited by J. Inciardi. NY: Greenwood Press, 1990b.

DeLeon, G. and Jainchill, N. "Circumstances, Motivation, Readiness and Suitability (CMRS) as Correlates of Treatment Tenure." *Journal of Psychoactive Drugs* (1986).

_____. "Residential Therapeutic Communities for Female Substance Abusers." *Bulletin of the New York Academy of Medicine* 68, no. 3 (1991): 277–90.

DeLeon, George and James T. Ziegenfuss. *Therapeutic Communities for Addiction: Readings in Theory, Research and Practice.* Springfield, IL: Chas. C. Thomas, 1986.

DeLeon, George and Mitchell S. Rosenthal. "Treatment in Residential Therapeutic Communities." In *Treatments of Psychiatric Disorders, Volume II*, edited by T. B. Karasu. Washington, DC: American Psychiatric Press, 1989.

Denning, Pat. *Practicing Harm Reduction Psychotherapy: An Alternative Approach to Addictions.* New York: Guildford, 2004.

Densen-Gerber, Judianne. *We Mainline Dreams: The Odyssey House Story.* Garden City, NY: Doubleday, 1973.

Denzin, Norman. *The Recovering Alcoholic.* Beverly Hills, CA. Sage Publications, 1987.

Douglas, Mary, ed. *Constructive Drinking: Perspectives on Drink from Anthropology.* Cambridge: Cambridge University Press, 1987.

_____. *Implicit Meanings: Essays in Anthropology.* London: Routledge & Kegan Paul, 1978.

_____. *Natural Symbols: Explorations in Cosmology.* New York: Vintage Books, 1973.

_____. *Purity and Danger: An Analysis of Concepts of Pollution and Taboo.* London: Routledge & Kegan Paul, 1966/1978.

Duneier, Mitchell. *Sidewalk.* New York: Farrar, Strauss, and Giroux, 1999.

_____. *Slim's Table: Race, Respectability, and Masculinity.* Chicago: Chicago University Press, 1992.

Durkheim, Emile. *The Division of Labour in Society.* Translated by George Simpson. New York: Macmillan, 1964.

_____. *The Elementary Forms of the Religious Life.* Translated by J. W. Swain. New York: Collier Books, 1961.

_____. *Suicide: A Study in Sociology*. Translated by John A. Spaulding and George Simpson. Edited with an introduction by George Simpson. New York: The Free Press, 1951.

Duster, Troy. *The Legislation of Morality*. New York: Free Press, 1970.

Ehrenreich, Barbara and Guy Ehrenreich. "Medicine and Social Control." In *Welfare in America: Controlling the "Dangerous Classes*," edited by B. Mandrell. Engelwood Cliffs, NJ: Prentice-Hall, 1975.

Elkins, Stanley M. *Slavery: A Problem in American Institutional and Intellectual Life*. Chicago: University of Chicago Press, 1968.

Empey, LaMar T. and Mark C. Stafford. *American Delinquency: Its Meaning and Construction*. 3rd ed. Belmont, CA: Wadsworth, 1982.

Endore, G. *Synanon*. Garden City, NY: Doubleday, 1968.

Epstein, Edward Jay, *The Agency of Fear*. New York: Putnam's Sons, 1977.

Erickson, Patricia G., Diane M. Riley, Yuet W. Cheung, and Patrick O'Hare. *Harm Reduction: A New Direction for Drug Policies and Programs*. Toronto: University of Toronto Press, 1997.

Erikson, Kai T. "Notes on the Sociology of Deviance. In *The Other Side: Perspectives on Deviance*, edited by Howard S. Becker. New York: Free Press, 1964.

_____ *Wayward Puritans: A Study in the Sociology of Deviance*. New York: John Wiley, 1966.

Faupel, Charles E. "A Typology of Heroin Users." *Social Problems* 34, no. 1 (1987): 54–63. Reprinted in Rubington and Weinberg.

Festinger, Leon, Henry W. Reicken, Jr., and Stanley Schachter. *When Prophecy Fails*. New York: Harper and Row, 1956.

Fingarette, Herbert. "Alcoholism: The Mythical Disease." *The Public Interest* 91 (1988a): 3–22.

_____ *Heavy Drinking: The Myth of Alcoholism as a Disease*. Berkeley, CA: University of California Press, 1988b.

Flinn, Frank K. "Criminalizing Conversion: The Legislative Assault on New Religions." In *Crimes, Values, and Religion*, edited by James Day and William Laufer. Westport, CT: Ablex Publishing, 1987.

Foucault, M. *Madness and Civilization*. New York: Random House, 1965.

Frankel, Barbara. *Transforming Identities: Context, Power and Ideology in a Therapeutic Community*. New York: Peter Lang Publishing, 1985.

Fuchs Ebaugh, H. R. *Becoming an EX: The Process of Role Exit*. Chicago: The University of Chicago Press, 1988.

Galanter, Marc. "Religious Experience and the Regulation of Drug Use." In Lowenstein and Ruiz (eds.), 1981.

Gamson, William A. *The Strategy of Social Protest*. Homewood, IL: Dorsey Press, 1975.

Garfinkel, Harold. "Conditions of Successful Degradation Ceremonies," *The American Journal of Sociology* 61 (1956): 420–24.

Geary, Frances R. "Evaluation." In Lowenstein and Ruiz (eds.), 1981.

Geertz, Clifford. *The Interpretation of Cultures*. New York: Alfred Knopf, 1973.

_____ *Local Knowledge: Further Essays in Interpretive Anthropology*. New York: Basic Books, 1983.

Gerrard, Michelle Decker, Greg Owen, and Patricia Owen. "Minnesota Teen Challenge follow-up study." Wilder Research Foundation, 2007. http://www.wilder.org/research.0.html

Gerstel, David. *Paradise Incorporated: Synanon*. Novato, CA: Presidio Press, 1982.

Glaser, Barney G. and Anselm Strauss. *The Discovery of Grounded Theory*. Chicago: Aldine Publishing, 1967.

Glasscote, Raymond M., James N. Sussex, Jerome H. Jaffe, John Ball, and Leon Brill. *The Treatment of Drug Abuse: Programs, Problems, Prospects*. Washington, DC: The Joint Information Service of APA and NAMH, 1972.

Glock, Charles Y. and Philip E. Hammond, eds. *Beyond the Classics: Essays in the Scientific Study of Religion*. NY: Harper and Row, 1973.

Glock, Charles Y. and Robert N. Bellah, eds. *The New Religious Consciousness*. Berkeley, CA: University of California Press, 1976.

Goffman, Erving. *Asylums*. Garden City, NY: Doubleday, 1961.

_____ "On Cooling the Mark Out." *Psychiatry* 15 (1952): 451–63.

_____ *The Presentation of Self in Everyday Life*. New York: Anchor Books, 1959.

Goode, David and Irving Kenneth Zola. *A World Without Words: The Social Construction of Children Born Deaf and Blind*. Philadelphia, PA: Temple University Press, 1994.

Goode. Erich. *Deviant Behavior*. 5th ed. Boston, MA: Allyn and Bacon, 1997.

_____ *Deviant Behavior*. 9th ed. Engelwood Cliffs, NJ: Prentice Hall, 2010.

_____ *Drugs in American Society*. New York: Knopf, 1993.

_____ *Drugs in American Society*. New York: McGraw-Hill, 2007.

_____, ed. *Social Deviance*. Boston, MA: Allyn and Bacon, 1996/2009.

Government Accounting Office. *Drug Abuse: Research Shows Treatment is Effective, but Benefits May Be Overstated*. USGAO Report to Congress (HEHS-98-72). Washington, DC: USGAO, 1988.

Greil, A. L. and D. R. Rudy. "Conversion to the World View of AA: A Refinement of Conversion Theory." *Qualitative Sociology* 6 (1983): 5–28.

_____ "'Social Cocoons': Encapsulation and Identity Transformation Organizations." *Sociological Inquiry* 54, no. 3 (1984a): 260–73.

_____ "What Have We Learned From Process Models of Conversion? An Examination of Ten Case Studies." *Sociological Focus* 17, no. 4 (1984b): 305–23.

Gusfield, Joseph R. and Jerzy Michalowicz. "Secular Symbolism: Studies of Ritual, Ceremony, and The Symbolic Order in Modern Life." *Annual Review of Sociology* 10 (1984): 417–35.

Habermas, Jurgen. *Toward a Rational Society: Student Protest, Science, and Politics.* Translated by Jeremy Schapiro. Boston, MA: Beacon Press, 1970.

Haley, Alex. *Roots: The Saga of an American Family.* New York: Vanguard, 2007.

Hamilton, Michael S. "The Dissatisfaction of Francis Schaeffer." *Christianity Today* 41, no. 3 (1997): 22–30.

Hammond, John L. *The Politics of Benevolence: Revival Religion and American Voting Behavior.* Norwood, NJ: Ablex Publishing, 1979.

Harrison, Lana and Arthur Hughes, eds. *The Validity of Self-Reported Drug Use: Improving the Accuracy of Survey Estimates.* Rockville, MD: NIDA Research Monograph 167, 1997.

Harrison, Michael I. "Preparation for Life in the Spirit." *Urban Life and Culture* 2, no. 4 (1974): 387–415.

Hawkins, J. David and Norman Wacker. "Verbal Performances and Addict Conversion: An Interactionist Perspective on Therapeutic Communities." *Journal of Drug Issues* (Summer 1983): 281–98.

Hebdige, Dick. *Subculture: The Meaning of Style.* London: Metheun, 1979.

Heirich, Max. "Change of Heart: A Test of Some Widely Held Theories about Religious Conversion." *American Journal of Sociology* 83, no. 3 (1977): 653–80.

Hess, Catherine B. "Research Summation Appendix." In Manuel, 1993.

Hirschi, Travis. *Causes of Delinquency.* Berkeley: University of California Press, 1969.

Hobsbawm, E. J. *Primitive Rebels.* New York: Norton, 1959.

Hoffman, Abbie (with Johnathon Silvers). *Steal This Urine Test: Fighting Drug Hysteria in America.* New York: Penguin Books, 1987.

Holloman, Regina. "Ritual Opening and Individual Transformation: Rites of Passage at Esalen." *American Anthropologist* 76 (1974): 265–79.

Hood, Daniel E. *Addiction Treatment: Comparing Religion and Science in Application.* New Brunswick, NJ: Transaction Publishing, 2011a.

_____. "Conversion as Treatment for Drug Abuse: A Comparison of Religious and Secular Residential Treatment Programs." Paper presented to Inter-University Seminar, New School for Social Research, New York, 1992.

_____. "Drug Myths and (Im)Moral Panics: Indications of Racism in American Anti-Drug Policy, 1914–1990." Paper presented at the Greater New York Conference on Social Research. New York, NY, 1995.

_____. "Harm Reduction as Treatment: An Ethnographic Consideration." A Research Grant Report presented to the Open Society Institute, New York, NY, 2001.

_____. *Redemption and Recovery: Further Parallels in Religion and Science as Addiction Treatment*. New Brunswick, NJ: Transaction Publishing, 2011b.

Hubbard, Robert L., et al. *Drug Abuse Treatment: A National Study of Effectiveness*. Chapel Hill, NC: University of North Carolina Press, 1989.

Hunter, James Davison. *American Evangelicalism: Conservative Religion and the Quandary of Modernity*. New Brunswick, NJ: Rutgers University Press, 1983.

_____. *Evangelicalism: The Coming Generation*. Chicago: University of Chicago Press, 1987.

Inciardi, James A. *The War on Drugs: Heroin, Cocaine, Crime, and Public Policy*. Palo Alto, CA: Mayfield, 1986.

Inciardi, James A. and Karen McElrath, eds. *The American Drug Scene: An Anthology*. Los Angeles: Roxbury Publishing, 1995.

Inciardi, James and Lana Harrison, eds. *Harm Reduction: National and International Perspectives*. Beverly Hills, CA: Sage Publications, 2000.

James, William. *The Varieties if Religious Experience: A Study in Human Nature*. New York: Mentor Books, 1958.

Johnson, Benton. "A Critical Appraisal of the Church Sect Typology." *American Sociological Review* 22 (1957): 88–92.

Johnson, Bruce D., Paul J. Goldstein, Edward Preble, James Schmeidler, Douglas S. Lipton, Barry Sprunt, and Thomas Miller. *Taking Care of Business: The Economics of Crime by Heroin Users*. Lexington MA: Lexington, 1985.

Johnson, Byron R. *Objective Hope: Assessing the Effectiveness of Faith-Based Organizations: A Review of the Literature*. Philadelphia, PA: University of Pennsylvania Center for Research on Religion and Urban Civil Society, 2002.

Johnson, Gregory. "Conversion As a Cure: The Therapeutic Community and the Professional Ex-addict." *Contemporary Drug Problems* 5 (1976): 187–205.

Johnson, Paul E. *A Shopkeeper's Millennium: Society and Revivals in Rochester,* New York: Hill and Wang, 1979.

Jonas, Hans. *The Gnostic Religion: The Message of the Alien God and the Beginnings of Christianity*. 2nd ed., enlarged. Boston, MA: Beacon Press, 1963.

Kaminer, Wendy. *I'm Dysfunctional, You're Dysfunctional: The Recovery Movement and Other Self-Help Fashions*. Reading, MA: Addison Wesley, 1992.

Kanter, Rosabeth Moss. *Commitment and Community: Communes and Utopias in Sociological Perspective*. Cambridge, MA: Harvard University Press, 1972.

Kearney, Margaret H., Sheigla Murphy, and Marsha Rosenbaum. "Mothering on Crack Cocaine: A Grounded Theory Analysis." *Social Science and Medicine* 18, no. 2 (1994): 351–61.

Kee, Howard Clark. *Miracle in the Early Christian World: A Study in Socio-historical Method.* New Haven, CT: Yale University Press, 1983.

Kennard, David. *An Introduction to Therapeutic Communities.* London: Routledge, 1986.

Kooyman, Martien. "The Psychodynamics of Therapeutic Communities for Treatment of Heroin Addicts." In DeLeon and Ziegenfuss (eds.), 1981.

Kurtz, Ernest. *Not-God: A History of Alcoholics Anonymous.* Center City, MN: Hazelden, 1991.

Laconte, Joe. "Killing Them Softly." *Policy Review* 90 (July–August 1998): 14–22.

Langrod, John, Herman Joseph, and Katherine Colgan. "The Role of Religion in the Treatment of Opiate Addiction." In *Major Modalities in the Treatment of Drug Abuse*, edited by Leon Brill and Louis Lieberman. New York: Behavioral Publications, 1972.

Langrod, John, Lois Alksne, and Efrain Gomez. "A Religious Approach to the Rehabilitation of Addicts." In Lowinson and Ruiz (eds.), 1981.

LeRoy Ladurie, Emmanuel. *Carnival in Romans.* Translated by Mary Feeney. New York: George Braziller, 1979.

_____. *Montaillou: The Promised Land of Error.* Translated by Barbara Bray. New York: George Braziller, 1978.

Leshner, Alan I. "Addiction Is a Brain Disease, and It Matters," *Science* 278, no. 5335 (1997): 45–47.

_____. "Why Shouldn't Society Treat Drug Abusers?" *The Los Angeles Times*, June 11, 1999, B7:1.

Levine, Harry Gene. "The Alcohol Problem in America: From Temperance to Alcoholism." *British Journal of Addiction* 79 (1984): 109–19.

_____. "The Discovery of Addiction: Changing Conceptions of Habitual Drunkenness in America," *Journal of Studies in Alcohol* 39, no. 1 (1978): 143–74.

_____. "Temperance Cultures: Concern About Alcohol Problems in Nordic and English-Speaking Cultures." In *The Nature of Alcohol and Drug Related Problems*, edited by M. Lader et al. New York: Oxford University Press, 1992.

Levine, Harry G. and Deborah P. Small. *Marijuana Arrest Crusade: Racial bias and Police Policy In New York City, 1997–2007.* New York: New York Civil Liberties Union.

Levinson, Jack. "Critical Humanism and the Reproduction of Professional Discourse: The Case of the Therapeutic Community Movement." Unpublished manuscript, 1994.

Link, Ann, producer and editor. *Lower East Side Needle Exchange Program Video Tape #1.* New York: Lower East Side Needle Exchange, 1993.

Littell, Franklin H. *The Origins of Sectarian Protestantism: A Study of the Anabaptist View of the Church.* New York: Macmillan, 1972.

Lofland, John. *Analyzing Social Settings: A Guide to Qualitative Observation and Analysis.* Belmont, CA: Wadsworth, 1971.

_____. "Becoming a World-Saver Revisited." *American Behavioral Scientist* 20, no. 6 (1977): 805–18.

_____. *Doomsday Cult: A Study of Conversions, Proselytization, and Maintenance of Faith.* Englewood Cliffs, NJ: Prentice Hall, 1966.

_____. *Social Movement Organizations: Guide to Research on Insurgent Realities.* New York: Aldine De Gruyter, 1996.

Lofland, John and Lyn H. Lofland. *Analyzing Social Settings: A Guide to Qualitative Observation and Analysis.* 2nd ed. Belmont, CA: Wadsworth Publishing, 1984.

Lofland, John and Rodney Stark. "Becoming a World-Saver: A Theory of Religious Conversion." *American Sociological Review* 30 (1965): 862–74.

Lowinson, Joyce H. and Pedro Ruiz, eds. *Substance Abuse: Clinical Problems and Perspectives.* Baltimore, MD: Williams and Wilkins, 1981.

Lowinson, Joyce H., Pedro Ruiz, Robert B. Millman, and John G. Langrod, eds. *Substance Abuse: A Comprehensive Textbook.* 3rd ed. Baltimore, MD: Williams and Wilkins, 1997.

Luckmann, Thomas. *The Invisible Religion: The Problem of Religion in Modern Society.* New York: Macmillan, 1967.

Lukes, Steven. *Emile Durkheim: His Life and Work.* Stanford, CA: Stanford University Press, 1985.

Lusane, Clarence. *Pipe Dream Blues: Racism and the War on Drugs.* Boston, MA: South End Press, 1991.

MacAndrew, C. and R. B. Edgerton. *Drunken Comportment: A Social Explanation.* Chicago: Aldine Press, 1969.

Manheim, Karl. *Ideology and Utopia: An Introduction to the Sociology of Knowledge.* Translated by Louis Wirth and Edward Shils. New York: Harcourt, Brace and World, 1936.

Manning, Nick P. *The Therapeutic Community Movement: Charisma and Routinization.* New York: Routledge, 1989.

Manuel, David. *The Jesus Factor.* rev. ed. Columbus, GA: Brentwood Christian Press, 1993.

Marlatt, G. Alan. *Assessment of Addictive Behaviors.* New York: Guilford Press, 1988.

Marlatt, G. Alan and J. R. Gordon, eds. *Relapse Prevention: Maintenance Strategies in the Treatment of Addictive Behaviors.* New York: Guilford Press, 1985.

Marlatt, G. Alan and John S. Baer. "Harm Reduction and Alcohol Abuse: A Brief Intervention for College-Student Binge Drinking." In edited by Patricia G. Erickson et al. (eds.), 1997.

Marlatt, G. Alan and Kim Fromme. "Metaphors for Addiction." In *Visions of Addiction,* edited by Stanton Peele. Lexington, MA: Lexington Books, 1988.

Massing, Michael. *The Fix.* New York: Simon and Schuster, 1998.

Matza, David. *Becoming Deviant*. Englewood Cliffs, NJ: Prentice Hall, 1969.

_____. *Delinquency and Drift*. New York: John Wiley, 1964.

Mauss, Marcel. *Sociology and Psychology: Essays*. Boston, MA: Routledge & Keegan Paul, 1979.

McCoy, H. Virginia, Christine Miles, and James Inciardi. "Survival Sex: Inner City Women and Crack-Cocaine." In James Inciardi and Karen McElrath (eds.). Los Angeles: Roxbury, 1995.

McGovern, Constance M. *Masters of Madness: Social Origins of the American Psychiatric Profession*. Hanover, NH: University Press of New England, 1985.

McGuire, Meredith. *Religion: The Social Context*. 2nd ed. Belmont, CA: Wadsworth, 1987.

_____. *Religion: The Social Context*. 3rd ed. Belmont, CA: Wadsworth, 1992.

_____. "Testimony as a Commitment Mechanism in Catholic Pentecostal Prayer Groups." *Journal for the Scientific Study of Religion* 16, no. 2 (1977): 165–68.

McKim, William A. *Drugs and Behavior: An Introduction to Behavioral Pharmacology*. 2nd ed. Englewood Cliffs, NJ: Prentice-Hall, 1997.

McLoughlin, William. *Modern Revivalism: Charles Gradison Finney to Billy Graham*. New York: Ronald Press, 1959.

Mead, George H. *Mind, Self, and Society: From the Standpoint of a Social Behaviorist (Works of George Herbert Mead, Vol. 1)*. Chicago: University of Chicago Press, 1967.

Mieczkowski, Thomas, ed. *Drugs, Crime, and Social Policy: Research, Issues, and Concerns*. Boston, MA: Allyn and Bacon, 1992.

Milgram, Stanley. *Obedience to Authority: An Experimental View*. New York: HarperCollins, 1974.

Miller, W. R. and N. K. Heather, eds. *Treating Addictive Behaviors: Processes of Change*. New York: Plenum, 1986.

Miller, Walter B. "Lower Class Culture as a Generating Milieu of Juvenile Delinquency." *Journal of Social Issues* 14, no. 3 (1958): 5–19.

Mills, C. W. *Power, Politics & People: The Collected Essays of C. Wright Mills*. Edited by Irving Louis Horowitz. London: Oxford University Press, 1939/1974.

_____. "Situated Actions and Vocabularies of Motive." In *Power, Politics, and People*, 1940.

_____. *The Sociological Imagination*. Oxford: Oxford University Press, 1959.

Mitchell, Dave, Cathy Mitchell, and Richard Ofshe. *The Light on Synanon: How a Country Weekly Exposed a Corporate Cult—And Won the Pulitzer Prize*. New York: Seaview Books, 1980.

Morgan, H. Wayne. *Drugs in America: A Social History 1800–1980.* Syracuse, NY: Syracuse University Press, 1981.

Morris, J. G. and B. N. Meltzer, eds. *Symbolic Interaction: A Reader in Social Psychology.* 2nd ed. Boston, MA: Allyn and Bacon, 1972.

Morris, Monica B. *An Excursion into Creative Sociology.* New York: Columbia University Press, 1977.

Moskos, Peter. *Cop in the 'Hood.* Princeton, NJ: Princeton University Press, 2004.

Muffler, John, John G. Langrod, James T. Richardson, and Pedro Ruiz. "Religion." In Lowinson, Ruiz, Millman, Langrod (eds.), 1997.

Murphy, Sheigla and Marsha Rosenbaum. *Pregnant Women on Drugs: Combating Stereotypes and Stigma.* New Brunswick, NJ: Rutgers University Press, 1999.

Musto, M.D., David. *The American Disease: Origins of Narcotic Control.* Exp. ed. Oxford: Oxford University Press, 1987.

Nadelmann, Ethan, Jennifer McNeely, and Ernest Drucker. "International Perspectives." In Lowinson and Ruiz (eds.), 1997.

Nadelmann, Ethan, Peter Cohen, Ernest Drucker, Ueli Locher, Gerry Stimson, and Alex Wodak. *The Harm Reduction Approach to Drug Control: International Progress.* New York: The Lindesmith Center, 1994.

Nash, George. "The Sociology of Phoenix House." In *Sociological Aspects of Drug Dependence,* edited by Charles Winick. Cleveland: CRC Press, 1974.

Nelson, Benjamin. *The Idea of Usury: From Tribal Brotherhood to Universal Otherhood.* 2nd ed., enlarged. Chicago: University of Chicago Press, 1969.

_____. *On the Roads to Modernity: Conscience, Science, and Civilizations.* Edited by Toby E. Huff. Totowa, NJ: Rowman and Littlefield, 1981.

_____. "Weber's Protestant Ethic: Its Origins, Wanderings, and Foreseeable Futures." In Glock and Hammond (eds.), 1973.

Nelson, Benjamin, ed. and Jerome Gittleman, trans. "Max Weber On Church, Sect, and Mysticism." *Sociological Analysis* 34, no. 2 (1973): 140–49.

New York Times. "The Drs Said Strike One…," April 26, 1998, 8:1.

NIDA. *Principles of Drug Addiction Treatment: A Research-Based Guide.* Washington, DC: National Institutes on Drug Abuse, 1999. (NIH Publication No. 99-4180.)

Nock, A. D. *Conversion: The Old and the New in Religion from Alexander the Great of Augustine of Hippo.* New York: Oxford University Press, 1972/1933.

Nolan, James L. Jr., ed. *Drug Courts: In Theory and Practice.* New York: Aldine DeGruyter, 2002.

_____. *Reinventing Justice: The American Drug Court Movement.* Princeton, NJ: Princeton University Press, 2001.

Office of Alcoholism and Substance Abuse Services, New York State. "OASAS Reviews Show Treatment Works." Press release, September 20, 1990.

Office of Technology Assessment. *The Effectiveness of Drug Abuse Treatment: Implications for Controlling AIDS/HIV Infection.* Washington, DC: U.S. Congress, 1990.

Ofshe, Richard and Ethan Watters. *Making Monsters: False Memories, Psychotherapy, and Sexual Hysteria.* Berkeley: University of California Press, 1996.

Olin, W. *Escape from Paradise: My Ten Years in Synanon.* Santa Cruz, CA: Unity Press, 1980.

Oliver, William. *The Violent Social World of Black Men.* New York: Maxwell MacMillan, International, 1998.

Onken, Lisa Simon, Jack D, Blaine, and John J. Boren, eds. *Beyond the Therapeutic Alliance: Keeping the Drug-Dependent Individual in Treatment.* Research Monograph 165. Rockville MD: National Institute on Drug Abuse, 1999.

_____. "Treatment for Drug Addiction: It Won't Work If They Don't Receive It." In Onken, Blaine, and Boren (eds.), 1999.

Orbuch, L. T. "People's Accounts Count: The Sociology of Accounts." *Annual Review of Sociology* 23 (1997): 445–78.

Otto, Rudolph. *The Idea of the Holy.* Translated by J.W. Harvey. New York: Oxford University Press, 1950/1917.

_____. *Mysticism, East and West: A Comparative Analysis.* New York: Macmillan, 1960/1932.

Ozment, Steven E. *The Reformation in the Cities: The Appeal of Protestantism to Sixteenth-Century Germany and Switzerland.* New Haven, CT: Yale University Press, 1975.

Pagels, Elaine. *The Gnostic Gospels.* New York: Vintage Books, 1981.

Paone, Denise and Julie Alperen. "Reframing the Debate: effective treatment for crack using women." Presented at the 8th International Conference on Harm Reduction, Paris, 1996.

Peele, Stanton. *Diseasing of America: Addiction Treatment Out of Control.* Boston, MA: Houghton Mifflin, 1989.

_____. *The Meaning of Addiction.* Lexington, MA: Lexington Books, 1985.

Perfas, Fernando B. *Therapeutic Community: Social Systems Perspective.* Lincoln, NE: iUniverse, 2004.

Preble, Edward and John Casey, "Taking Care of Business - The Addict's Life on the Street." *The International Journal of the Addictions* 4 (1969): 145–69.

Pritchard, L. K. "Religious Change in Nineteenth Century America." In Glock and Bellah (eds.), 1976.

Psychology Today, September/October, 1994, [entire issue].

Rambo, Lewis R. *Understanding Religious Conversion.* New Haven, CT: Yale University Press, 1993.

Ray, Marsh B. "The Cycle of Abstinence and Relapse among Heroin Addicts" in H. Becker (ed.), 1964.

Reinarman, Craig. "The Social Construction of Drug Scares." In Goode (ed.), 1996/1994.

Reinarman, Craig and Harry G. Levine. *Crack in America: Demon Drugs and Social Justice.* Berkeley: University of California Press, 1997.

Reuter, Peter and Harold Pollack. "How Much Can Treatment Reduce National Drug Problems?" *Addiction* 101, no. 3 (2006): 341–47.

Richardson, James T., ed. *Conversion Careers: In and Out of the New Religions.* Beverly Hills, CA: Sage Publications, 1978.

Ritzer, George. *Contemporary Theory and its Classical Roots: The Basics.* New York: McGraw-Hill, 2003.

Robbins, Thomas. *Cults, Converts and Charisma: The Sociology of New Religious Movements.* Beverly Hills, CA: Sage Publications, 1988.

Robinson, Matthew and Allan Scherlen. *Lies, Damned Lies and Drug War Statistics: A Critical Analysis of Claims Made by the Office of National Drug Control Policy.* Albany, NY: State University of New York Press, 2007.

Roman, Shadi. "The Treatment of Drug Addiction: An Overview." In Mieczowski (ed.), 1992.

Rose, Arnold M., ed. *Human Behavior and Social Processes: An Interactionist Approach.* Boston, MA: Houghton Mifflin Company, 1961.

Rosenbaum, Marsha, Sheilga Murphy, Jeanette Irwin, and Lynn Watson. "Women and Crack: What's the Real Story?" in *Drug Prohibition and the Conscience of Nations*, edited by Arnold S. Trebach and Kevin B. Zeese. Washington, DC: The Drug Policy Foundation, 1994.

Rothman, David J. *The Discovery of the Asylum: Social Order and Disorder in the New Republic.* Boston, MA: Little, Brown and Co, 1971.

Rubington, Earl and Martin S. Weinberg. *Deviance: An Interactionist Perspective.* 7th ed. Boston, MA: Allyn and Bacon, 1999.

Ryan, William. *Blaming the Victim.* rev. and updated ed. New York: Vintage Books, 1976.

Schoket, David. "Circumstances, Motivation, Readiness and Suitability for Treatment in Relation to Retention in a Residential Therapeutic Community: Secondary Analysis." Unpublished dissertation. CUNY, 1992.

Schroyer, Trent. *The Critique of Domination: The Origins and Development of Critical Theory.* Boston, MA: Beacon Press, 1975.

Schur, Edwin M. *Labeling Deviant Behavior.* NY: Harper and Row, Publishers, 1971.

Schweitzer, Albert. *The Problem of the Lord's Supper.* Translated by A. J. Mattil, Jr. Edited and introduced by John Reuman. Macon, GA: Mercer University Press, 1971.

Scott, James C. *The Moral Economy of the Peasant.* New Haven, CT: Yale University Press, 1976.

Scott, Marvin B. and Stanford M. Lyman. "Accounts." *American Sociological Review* 33 (February 1968): 46–62.

Shelden, Randall G. *Controlling the Dangerous Classes: A History of Criminal Justice in America.* 2nd ed. Boston, MA: Allyn and Bacon, 2007.

Skoll, Geoffrey R. *Walk the Walk and Talk the Talk: An Ethnography of a Drug Abuse Treatment Facility.* Philadelphia, PA: Temple University Press, 1992.

Snow, David A. and Richard Machalek. "The Sociology of Conversion." *Annual Review of Sociology* 10 (1984).

Stark, Rodney and William Sims Bainbridge. *The Future of Religion.* Berkeley: University of California Press, 1985.

_____. "Networks of Faith." *American Journal of Sociology* 86 (1980): 1376–95.

Steinberg, Stephen. *The Ethnic Myth: Race Ethnicity, and Class in America.* Boston, MA: Beacon Press, 1989.

Stone, Olive M. "Cultural Uses of Religious Visions: A Case Study," *Ethnology* 1 (1962): 329–48.

Straus, R. A. "Changing Oneself: Seekers and the Creative Transformation of Life Experience." In *Doing Social Life*, edited by J. Lofland. New York: Wiley, 1976.

_____. "Religious Conversion as a Personal and Collective Accomplishment." *Sociological Analysis* 40 (1979): 158–65.

Sugarman, Barry. "Structure, Variations, and Context: A Sociological View of the Therapeutic Community." In DeLeon and Ziegenfuss (eds.), 1981.

Sykes, Gresham M. and David Matza. "Techniques of Neutralization: A Theory of Delinquency." *American Sociological Review* 22 (December 1957): 664–70.

Tatarsky, Andrew. *Harm Reduction Psychotherapy: A New Treatment for Drug and Alcohol Problems.* Lanham, MD: J. Aronson, 2007.

Thompson, E. P. "The Moral Economy of the English Crowd in the Eighteenth Century." *Past and Present* 50 (1971): 76–136.

Thompson, Roger D. "Teen Challenge of Chattanooga, TN: Survey of Alumni." University of Tennesee, Chattanooga, Unpublished manuscript, 1994.

Tillich, Paul. *The Protestant Era.* Edited by James L. Adams. Chicago: University of Chicago Press, 1948.

Tims, Frank and J. P. Ludford, eds. *Drug Abuse and Treatment Evaluation: Strategies, Progress, and Prospects.* Rockville, MD: NIDA Research Monograph 51, 1984.

Tims, F. S., George De Leon, and Nancy Jainchill, eds. *Therapeutic Community: Advances in Research and Application.* Rockville, MD: NIDA Research Monograph 114, 1994.

Trebach, Arnold S. and Kevin B. Zeese. *Drug Prohibition and the Conscience of Nations.* Washington DC: The Drug Policy Foundation Press, 1990.

Trice, H. M. and P. M. Roman. "Delabeling, Relabeling, and Alcoholics Anonymous." *Social Problems* 17, no. 4 (1970): 538–46.

Turner, Victor. *The Ritual Process.* Chicago: Aldine, 1969.

Van Gelder, Lawrence. "Charles Dederich, 83, Synanon Founder, Dies." *New York Times,* March 4, 1997. http://www.nytimes.com.

Van Gennep, Arnold. *The Rites of Passage.* Translated by M. Vikedorn and G. Coffee. Chicago: Chicago University Press, 1960.

Waldorf, Dan. *Careers in Dope.* Englewood Cliffs, NJ: Prentice Hall, 1973.

_____. "Life without Heroin: Some Social Adjustments During Long-Term Periods of Voluntary Abstention." *Social Problems* 18, no. 2 (1970): 228–43.

_____. "Natural Recovery from Opiate Addiction: Some Social-psychological Processes of Untreated Recovery." *Journal of Drug Issues* 13, (Spring 1983): 237–80.

Waldorf, Dan, Craig Reinarman, and Sheigla Murphy. *Cocaine Changes: The Experience of Using and Quitting.* Philadelphia: Temple University Press, 1991.

Waldorf, Dan and Patrick Biernacki. "The Natural Recovery from Opiate Addiction: Some Preliminary Findings." *Journal of Drug Issues* 11 (Winter 1981): 61–74.

Walton, John. *Sociology and Critical Inquiry: The Work, Tradition, and Purpose.* 2nd ed. Belmont, CA: Wadsworth, 1990.

Weber, Max. *Economy and Society.* Vols. 1 and 2. Edited by G. Roth and C. Wittich. Berkeley, CA: University of California Press, 1978.

_____. *From Max Weber: Essays in Sociology.* Translated and edited by H. H. Gerth and C. W. Mills. New York: Oxford University Press, 1969.

_____. *The Sociology of Religion.* Translated by Ephraim Fischoff. Introduction by Talcott Parsons. Boston, MA: Beacon Press, 1964/1922.

Weil, Andrew. *The Natural Mind: A New Way of Looking at Drugs and Higher Consciousness.* Boston, MA: Houghton Mifflin, 1986.

Weppner, R. S. *The Untherapeutic Community.* Omaha, NB: University of Nebraska Press, 1983.

Whiteacre, Kevin. *Drug Court Justice: Experience in a Juvenile Drug Court.* New York, NY: Peter Lang Publishing, 2008.

White, William L. *Slaying the Dragon: The History of Addiction Treatment and Recovery.* Bloomington, IL: Chestnut Health Systems, 1998.

Wilkerson, David (with John and Elizabeth Sherrill). *The Cross and the Switchblade.* New York: Pyramid, 1964.

Williams, George H. *The Radical Reformation.* Philadelphia, PA: Westminster.

Williams, Terry. *Cocaine Kids: The Inside Story of a Teenage Drug Ring.* Reading, MA: Addison-Wesley, 1989.

_____. *Crackhouse: Notes form the End of the Line.* New York: Penquin Books, 1992.

Wineburg, Robert J. *Faith-based Inefficiency: The Follies of Bush's Initiatives.* Westport CT: Praeger Publishers, 2007.

Winick, Charles. "The Counselor in Drug Abuse Treatment." *The International Journal of the Addictions* 25, no. 12A (1990–91): 1479–502.

_____. "An Empirical Assessment of Therapeutic Communities in New York City." In *The Yearbook of Substance Use and Abuse*, Vol. II, edited by Leon Brill and Charles Winick. New York: Human Services Press, 1980.

_____. "Maturing Out of Narcotic Addiction." *United Nations Bulletin on Narcotics* 14, no. 1 (1962): 1–7.

_____. "Physician Narcotic Addicts." In Becker (ed.), 1964.

_____. "Retention and Outcome at ACI: A Unique Therapeutic Community." *The International Journal of the Addictions* 25, no. 1 (1990): 1–26.

_____. "Social Behavior, Public Policy, and Nonharmful Drug Use." *The Milbank Quarterly* 69, no. 3 (1991): 427–59.

_____. "Some Aspects of the Careers of Chronic Heroin Users." In *Drug Use: Epidemiological and Sociological Approaches*, edited by Eric Josephson and Eleanor E. Carroll. Washington, DC: John Wiley, 1974.

_____. "Therapeutic Communities for Addictions (A Review)." *Social Policy* 17 (Spring 1987): 61–62.

Worsley, Peter, ed. *The New Introducing Sociology.* rev. ed. London: Penguin Books, 1992.

Wrong, Dennis. "The Oversocialized Conception of Man in Modern Society." *American Sociological Review* 26 (1961): 183–93.

Wuthnow, Robert. *Poor Richard's Principle: Recovering the American Dream Through the Moral Dimension of Work, Business, and Money.* Princeton: Princeton University Press, 1996.

_____. *Saving America: Faith-Based Services and the Future of Civil Society.* Princeton, NJ: Princeton University Press, 2004.

Wuthnow, Robert, James Davison Hunter, Albert Bergesen, and Edith Kurzweil. *Cultural Analysis: The Work of Peter L. Berger, Mary Douglas, Michel Foucault, and Jurgen Habermas.* London: Routledge & Kegan Paul, 1984.

Yablonsky, Lewis. *Synanon: The Tunnel Back.* Baltimore, MD: Pelican Publishing, 1967.

_____. *The Therapeutic Community.* New York: Gardener Press, 1989.

Zimmer, Lynn and John P. Morgan. *Marijuana Myths Marijuana Facts: A Review of the Scientific Evidence.* New York: The Lindesmith Center, 1997.

Zinberg, Norman E. *Drug, Set, and Setting: The Basis for Controlled Intoxicant Use.* New Haven, CT: Yale University Press, 1984.

Author Index

Subject Index

Resident and Staff Index